NARCISSISTIC LEADERS

NARCISSISTIC LEADERS

Who Succeeds and Who Fails

Michael Maccoby

A hardcover edition of this book was published in 2003 by Broadway Books, a division of Random House. First Harvard Business School Press edition published in 2007. Copyright 2003, 2007 by Michael Maccoby.

Printed in the United States of America

11 10 09 08 07 5 4 3 2 1

Book design by Richard Oriolo

ISBN: 978-1-4221-0414-9

Library of Congress Cataloging in Publication data for this title is available.

And liberty cannot be preserved without a general knowledge among the people. . . . But besides this they have a right, an indisputable, unalienable, indefeasible divine right to the most dreaded and envied kind of knowledge, I mean the character and conduct of their leaders.

—JOHN ADAMS
A Dissertation on the Canon and Feudal Law, August 12, 1765

The third type (is) justly called the narcissistic type. . . . There is no tension between ego and super-ego (indeed, on the strength of this type one would scarcely have arrived at the hypothesis of a super-ego), and there is no preponderance of erotic needs. The subject's main interest is directed to self-preservation; he is independent and not open to intimidation. His ego has a large amount of aggressiveness at its disposal, which also manifests itself in a readiness for activity. In his erotic life loving is preferred above being loved. People belonging to this type impress others as being "personalities"; they are especially suited to act as a support for others, to take on the role of leaders and to give a fresh stimulus to cultural development or to damage the established state of affairs.

—SIGMUND FREUD
"Libidinal Types," 1931

To Sandylee

ACKNOWLEDGMENTS

This book grew out of an article in the January 2000 *Harvard Business Review*, "Narcissistic Leaders: The Incredible Pros, the Inevitable Cons." Diane Coutu and David Champion encouraged me to write the article and guided it into publication. Shortly thereafter, I received a call from Charlie Conrad of Broadway Books, who was enthusiastic about my writing this book. As my editor, Charlie has been continually supportive and helpful with his suggestions.

Most of the research for this book has come from my experience as a consultant, business coach, and psychoanalyst combined with the interviews, books, and articles noted in the text. I have also benefited by conversations with Jim Moore, an author and consultant to high-tech leaders; Mark Liebovich, who interviewed a number of productive narcissists for his book *The New Imperialists,* and Karen Southwick, who is writing a book about Larry Ellison.

Richard Margolies, Ph.D., and Mauricio Cortina, M.D., were helpful in discussions about psychoanalytic theories of narcissism.

I appreciate support over twenty-five years from Mike Wolff, editor of *Research Technology Management,* which first published some of the ideas that have been developed in this book. Goran Collert and Sidney Harman helped by reading and commenting on drafts of Chapter 4. A number of executives provided material about their narcissistic bosses, but I would not be doing them a favor by thanking them publicly.

I owe special thanks to my assistant, Maria Stroffolino, who has helped in many ways, both preparing the manuscript and as a researcher.

Lydia Wills has been much more than a literary agent. She has challenged me to develop and clarify my ideas, to translate technical psychoanalytic thinking into common language, and she has shared in a two-year dialogue developing the themes of this book. I very much appreciate her contribution.

CONTENTS

In a time of historic changes in the way we live and work, the opportunities before us, and the threats we face, visionary business leaders have spearheaded these changes with their ideas, revolutionary technology, and organizational innovations. But visionary leaders in both business and government have also been destructive pied pipers, ruining investors who believed in their shady businesses and leaving a legacy of hatred in people left behind in the wake of history. This book is about understanding both the good and the bad visionary leaders—the type of personality that Sigmund Freud, who identified himself as one, termed *narcissistic*.

As the business world changes, so do popular styles of leadership. When this book was first published in 2003, the stock of narcissistic business leaders had plummeted owing to the dot-com crash and Enron- and Tyco-type scams. Formerly admired narcissistic leaders were unmasked as failures, frauds, and fabricators. Even successful narcissists were frowned on as too greedy and self-promoting. While throughout the 1990s, bigger-than-life narcissists decorated the covers of *Fortune*, *BusinessWeek,* and even *Time* and *Newsweek*, in 2003 we saw a shattered marble bust of Jack Welch on the cover of *The Economist*.

For a while, the new twenty-first century ideal became the determined, methodical but "self-effacing, quiet, reserved, even shy" obsessive business leaders celebrated by Jim Collins in *Good to Great*. Even narcissistic bosses began to spout the self-deprecating talk we invariably hear on TV from the winners of golf tournaments. ("It's a tough course, but I had a few lucky breaks, etc.") But of course there's a big difference between talking and acting humble. On May 20, 2006, at an Economist Leadership Forum on Narcissistic Leaders, in Rome, Fausto Bertinotti, president of the Chamber of Deputies, made the astute point that while only narcissists can be visionary leaders, they'd be wise to learn to act humble.

Then, in 2006, *Fortune* did an about-face. Steve Jobs, a prototypical productive narcissist, was named "the model CEO for the twenty-first century." Why turn the spotlight from the modest but driven obsessives heralded a few years before? Was *Fortune* just reflecting the fact that Jobs had hit it big with the iPod—or was there a dawning awareness that to sustain business success, you need bold innovators, productive narcissists? Of course, the problem with narcissists is that while some—like Jobs, Bill Gates, Larry Ellison, Howard Schultz, and Oprah Winfrey—keep on innovating and producing what people want to buy, some—like Steve Case or

Jean-Marie Messier—flare out, and others—like Bernie Ebbers, Kim Woo Chong, and Dennis Kozlowski—turn out to be crooked.

To understand differences among narcissists and even predict which visionaries will succeed and which are likely to fail, this book dissects narcissistic personalities and contrasts narcissists with the other psychoanalytic personalities: the careful obsessives, caring erotics, and adaptive marketing types. I've changed the original title of this book from *The Productive Narcissist: The Promise and Peril of Visionary Leadership* to focus on the themes that have most interested readers. (This new title is also close to the one used in the Spanish translation, *El Lider Narcisista*.) The English translation of the Japanese title is *Why Nasty Guys Advance in Their Careers.* But unlike the Japanese, who consider all self-promoting narcissists as nasty, I take a more differentiated view and recognize the positive contributions of some narcissistic leaders.

Are narcissistic leaders really better than the obsessives? Not necessarily. Are we just seeing changes in business leadership fashion? Yes, to some extent. But in the thirty-five years I've studied business leaders I've seen that different personality types fit better in certain roles, and the importance of these roles continually changes. The fashions aren't arbitrary. It's a matter of *context*, not that one type is better or worse than another. Sometimes mature businesses led by obsessives outperform the innovative businesses led by narcissists and sometimes it's the reverse. The obsessive business leaders are great at cutting costs, throwing nonperformers off the corporate bus, and putting in place the right processes for productivity in manufacturing, marketing, and retail companies. But their innovations are generally improvements on existing products, like Gillette's next new razor blade. Obsessives want to win the game they're in, even break records, like Tiger Woods chasing Jack Nicklaus's record number of wins in golf majors. But productive narcissists want to create new games, changing the way we live and work. While Henry Ford, the narcissist, was realizing his vision of making a car most Americans could afford, Collins's exemplary obsessives might have been making better and cheaper buggy whips for horse-drawn carriages or breeding faster horses.

Some of the most effective managers intuitively know they have to fit personality to the role. Jack Welch writes that he picked a head for a commodity product business who was "in his element with people who sweated the nitty-gritty details like he did, talking about ways to squeeze efficiencies out of every process." This is a productive obsessive. For the head of an innovative, risky business, he picked someone who "hated the nuts and bolts of management . . . But he sure did have the guts and vision to place the big bets." This is a productive narcissist.

Using the personality questionnaire you'll find at the end of chapter 1, my colleagues and I have tested the theories presented in this book. I've used the questionnaire with hundreds of managers in workshops on leadership and discussed the results with them. For example, production managers at Volvo-Mack trucks are productive obsessives, as are managers in the U.S. Army Corps of Engineers; most of the business media managers at VNU have marketing personalities. Matt Downs and Michael Anderson, students at Stanford Business School, gave the questionnaire to thirty-six executives of Bay Area businesses. As the theory predicted, nine of ten high-tech entrepreneurs with the guts and vision to place the big bets were narcissists, while six of seven manufacturers who squeezed the efficiencies out of every process were obsessives.

Executives in sales or professional services fell almost evenly in the marketing, narcissistic, and erotic buckets.

I've found the same patterns in business executives I've taught at Oxford's Said School of Business and the Brookings Institution's programs for federal managers. Effective executives usually have personalities that fit their role. Furthermore, some CEOs I've coached have used the questionnaire with their own teams and with candidates for executive jobs. They find the personality profile useful, not only for improving chances of hiring someone who fits the role but also for enlivening a recruiting interview.

In contrast to my approach, some management writers contend that personality doesn't matter, that leaders can tailor their style to fit the situation they're faced with. Obviously this is true to some degree. Depending on the situation, practically any leader can be commanding or consultative. Any leader can learn when to be close and when to increase distance from the troops. But as Heraclitus wrote twenty-five hundred years ago, character is man's fate. There are limits to behavioral plasticity, and in time of stress, personality prevails. A CEO put it neatly when I asked his view of situational leadership: "Most of my interactions are taking place in chaos. I can't stop and think about what my style should be with different people. My style is my personality." Naturally, some personalities are more flexible and others are more rigid. Of all the personality types, the marketing type is the most elastic; these people can seem so chameleonlike that we might believe they have no personality. But this quality of adaptability is exactly what defines the marketing personality.

By emphasizing context, I'm not eliminating the idea that some leadership styles are better than others. But my leadership hierarchies are different from the one Collins presents. He puts the selfless obsessives at the top of his hierarchy and even the best of the self-promoting narcissists a step below them. While I look for the personality that fits the role and don't place any type above another, I do recognize that all types have positive and negative potentials that can be described in terms of two hierarchies viewed within, not between, personality types. These are levels of productiveness (chapter 3) and levels of moral reasoning.

These two hierarchies are different and don't always correlate with each other. I use the contrast of productive versus unproductive to describe healthier versus less developed or even disturbed personalities. A productive person is active and enthusiastic— someone who bounces back from failure and perseveres to achieve a reasoned purpose. In contrast, unproductive people are less free and therefore reactive rather than active, without a clear purpose and driven by addictive needs that make them fearful and dependent.

Of course, higher levels of moral reasoning don't guarantee that actions will always have the intended benefit, but clearly we want leaders who seek to achieve a common good, not just to feather their own nests. Although morally developed people are almost always productive, there are active, enthusiastic productive people who cut corners or worse and don't score highly on the scale of moral reasoning. In other words, being productive doesn't necessarily mean being good.

In other words, when productive narcissists are morally good, they can be very, very good and when they are bad, they can be horrid. This is because unlike the obsessives, they don't respect the existing cultural norms and want to impose their own vision and values, which can be morally good or bad. As Freud described the narcissistic personality, its defining quality is a lack of a strong pro-grammed conscience or what he termed the super-ego. For what-ever reason, as children, narcissists did not internalize the ethical commands of a parent, and therefore they are free either to design their own conscience or to leave the space blank. Narcissists want to change the world to fit their view of how things should be, and they have little or no sense of guilt to constrain them from radical, risky ventures that can be creative or destructive at either a high or low level of moral reasoning.

In support of Freud's theory, many well-known male narcissistic leaders had weak or absent fathers who were not admired models—the basis for internalizing strong norms, especially for boys. Ac-cording to Lyndon B. Johnson's brother Sam, "the most important thing for Lyndon was not to be like his daddy" who was a bankrupt rancher. Ronald Reagan's father was an alcoholic shoe salesman and Bill Clinton's father died before he was born. But all three, like a number of productive narcissists, had strong mothers who gave them unconditional love and a sense of invulnerability. An excellent film portrayal of a narcissist is *Citizen Kane,* written, produced, and directed by Orson Welles (himself a creative narcissist who also played the lead role) and based on the life of William Randolph Hearst. Charles Kane's father is a weak failure, and his strong mother sends him off as a child to be raised as the heir to a fortune. He starts his career as a visionary, crusading newspaper publisher, but ends up disgraced and isolated, done in by his grandiosity and unwillingness to heed the advice of his best friend.

Since narcissists don't grow up with a programmed conscience; forming their views of right and wrong or finding a purpose in life requires an internal dialogue that can take time. Some narcissists,

Hamlet-like, never fully decide. Some we now honor as great leaders—Abraham Lincoln, Franklin Delano Roosevelt, Mohandas Gandhi, and Winston Churchill—didn't start out with a clear, inspiring purpose for the common good. Lincoln was an ambitious country lawyer who only matured into the visionary of the Gettysburg Address after sleeplessly struggling with the meaning of the Civil War, finally coming to the view that it was not just to preserve the Union, but to realize the promise of the Declaration of Independence—that all Americans shared the unalienable right to liberty. Roosevelt was a rich and charming politician who transcended his crippling polio, affirmed the power of the individual spirit, and gave hope to a nation mired in economic and psychic depression. Gandhi wanted to be a respected barrister but, humiliated by British racists, defied them with principled civil disobedience that shamed the British public and eventually inspired an oppressed people to become a great nation. And Churchill, viewed as lacking judgment in his early public life, then rejected by his party and country as he warned against Hitler, became the invincible leader resisting Nazi forces and inspiring Britain to persevere when it was at its lowest ebb.

These leaders forged their own unique views of what needed to be done to make their world a better place. Unlike other personality types who try to please parents, peers, or the public, they fought to be true to their own developing conception of the right. This is not to say that they were particularly caring. Like most narcissistic leaders, they could be arrogant and bullying, running roughshod over naysayers. And they did not obsess over decisions resulting in the deaths of thousands, when they believed this was the price for achieving the common good.

Narcissists need followers or else they become isolated, and both good and bad narcissistic leaders have been effective recruiters. The difference is that the bad ones invariably make their change-the-world visions into excuses to grab unlimited power at the expense of any common good. Immoral monsters like Napoleon, Hitler, Stalin, and Mao began their leadership careers spouting idealistic visions and ended up devastating their own countries and revealing that their ultimate priority was at the bottom of the scale of moral reasoning—unlimited personal power.

To be sure, the good narcissistic leaders were at times kept in check by the countervailing forces of democratic societies. Roosevelt failed to pack the Supreme Court and Churchill was voted out of power after the war was over. But unlike the tyrants who crushed democratic institutions, the good narcissists believed in and defended democratic institutions.

Narcissists Versus Psychopaths

Since the publication of this book, I've been asked whether there is any difference between narcissists and psychopaths. The answer is that some narcissists are similar to psychopaths or, put another way, psychopaths can be considered an extreme and malignant version of the narcissistic personality.

Both psychopaths and narcissists can be extremely seductive when they need something from people. Both can be glib, charming, manipulative, deceitful, and ruthless. Both use people, squeeze them like oranges, and throw them away once they've drunk the juice.

The difference then is that psychopaths, unlike some productive narcissists, always operate at the lowest level of moral reasoning with no concern for the common good, much less remorse or guilt for self-serving actions that harm other people. Psychopaths can be brilliant, but they build no lasting relationships. Narcissists sometimes do.

Furthermore, whatever their faults, and there were some big ones, narcissistic leaders like Andrew Carnegie, John D. Rockefeller, Henry Ford, and Bill Gates not only created great companies employing thousands, with products that millions have found useful, but they also gave huge sums to fund programs for human betterment. Unlike psychopaths such as Al Dunlop ("Chainsaw Al" of Sunbeam) and others who trash companies and sneak away with the loot or the shady book-cookers like Japanese Internet mogul Takafumi Horei, these philanthropic narcissists linked their own success to the success of the companies they built. Also, to sustain successful companies, they had to be trusted by employees, customers, and suppliers. They had to honor commitments and set a good example, or else in each case the company's spirit would have been eroded by cynicism, with employees just looking out for themselves. That's what happens when psychopaths are in charge. But it also happens when productive narcissists become so puffed up and isolated that they lose their judgment and sense of reality.

Who Succeeds and Who Fails

Some narcissistic leaders who light up the sky like summer fireworks also quickly flare out, while others sustain their initial success. The difference has to do with the character and intelligence, personality and brains, of the narcissistic leader.

Richard Nixon and Bill Clinton are examples of narcissists whose character flaws did them in. Both lacked strong internal checks to their self-defeating impulses: Nixon's dirty political tricks and Clinton's combination of uncontrolled lust and lying about it.

As I write this, Italy's Silvio Berlusconi has narrowly lost the national election. For years he has teetered on the edge of disaster, dodging accusations of bribery and corruption while claiming he is "the Jesus Christ of politics," tormented by his enemies and sacrificing himself for all Italians. Other narcissists like Napoleon and Henry Ford have failed to control their grandiosity and ended up not only harming themselves but also the people who followed them.

The difference between narcissistic business leaders who have sustained success and those who haven't also has to do with the quality of their thinking, their kind of intelligence. Clearly, anyone who gets to the top of a major business would score well on a traditional IQ test. But that would only indicate one kind of intelligence, essentially a combination of good memory and analysis. During the past twenty years, psychologists have demonstrated that while traditional IQ is correlated with doing well in school, it doesn't predict success in business. This means you can have a high IQ and do poorly in business. Other kinds of intelligence—street smarts, imagination, emotional intelligence, systems thinking—can be even more important to business success.

When I compared those narcissistic business leaders who sustained success with those who did not, I found the eventual failures—including William Durant, founder of General Motors; Jean-Marie Messier of Vivendi; Carly Fiorina of HP; and others—all built their empires by buying companies, often accumulating heavy debt, rather than growing their company. The successful ones who bought many companies, like Jack Welch, showed exceptional ability in integrating the acquisitions into a strong corporate culture. That's because these successful leaders shared a kind of intelligence that was missing in those who flamed out. I call it *strategic intelligence*. It applies elements of analytic intelligence, street smarts, and creative intelligence in five interrelated qualities: foresight, systems thinking, visioning, motivating, and partnering. (See chapter 4.)

A group of consultants who read this book were stimulated enough to contact me about learning more about strategic intelligence (SI). They joined me to interview more than thirty top executives on their level of SI and its importance to them in developing and implementing strategy.

These executives all agreed that SI was essential for top leadership effectiveness. Typically, Lydia Thomas, CEO of Mitretek, pointed out that foresight—scanning for future trends, developing alternative scenarios, sensing opportunities and threats—was an essential CEO responsibility. As for the other elements of SI, she agreed, "You can't be successful without them."

Not surprisingly, how leaders use their brains is connected to their personality type. Narcissists, more than the other types, are natural visionaries and tend to think holistically about what they want to create, while obsessives are more likely to make lists of what they plan to do. However, for many of the executives we interviewed, systems thinking is the most difficult SI element. Their knee-jerk approach to a problem is to attack and analyze, to break it into clearly manageable pieces that are more likely to be stacked than integrated. Furthermore, they've learned in business school to construct bureaucracies by splitting work roles into hierarchically ordered chunks. And that's a big reason why organizations end up with silos that block people from collaborating and learning from each other.

The kind of systems thinking most lacking in Western managers combines social, technical, and economic factors. A disastrous example of this weakness has been the inability of American auto companies and, for that matter, researchers and business school professors to understand the Toyota "humanware" system even when it's been explained to them. Toyota organizes work to cut costs, incentivize innovation at all levels, and encourage continuous development of employees as well as continuous improvement of production. It is well known that when Toyota took over management of a poorly performing GM plant in Fremont, California, productivity jumped and union grievances disappeared. GM sent a string of managers to learn how Toyota did it, but even those who learned were unable to recreate anything similar back at their home factories. That's because it wasn't a matter of changing this or that practice, such as just-in-time delivery of parts, but of redesigning a whole socio-technical-business system, which at Toyota keeps evolving.

When I visited Japanese auto companies, I found a greater understanding and application of systems thinking than in the United States or Europe. Why is this so? I'm not sure of the answer, but my hunch is that Asian philosophy and cultural traditions play a role. Chinese philosophy is holistic, relating opposites like *yin*, the female principle, and *yang*, the male principle. The Japanese *daimyo* tradition of feudal knighthood combined the way of *bu* (the arts of swordsman, archery, horsemanship) with the way of *bun* (the arts of calligraphy, poetry composition, painting). In the West, these arts were separated; warriors and artists had totally different career paths.

In the exhibition of Daimyo Culture presented at the National Gallery of Art in Washington, D.C., it was suggested that modern Japanese industrialists were influenced by this tradition, that they combined a warlike business strategy with a sense of elegant design. Whatever the reason, education in Japan, Taiwan, China, and Korea appears a factor in developing systems thinking.

However, there have also been notable systems thinkers in the West. Furthermore, SI doesn't have to depend on a single leader. The qualities of SI can be shared in a group, as was the case with the framers of the U.S. Constitution. They envisioned a great nation that needed the strength that could be gained only by partnering among the thirteen original states. They foresaw new states joining the union and prepared for their entry. And they recognized that to motivate Americans to support this new government, the Constitution had to protect individual liberty. That's what the revolution was all about, and Americans feared a new, overweening national government. Although it took the first ten amendments—the Bill of Rights—to fully establish this principle of civil rights; the Civil War, the fourteenth amendment, and the civil rights legislation of the 1950s and 1960s to expand these rights to African-Americans; and the nineteenth amendment to grant women's suffrage, the framers had been thinking systemically about the constitution as they prepared for the convention that drafted it. James Madison, in particular in the *Federalist* Number 10, emphasizes that a system of checks and balances—what eventually became the executive, legislative, and judicial branches—would be necessary to protect individual liberty. Without this system, democracy could lead to oppression of individuals and minorities by majority factions.

Can systems thinking and the other elements of SI be taught? Yes, but only if managers are willing first to unlearn the bureaucratic logic they've been practicing.

How About Emotional Intelligence (EI)?

A number of readers believe that this book shows that successful leaders are tough guys without emotional intelligence. That overstates what I've written.

While it's true that many successful narcissistic leaders lack EI, the issue is complex. Keep in mind that elements of EI like empathy are talents, not values. Being sensitive to others' feelings doesn't mean you care about them. Bill Clinton used empathy to charm and seduce, while Abraham Lincoln used empathy to manage a cabinet of big egos. Does a narcissistic leader's lack of emotional sensitivity indicate an inability or does it result from a decision to tune out diverting emotions? Some narcissists tell me they are protecting themselves from doubts and bad feelings by ignoring emotions. However, in so doing, they are losing the ability to better understand themselves and others. EI doesn't necessarily keep a leader from making tough decisions that hurt some people. Decisive leaders can be hard-hearted, have a well-protected heart, or, like Lincoln, have a brave heart, but they don't have flabby or bleeding hearts.

The Future for Narcissistic Leaders

As long as we remain in a period of continual technological and social change, productive narcissists will inevitably emerge to grasp opportunities with new visions that pull in followers who hope for riches or to be part of something great.

A prime example: Craig Venter, who first mapped the human genome, may have failed at Celera, but after a three-year yacht trip around the world, he now promises to cure our addiction to oil by creating a designer microbe with "genes culled from the ocean to turn crops such as switch grass and cornstalks into ethanol." So he told the *Washington Post*'s Michael S. Rosenwald, adding, "We are on a crusade as much as it is an economic goal. This is one of those crusades that only works if it becomes profitable." You won't hear anything like that from the humble level 5s.

While the past few years have seen a pendulum swing back and forth from narcissistic to obsessive leaders, business researchers are now reporting that large companies need to be what Charles O'Reilly and Michael L. Tushman call *ambidextrous organizations*, combining mature operations with risky innovation. But where will they find the entrepreneurial productive narcissists who drive innovation? And how can narcissists survive in large, bureaucratic companies?

Bala Chakravarthy and Peter Lorange of IMD International, who have studied successful ambidextrous companies like Medtronics and Nestlé, find that young entrepreneurial visionaries survive only when sponsored by a courageous senior executive who puts his own credibility on the line. As noted in chapter 4, this kind of mentor kept Jack Welch at GE when he was a division manager. Without such a mentor, Welch would have either left or been shelved as too rebellious and abrasive for promotion.

There are other solutions for ambidextrous companies. Smart marketing types can buy a company to get the innovators. That's what Bob Iger of Disney did when he bought Pixar, getting John Lasseter as Chief Creative Officer and Steve Jobs as a board member.

All personality types with SI will find a way to partner with talent that complements their strengths. HP shareholders should hope that Mark Hurd, a productive obsessive who has succeeded in paring away the fat at HP, recruits innovative narcissists. By cost cutting and aggressively moving product, he has dramatically improved profitability, but all that can't create great new products that grow the company.

Questioning Popular Theories

As you read this book, you'll find that I question, explicitly or implicitly, four popular fashions in management theorizing: situational leadership, level-5 self-effacing leadership, emotional intelligence, and focusing solely on people's strengths.

These theories aren't all wrong, but I believe they are incomplete and can limit your ability to understand people and make wise decisions about them. The appeal of these theories is that they're optimistic and idealistic. It would make life easier if we could always change our style of leadership to fit the situation, but we can't. It would be inspiring if all the best leaders were humble and self-effacing, but they aren't. Employees would be happier if all the most successful leaders demonstrated emotional intelligence, but they don't. And it would make life more pleasant if we didn't have to pay attention to people's weaknesses, but we do. And the reason is that by viewing the whole person, not just strengths, we expand our knowledge and become better able to develop strengths in ourselves and others. We also are better equipped to avoid getting hurt by toxic leaders.

It's good to accentuate the positive, particularly if it helps to eliminate the negative. Notably, a number of narcissistic leaders have thanked me for emphasizing the positive potentials of their personalities, and a few have sought my help in building on those strengths, because when they do that, the negatives seem to lose their bite. In other words, when you coach narcissists who do want to improve themselves, the best strategy is to focus on growth, not their faults.

To conclude, I'm proposing that management theories need to take account of personality and context. Different personality types shine in different settings. Their approach to leadership may be right for one context but not another. But little attention has been paid by business theorists to understanding personality, and what little there is has focused on behavioral traits. After the publication of this book, Gerhard Gschwandter and I published an article in *SellingPower* describing how the different personality types typically deal with customers. In that piece, we introduced the concept of *Personality IQ*, the ability to understand personality, to see how people relate to others, and to perceive their strengths and weaknesses. This book can help you to improve your Personality IQ, but knowledge of types is only one part of the equation. It doesn't tell you the level of a person's productiveness and moral reasoning or emotional attitudes such as enthusiasm, envy, anger, fear, sadness, optimism, and so on. That requires a combination of intellect and emotional awareness or what I'd rather call a heart that listens—the ability to experience and recognize emotional attitudes.

In my next book, forthcoming from Harvard Business School Press, I'll write more about the role of personality in both leaders and followers in the changing context of our time.

Appreciation

This edition would not have been published without the support of enthusiastic readers. In particular, I appreciate the efforts of Jeff Kehoe, who championed the book at the Harvard Business School Press. He made the case for publication with testimony from Charles O'Reilly, Charles Handy, and Dr. Donald L. Nathanson, all of whom have made significant contributions to understanding people and organizations in their own writings. Thanks to Julia Ely, who edited this preface, and to Maria Stroffolino, who has patiently typed the many drafts.

Washington, D.C.
April 2006

NARCISSISTIC LEADERS

THE "CHANGE THE WORLD" PERSONALITY

C all to mind all the people you know—your business colleagues, your social set, even some of your heroes—and ask yourself this question: How many of them say that it's their personal goal to change the world? Plenty of people aspire to invent a product or start a new company or make a difference in their customers' lives, but to actually say you want to change the world? That's an extraordinary goal. What kind of person believes that he, through his ideas and the force of his own personality, can bring about the kind of changes that affect how people live and work? As it turns out, it takes a very unusual person.

I first noticed *how* unusual when I met Sidney Harman. Although I had studied and worked with thinkers who wanted to change the world, I was never convinced about their vision—that is, until Sidney Harman. Harman was a technology pioneer who manufactured stereo equipment and auto parts, eventually combining the two to create upscale audio systems for cars. It was 1973, and I was fresh from my experience interviewing managers at high-tech companies like Hewlett-Packard, DuPont, Intel, Texas Instruments, and IBM for my book *The Gamesman*. I thought I had heard the full range of corporate goals—satisfy customers, build better products, keep shareholders happy, increase profits, grow the company, even contribute to the social good. But I was unprepared for a CEO with a vision of such scope. Harman told me straight out during our first meeting: Just making profitable new technology and producing it cheaply wasn't enough; he had big ideas about how to humanize factory life. As he saw it, the entire relationship between labor and management, which was predicated on inequality and artificial hierarchies for the past hundred years, should be thrown out. He was thinking about a new system that would revolutionize the social structure of the factory. And then he said the words: He wanted to change the world. Did I want to help him do it?

I must have needed some work on my poker face back then, because right after he made his grandiose statement, Harman said: "You don't like me, do you?" I told him that it wasn't a question of like or dislike, I was just skeptical. I thought he sounded, at best, like a bleeding-heart liberal, and at worst like a pompous blowhard, and I told him so. But the funny thing is that I was hooked. My training is in psychoanalysis and anthropology, and I had been looking for a way to study how to improve the dehumanizing effects of factory life, so working with Harman was an opportunity I couldn't pass up. I ended up working with Harman on a groundbreaking study of the humanization of his factory in Bolivar, Tennessee.

Harman went on to create an international audio industry. And I filed away that phrase—"I want to change the world"—for years.

The next time I heard that statement from a CEO was in 1984. Pehr Gyllenhammar, the CEO of Volvo, set out to do away with the assembly line and replace it with teams of craftsmen. He had no intention of limiting this dramatic reorganization to Volvo; he wanted it to take place on a broad international scale that would change the factory forever. Soon after, I met Robert Johnson, now the richest African-American CEO, who told me that he was going to create an empire that would change the face of black entertainment. And all over the press in 1986, Steve Jobs made it clear that his new company, Next, wasn't just producing a simple desktop computer that kids could tap away at; he was creating a vehicle for students to have the greatest possible impact on society. A consultant to Next said, "We signed up with Steve because we were going to revolutionize education. . . . In the early days at Next, there was a sense of mission and crusade." At the time, these were scattershot examples, and I didn't really make any connection between them. But in the following decade, I began hearing more and more CEOs proclaiming that what they were doing wasn't making a better computer interface, creating new telecommunications systems, or bioengineering cheaper corn; what they were doing was changing the world.

In the mid to late '90s, a dramatic shift occurred, one that was impossible to ignore. The traditional corporate CEO who cut costs, improved productivity, and increased profitability was pushed aside by a new breed of visionary leader. The "change the world" personality went from being an interesting oddity, an anomaly, to a dominant player in the business community. What was once an extraordinary statement, the kind that landed Jeff Bezos on the cover of *Time,* was now a standard business-page pronouncement. Just consider how these high-profile leaders describe their corporate mission: Larry Ellison compares his misunderstood vision at Oracle to that of Galileo; Steve Case says that his special skill is "really believing in the medium and its possibilities and ability to change the world"; Bill Gates rarely discusses profits with his staff and the public, preferring to say: "What we aim to do is to make tools to make people's lives better"; and Robert Shapiro, formerly CEO of Monsanto, described his vision of genetically altered crops as "the single most successful introduction of technology in the history of agriculture, including the plow."

As new examples tumbled out, whether in my practice as a consultant to CEOs or in the business press, it became clear that this heralded a major change in the personality of the strategic leaders at the top. The personality type that so startled and fascinated me when I worked with Sidney Harman in the 1970s was now running the most innovative and influential companies. A new kind of visionary leader dominated our business landscape, and since business plays a much bigger role in our lives, so did these CEOs. Were you to review the cover of *Fortune* magazine over the years, the rise of the visionary CEO would be starkly evident. A composite of routine work life—the inner machinery of a factory, oil drums, a nameless worker, the VW logo—usually appears on the cover throughout the magazine's first fifty years after its launch in the 1930s. But as the millennium approaches, more CEOs make it on the cover solo, the logo or actual product of a corporation giving way to the CEO's well-known persona. The last five years of *Fortune* is a who's who of superstar CEOs—Jeff Bezos, Jim Clark, Bill Gates, Steve Jobs, Jack Welch, George Soros, Jürgen Schrempp, Michael Saylor, Craig Venter, Robert Shapiro, Robert Johnson, Andy Grove, Ross Perot,

Larry Ellison, Steve Case, Martha Stewart, Oprah Winfrey, Esther Dyson—all of whom, at one time or another, have been quoted inside the magazine's pages as saying, in one way or another, that they want to change the world.

When I first noticed the "change the world" personality growing in numbers and importance in the business community in the early '90s, I began to investigate the shared traits that distinguish these leaders from the CEOs of the past. I was also curious about what societal changes were taking place that encouraged and rewarded the "change the world" personality, pushing them to the top of the corporate hierarchy. Throughout my career as a student of human development and its relation to work, I've used an interdisciplinary approach, combining concepts from psychoanalysis, sociology, anthropology, economics, and history. My background as a psychoanalyst teaches me to look for patterns of behavior, drawing on family history and dynamics, peer relations, the factors that influence personality development, and, in particular, what I call productiveness or living up to one's potential. My training as an anthropologist directs me to observe the context in which certain personalities develop over time, cultural factors interacting with economic events and market forces. Over the years, I've used a variety of clinical methods, including structured interviews, Rorschach tests, detailed questionnaires, and psychotherapy. I began my work in companies as a participant observer of the anthropological "tribe" of the business community, and over time have become an observing participant as a business consultant to CEOs and managers.

The emergence of a new kind of leader caused me to reexamine all of my theories about leaders and personality. I went back to the psychoanalytic teachings of Sigmund Freud and the psychoanalyst and social philosopher Erich Fromm (1900–1980) and sifted through thirty years of experience inside corporations, working with CEOs both as a consultant and psychoanalyst. I rethought my understanding of historical figures and literature. What emerged surprised me. The psychological portrait of today's business leaders that takes into account their personality traits, describing how they achieve innovations, engage followers, and react to the euphoria of success as well as the stress of setbacks, most closely fits the normal personality type that Freud called narcissistic: "People belonging to this type impress others as being 'personalities'; they are especially suited to act as a support for others, to take on the role of leaders and to give a fresh stimulus to cultural development or to damage the established state of affairs." In other words, these are the type of people who are most likely to say that they want to change the world.

I'm using the term "narcissism" to describe some of the most important business leaders in the world; but how could a word that's become synonymous with all sorts of self-centered behavior—a sense of overall superiority and entitlement, a lack of empathy or understanding of others, the need for constant attention and admiration, and overall arrogance—apply to them? These days, in both the psychiatric field and in colloquial conversation, "narcissism" has become a term for egoism, egocentricity, or just plain bad manners. But I believe the concept of narcissism has been widely misunderstood ever since Freud coined it after Ovid's pathologically self-involved creature from Greek mythology. I want to bring about a radical new definition of the term and the way we think about leadership, and show you how your understanding of productive narcissism can help you.

If some of today's successful CEOs exhibit traits of narcissism but don't fully fit the negative stereotype, how would I describe them? The characteristic that I first noticed about them—the desire to change the world—is not necessarily a requirement of this type, but it is representative. Others may look at the world as a place that *needs* changing, but only a narcissist believes he can change it. The narcissistic personality, as I am defining it here, rejects how things *are* for how things *should be*. Narcissists do not react to the external world so much as they try to create it. I first thought about this when a narcissistic CEO I was counseling told me, "I didn't get here by listening to people." As soon as he said it, I realized that he was absolutely right. When he said "here," he didn't necessarily mean the top of a billion-dollar health care company (although that's exactly where he was); what he meant was that his entire life had been an exercise in shutting out the chorus of voices that told him what, or what not, to do. This is the best way I can describe the narcissist without going into a full psychoanalytic portrait: They never listen. Narcissistic vision always starts with a rejection of the status quo. Most of us are told what to do by various authority figures throughout our lives—go to school, get good grades, wear the right clothes, watch certain TV shows and movies, adopt the right mannerisms and language, learn a marketable skill, go to college, date and eventually marry the appropriate person, go to the "in" spot, network in a certain social set—and most of us do these things in order to fit into society or get ahead at work. Narcissists simply don't listen to or hear the demands of authority.

This is one way of explaining Abraham Lincoln's early form of rebellion—reading. With the perfect vision of hindsight, we look at

Lincoln's disciplined self-education and reading as a sign of his ambition, a desire to raise himself above the family business. But he came from an agrarian culture that placed a high value on farm labor and skills and almost no stock in reading or book learning. There was no reason for Lincoln to think that he was improving himself by reading; in fact, the historian Douglas Wilson's research shows that his contemporaries thought of his constant reading as a combination of laziness and defiance, a way of avoiding the labor of the family farm. His cousin said: "Lincoln was lazy—a very lazy man—He was always reading—scribbling—writing—Ciphering— writing Poetry." A neighbor and former boss said: "Abe was awful lazy: he worked for me—was always reading & thinking—used to get mad at him." His friends and family saw him as a rebel who didn't listen to his father or boss; I see him as a narcissist who rejected the social demands in favor of his own vision, one that wasn't reinforced or encouraged by his peers. Lincoln had his own idea of how he should live his life, and he went about achieving it in spite of the early, negative consequences. There's a long list of contemporary narcissists who dropped out of school. Jim Clark was kicked out of high school for telling his teacher to "go to hell"; Bill Gates left Harvard without graduating; Steve Jobs talked his way into Reed College (without paying for tuition or room and board) and then never went to class—all of which is usually misunder- stood as "youthful rebellion." But narcissists like Lincoln are *beyond* rebellion—they simply don't recognize any authority to rebel *against*.

Whenever I lecture on narcissistic leaders, I throw out some examples of narcissists, mixing contemporary business leaders with historical figures. Even after hearing the way I define "narcissism," people still revert to the old stereotype. Abraham Lincoln? He can't be a narcissist—he was an even-tempered altruist, a model of humility and presidential decorum. Bill Gates? Sure, we know he's got a huge ego and a tendency to put other people down, but look at him. He's such a geek—not at all vain or concerned with his image. And he gives so much of his money away to charities. Oprah Winfrey? She's so open about her doubts and fears, letting everyone know about her personal struggles with sexual abuse and her own body image.

Every time I hear reactions like this, I realize how hard it is for people to think of narcissism as anything but a negative. If you're like most people, you think a narcissist is a vain, self-centered egomaniac. But this is a description of behavior—and most likely, bad behavior—rather than a portrait of a personality type. For example: Your boss runs a small service company. He's an insecure jerk who has a tendency to check himself out in the mirror while fixing his thinning hair, makes you pick up his dry cleaning, and is constantly screaming: "How come I'm the only one who does anything right around here?" This person is probably not a narcissist; he's a rude, selfish egotist.

A true narcissist is the kind of person who (1) doesn't listen to anyone else when he believes in doing something and (2) has a precise vision of how things should be. A narcissist possesses this dual combination of traits, not one or the other; plenty of people who aren't narcissists never listen to anyone else (they are negativistic, closed-minded, or arrogant), and plenty of people have an idea of how things should be (they are often just know-it-alls or big talkers). It is the *combination* of a rejection of the status quo, along with a compelling vision, that defines the narcissist.

But what about people who fit this characterization yet are unable to follow through on any of their big ideas and dreams, never rising to the top? The answer: A narcissist may be either productive or unproductive. The difference is that the most productive narcissists, the ones who do change our world, have the charisma and drive to convince others to buy in to their vision or embrace a common purpose. They communicate a sense of meaning that inspires others to follow them, whereas the unproductive types retreat into their own world and blame others for their isolation. The three leaders I cited above—Lincoln, Gates, and Winfrey—clearly fit the model of the productive narcissist, creating new things and motivating others, whether it's recasting the meaning of the Civil War at Gettysburg, or generating more wealth and jobs than can be counted, or single-handedly revitalizing reading and teaching people to take control of their lives. In other words, productive narcissists have the ability to change society. They are the people who take the risks that others can't, or won't, dare; the most productive transform our world through politics, business, social action, or the arts. Throughout history, narcissistic leaders have emerged during periods of great upheaval, creating new order often out of chaos, with both positive and negative outcomes. During turbulent political and social times, narcissists such as Franklin Delano Roosevelt, Napoleon Bonaparte, Charles de Gaulle, Mao Tse-tung, and Mohandas Gandhi have brought about sweeping changes. Productive narcissists are wired for periods of rapid and disruptive change.

In fact, I believe that productive narcissists already play an important role in the daily working life of a great number of people; many of us work around, with, or for narcissists—and, just maybe, are narcissists ourselves. However, most people aren't aware of this, and the popular misconceptions about leadership don't help. In the '80s and '90s, a whole school of leadership thought emerged that can be summed up by Daniel Goleman's concept of "emotional intelligence." This leadership theory, strains of which can be found in business literature from Stephen Covey to Jim Collins, equates successful leadership with empathy, listening to others, sensitivity to feelings, anger and impulse control, and working through consensus. This is the business equivalent of wishful thinking—I've found that it may make for a nicer place to work, but emotional intelligence does not guarantee success, and in many cases actually hinders successful leadership, especially when leaders have to make tough decisions that hurt some individuals.

What these theories of leadership lack is an understanding of personality type and how it plays out in different kinds of businesses. Successful leadership can't be considered separately from its context; the type of leader who is effective in one kind of business often runs another into the ground. There is no one-size-fits-all formula for successful business leadership. The solid, down-to-earth, and empathetic CEOs who are praised by Goleman and Collins as leadership models are successful in essentially conservative companies that focus on retail, manufacturing, and cutting costs. I contend that an innovative, change-oriented business requires a different kind of leader, one who is willing to take risks in order to realize the potential inherent in new technologies, globalization, and the information age. The current disdain for celebrity leaders such as Jack Welch obscures his brilliant leadership lessons—his ability to make tough decisions about evaluating divisions, to fire people who can't keep up, and to indoctrinate the organization—all skills that are ill suited to a humble, empathetic, and self-effacing leader. As one CEO said to me, "If I opened myself to everyone, I'd be eaten alive."

To be fair to these business theorists, I was also guilty of wishful thinking about leadership for many years. Throughout the '70s and '80s, I wrote extensively about the personality type of the ideal leader to carry the workforce into this new era of technological change and knowledge workers. In my books *The Gamesman* and *The Leader*, I argued that effective leaders had to develop their hearts along with their heads. "If I had to choose one quality to distinguish the best new leaders, it is openness to criticism, the passion for continual self-development, which teaches the leader to value the development of others," I wrote in *The Leader* (1981). It wasn't until I worked with Pehr G. Gyllenhammar (CEO of Volvo) and Jan Carlzon (CEO of SAS) that I saw productive narcissism in the most innovative leaders. It was then that I realized that the ideal leader I wrote about in my books and articles was different from the CEOs I was counseling.

The dissonance between what business theorists, including myself, were saying and what was actually happening in the business world raised a lot of questions that I, frankly, was unable to answer. Why, in the late '80s and early '90s, were we seeing so many "change the world" personalities dominating the business environment? Why was their personality so different from the personality of business leaders as recently as a decade before? What traits distinguished them from the other personality types? When I started to piece together the characteristics that are common to this personality, I noticed that not only were people of this type extremely successful, making it to the top of the most innovative companies, but they were also prone to sudden failure, bringing the company down with them. Why did so many of them fail?

I was unhappy with the answers I came up with, and skeptical of the current business literature. I struggled to find a workable theory, one that matched what was going on inside innovative companies, where "emotional intelligence" was nowhere to be found in upper management. I listened to the frustration of people who worked with narcissists, the most intelligent of whom knew, intuitively, that the advice of the day didn't apply to their boss and gave them little or no help in dealing with this unique personality type. I saw board members and executive committees who had no clue what to do with their narcissistic CEOs: leaders who regularly made it into the press with their high-profile and controversial comments, dramatic turnaround strategies, and big claims for the future. Shareholders might be excited about the share price, but those close to the CEO were concerned about his erratic behavior, disregard for others, and inability to listen to anyone. As we approached the millennium, many innovative companies knew that they needed to change with the times or confront competitive failure. Boards of directors were faced with the challenge of placing their companies in the hands of CEOs whose personality, vision, and strategy was in tune with the times. But how did they know if their CEO would bring about the kind of change that propels the company into the future or brings it tumbling down? Was he a visionary or just slightly unhinged? Would it be better to go with a steady, no-nonsense helmsman like Warren Buffett or perhaps a strong relationship-builder like John Chambers?

This book is the result of my endeavor to formulate a theory of leadership that actually works in today's business environment, that takes into account the realities of singular personalities at the helm of corporations and other organizations who have created entire industries and philosophies, with their own persona serving as their driving force. The narrative structure of the book chronicles my own process of understanding not only the personality type of these visionary leaders but the impact they have on their organizations in particular and society in general. Each chapter is organized around a question or series of questions I asked myself in my work with leaders and their organizations: What are the various personality types? What are the strengths and weaknesses of each type in the workplace? What are the personality types of today's leaders? To help you understand personality types, I have provided a comprehensive questionnaire to evaluate your own type and those of your colleagues and boss. What is the narcissistic type, and why do I think it has been so misunderstood? What does it mean to be productive, to live up to your potential at work? How do productive narcissists mobilize their strengths to achieve their vision—and how are their weaknesses often an exaggeration of their strengths?

Equipped with a better understanding of the qualities that make the "change the world" personality such a compelling business leader, I began to question the relationship between these qualities and long-term success. Over the past five years, we've seen many narcissistic leaders assume high-profile CEO positions with their overarching vision and turnaround strategies; but all too often, they have been incapable of convincing their organizations to embrace their vision or turning their promises into a profitable and successful business. What does it take for this "change the world" personality, or any personality type for that matter, to *sustain* leadership in times of rapid and unpredictable change? To answer this question, I took a closer look at the long-term success stories in my own work, as well as leaders throughout history, across countries, cultures, and industries, who build sustained empires. I found little correlation between long-term success and the criteria that have been popularized by business theorists for predicting and measuring success. Take, for example, appointments based on stellar résumés. Too often, corporate board members look to someone who has succeeded in the past, but they fail to take into account the size, complexity, and type of the previous company and industry, and whether the CEO can translate a successful strategy to a different culture and organization. This was the case with C. Michael Armstrong, who produced immediate results at Hughes with DirecTV, results that did not predict his failure at the much larger, more complex, and differentiated culture of AT&T. Or they may gauge a CEO's success in an industry that is buoyed by a profitable business tide, making that company's executives look like stars. Carly Fiorina was tapped by HP when her previous company, Lucent, was on the rise; but would she have been given the CEO position when Lucent bottomed out? I don't think so.

I've come to believe that we're looking at leadership in the wrong way, that the leadership literature is seriously flawed, skewed toward the one-on-one relationships between leaders and individuals, such as the ability to connect to others with emotional support and listening skills promoted by *Emotional Intelligence* and *The 7 Habits of Highly Effective People*. Sustainable corporate leadership is not just a matter of personality and attitude toward workers and colleagues, as so many business theories maintain. When you take a look at the success stories, the common thread is not emotional intelligence, IQ, a proven track record at a different corporation, or similar personality traits. Instead, long-term success is best judged by the set of interrelated skills that I call strategic intelligence.

Rather than focusing on a leader's interpersonal relationships or how someone interacts with individuals, strategic intelligence looks at the ability of a leader to think systemically: to develop a systemic vision that takes into account the confluence of present and future social and economic trends; to partner with people and corporations that complement and further corporate goals; to implement a vision by developing and motivating a complex social and business system. Strategic intelligence gives employees, board members, and investors a new set of criteria for gauging the ability of leaders, to put aside seductive promises, a track record in an unrelated industry, and overall charisma in favor of the skills needed to both construct a strategic vision and turn it into a reality. Strategic intelligence takes the emphasis away from interpersonal skills and places it squarely on the difficult and often messy job of motivating a workforce to share the same goals, values, and vision of the CEO. I find it odd that, in an era of increasingly complex organizations and multinational corporations, business theorists and leaders have turned so readily to advice that stresses one-on-one relationships rather than the difficult task of building productive organizations and motivating today's workforce. A hundred years ago, Henry Ford showed his considerable strategic intelligence with a vision of an industrial social-business system, a functional hierarchy of an integrated production team and sales network. What motivated Henry Ford's frontline workers? The $5-a-day wage, the highest industrial pay scale for assembly-line jobs that were timed down to the second. Needless to say, times have changed; what worked for Henry Ford does not work in today's business environment. Strategic intelligence takes into account a workforce that isn't as malleable as we're led to believe—leaders can't just point employees to new piles of cheese or get them to be more productive by making the office a more pleasant place to "share." The traditional incentives of money, stock options, inspirational speeches, flexible hours, and a caring environment are not enough to motivate today's highly educated workforce. Strategic intelligence speaks directly to the challenges facing CEOs in an era dominated by complex global corporations made up of knowledge and service workers who must be motivated to think as well as to act, who have to be convinced about the corporate vision and their particular role in it.

For those of us who work for productive narcissists or are asked to advise them, what are some strategies for dealing with them in a business setting? And finally, should you even worry about working for a productive narcissist in the future, or have they gone the way of the wild tech wars of the late '90s? It is only through a thorough understanding of personality type that we are equipped to answer these questions and make decisions about the leaders we choose to elect, work for, and follow. During these turbulent times, it is essential that we have the tools to evaluate our leaders, especially the visionaries who have the ability to create sweeping social and economic reforms, bringing with them the promise of great change as well as the possibility of great danger.

ONE

RECOGNIZING
PERSONALITY TYPES

Let's start out with a question I have asked hundreds of people at work: Can you describe your personality? If you're like most people, you don't have a ready answer. You may cite temperament traits such as "upbeat," "reserved," and "outgoing," or behavioral traits such as "dependable," "caring," and "hardworking." Some people focus on a key part of who they are, like "I play to win" or "I never give up." You may type yourself according to a work role—engineer, designer, manager—or a lifestyle label—parent, spouse, single. Very few people think of themselves as having a personality type that encompasses how they habitually meet the challenges of work and social relationships, the deep-rooted way they resolve the human needs to survive and prosper physically and emotionally, to make life satisfying and meaningful.

Imagine that you work in a small, successful technology company. You report to a manager who is known throughout the office as the "numbers guy." He sets the budget for your department, keeps an eye on the bottom line, and runs the office infrastructure. If you have a proposal for a new initiative, you know you won't get anywhere with him unless you've done your financial homework—worked up a spreadsheet or a detailed profit-and-loss report. How do you know this? Because you've seen how he reacts whenever he's approached without the financials in place; he can be rude, dismissive, even blow up at anyone who ignores his need for facts and figures. You and your colleagues like to complain about him, thinking that his obsession with the numbers gets in the way of more creative or spontaneous ideas. Nevertheless, you take his concerns into account whenever he pops into your office to ask a quick question, or when you need something from him, or whenever you're called upon by him to make a snap decision at a staff meeting. There's a pattern to his behavior, a typical, habitual response that you and your colleagues have noticed over time. He's not just playing a role; you think he's expressing his personality. You may even have a name for his behavior, calling him "anal," or a "little picture" person, behind his back.

You are already engaged in personality typing; in fact, you use these "typing" skills all the time, without even being aware of them. You may not have a manager or colleague who is exactly like this "numbers man" (although many people do), but surely you have a boss, coworker, or colleague whose behavior you can predict with a degree of accuracy. You have a good idea of what certain people will do in any given situation, how some of your colleagues will react to the stress of a group meeting, the demands of a deadline, or a particularly hard-driving boss. You might say about one of your coworkers, "She would *never* disagree with our boss," meaning that, in your experience, it's not in her nature; you've never seen her do it, and you can't imagine her acting differently. You notice the little smile of pleasure she shows when the boss nods approvingly at her positive statement—or how she turns off when a colleague looks for support to challenge the boss. Even if you can't come up with a label for her behavior, you've done some mental accounting of her personality, and this unconscious typing plays a part in all of your encounters with her.

Each and every day, we are confronted with a flood of people whose personality quirks and qualities baffle and intrigue us, challenging our own ability to "deal" with them, to decide, in a moment, how to act and react in a variety of settings—at home, in school, on the job, and even on the street. We intuitively recognize that there are different personality types, but there is a much better way of looking at people, a deeper and more precise understanding of personality type that can make you more effective in handling all of your relationships, especially in your career. This book is the result of my own endeavors to make sense of personality type, to provide diagnostic and conceptual tools for recognizing and understanding the different types. This "typing" is not a mere intellectual pursuit or parlor game to be played for fun, nor is it meant to be reductive; I believe that a better way of seeing personality can have a profound effect on our view of human nature and the way we interact with people. The example I opened with was meant to show just how much we use this information to bring order and sense to the profusion of personalities we encounter on a daily basis.

Since information about type influences your own behavior, it can only be to your benefit to have a greater understanding of personality type when managing your relationships. The ability to recognize personality type can be learned, and so can applying these insights to your career. When people come to me for coaching, they usually ask: What should I do? What steps should I take to be more successful? I never give advice without first determining an individual's personality type, then exploring the qualities of that type; once a client has a better grasp of his or her own type, we can strategize together. There is no one-size-fits-all career advice. It depends on personality type. Before you can fully understand your own potentialities and shortcomings, how they can work in concert with the personalities of others, and how you can become more productive, you need to define and understand your own personality.

An example from my own work makes clear that an understanding of personality type can have dramatic and lasting effects on your work life. I've been working for the last year with a businesswoman—the Professional Woman—and recently asked her to describe the effect that fresh insight into personality has had on her career. She immediately said that it had changed "everything," that she now sees personality type in everyone, including herself, and that this rush of readily usable data had sharpened her judgment and impacted how she handles a multitude of situations. She told me one particular story about her partner, a difficult and self-centered manager, who was arguing with one of her colleagues. After a few strained exchanges, the boss shouted in frustration, "Why can't you be more like the Professional Woman and just ignore what I say!" The Professional Woman used to be the one who had a contentious relationship with her partner, always sparring with him over the right way to handle the business. She used to spend a lot of time trying to change her partner's personality, to fight it, always hoping he would conform to her expectations. No longer: She has become the office model of how to deal with the boss and his personality. This important shift in office dynamics didn't come about through self-help books or psychotherapy (although she had tried those in the past); it was a result of learning more about her own type and that of her partner, and applying some of the lessons of typing to her day-to-day encounters. Only in the last year has she figured out, with a better knowledge of personality, that it is in her strategic interest to ignore a lot of what her partner says in the moment and phrase her own ideas and concerns in a way that allows him to respond positively. Knowledge of personality has allowed her to be a much better partner, a collaborator in the true sense of the word.

This is the kind of result I've seen in most of the people I've counseled. A psychoanalytic understanding of personality type brings something that was only dimly seen into sharp focus. Many of my clients have moments of "aha," when they recognize a pattern or dynamic. Then they don't have to be told how to react to or deal with people; it becomes obvious. I'm confident about the usefulness and importance of personality types because I have seen case after case when a know-it-all CEO starts to listen, when a needy and dependent human resource manager starts to stand up for himself, when a consultant who always checks the way the wind is blowing challenges the client—when certain personalities take the best of what their type has to offer and become more productive. These are the moments when a client realizes that he can change more than his behavior—that his new knowledge about personality can change his entire way of dealing with life.

When I began my psychoanalytic career in 1961, I was a skeptic about personality type, even with my academic background in

Freudian psychology. It was true that I could spot temperamental differences, how some people could be called outgoing and others shy, or how typical pathologies, such as obsessive worrying, were woven into the fabric of certain people's character. But I thought that "typing" people, breaking the seemingly limitless personalities into rigid and narrowly defined categories, stripped human beings of their individuality, took away the qualities that made them irreducibly, ineffably, *them*. It wasn't until I worked with the psychoanalyst Erich Fromm, whose books *Escape from Freedom* and *Man for Himself* dealt with personality types, that I began to challenge my own thinking. Fromm and I had long discussions about personality types—Fromm speaking in favor of them, I against. No matter how much he tried to persuade me of the importance of personality type, I remained unconvinced, unwilling to see personality types as anything but robotic categories that deprived people of the freedom to choose who and what they wanted to be. While late-night conversations and theorizing didn't sway me, my fieldwork, the systematic interviews that I helped conduct with 850 people in a Mexican village, did. Fromm sent me out with a questionnaire that asked people what they most liked and disliked about their work, their concept of love, how they thought a father and a mother should experience love, the people they most admired and why. I also asked them to describe their dreams, their children, and what they thought about disobedience or stealing. I spent about two hours with each person, and once the people believed I was really interested in understanding them, they opened up. Most of them had never considered these questions, but once they did, they started to learn about themselves and their values. It was only against the background of the extensive interviews that I saw distinct patterns of behavior emerge, take shape. I also observed how children were raised and began to understand why different types develop early in a child's life. It took observing, questioning, and talking to many people who lived and worked and grew up in almost exactly the same environment for me to see that different types continually, habitually react in similar ways, especially to the challenges of work and social relationships. I realized that my old way of thinking was akin to calling every single color simply "color," rather than recognizing the distinctive hues of blue, red, and yellow. The comparison to color is not chosen lightly, because while people, like colors, are often a mix of different types, one usually predominates.

In my consulting work, I've found that the best way to illustrate to clients that personality type actually exists is for them to determine their *own* personality types with the questionnaire on page 26. I've used this questionnaire with executives to begin a conversation about how personality plays out in the workplace and influences leadership. Toward the same end, I encourage you to complete the questionnaire to determine your own type. To get the most out of this questionnaire, try to put aside your ideas about the categories or behaviors that you usually label successful or good or desirable. Think carefully about each question, and respond in a way that reflects how you, not some idealized version of you, actually behave. This is by no means easy. As a psychoanalyst, I'm a participant in people's struggle to see themselves as they really are. Those who are better equipped usually have spent some time and work on self-reflection and honesty, and the questionnaire is meant to aid that process. The description of personality types that I present later in the book will allow you to interpret the results.

That said, it's still hard to see yourself as others do. Even if you're as honest as possible, your coworkers or colleagues might have other ideas about you. The way to get around this is to complete the questionnaire first, then ask a colleague or friend whom you trust to complete it "for you"—that is, to answer the questions as they see you. You can then compare the results and see exactly where you may be lacking in self-knowledge, which will help you to arrive at an honest appraisal of your behavior and its strong and weak points. People who do this are often surprised by the results, motivated to learn more about themselves, and interested in how they can become more productive. Helping people to understand themselves and become more productive has been my professional purpose throughout my career: working as a child therapist in Boston, coaching teenage boys in a Mexican village, practicing as a psychoanalyst in Mexico City and Washington, D.C., and finally working with all levels within organizations, from factory workers and telephone operators to middle managers and CEOs. In every case, the people who were open to seeing themselves clearly, including their defects, were best able to free themselves from their hard-wired past and develop and grow into the people they wanted to be, to determine their future. A goal of this book is to facilitate your quest for self-knowledge as well as your understanding of the people you work with.

A note on the methodology: The questionnaire breaks personality or character into four types that I've adapted from the work of Sigmund Freud and Erich Fromm. The questions are based on hundreds of interviews I've conducted with managers in more than twenty countries, particularly in my work with Hewlett-Packard, IBM, AT&T, Asea Brown Boveri (ABB), and Volvo, as well as professional managers in health care, the federal government, and local law enforcement. The evaluation of the responses is in the appendix, and more complete descriptions of each type are laid out in the next chapter.

Circle the number that represents your answer to each question:

HOW WELL DOES THIS DESCRIBE YOU?

NEVER	ALMOST NEVER	SELDOM	SOMETIMES	FREQUENTLY	ALMOST ALWAYS

1. I want my work to further my own development.

0	1	2	3	4	5

2. I try to develop a vision for the ideal future of the business or organization.

0	1	2	3	4	5

3. I am an idealistic person.

0	1	2	3	4	5

4. I am satisfied at work if my job allows a great deal of autonomy.

0	1	2	3	4	5

5. I follow the rule that practice makes excellence.

0	1	2	3	4	5

6. I adapt easily to people I like.

0	1	2	3	4	5

7. I've developed my own view about what is right and wrong.

0	1	2	3	4	5

8. I see myself as a free agent.

0	1	2	3	4	5

9. I make my bosses into colleagues.

0	1	2	3	4	5

10. I adapt myself to continual change.

0	1	2	3	4	5

11. I believe I should take the initiative more.

0	1	2	3	4	5

12. Whatever my job, I try to provide high-quality work.

0	1	2	3	4	5

13. I try to keep my skills marketable.

0	1	2	3	4	5

14. I have a lot of aggressive energy I need to direct.

0	1	2	3	4	5

15. I keep my views to myself because I want to avoid an argument.

0	1	2	3	4	5

16. I put so much energy into responding to others that I feel I lose my sense of self.

0	1	2	3	4	5

17. The best boss for me is a good facilitator.

0	1	2	3	4	5

18. I try to be tough so I won't seem too soft.

| 0 | 1 | 2 | 3 | 4 | 5 |

19. I am bothered when there is a lack of neatness.

| 0 | 1 | 2 | 3 | 4 | 5 |

20. I find that the market gives me feedback on my value.

| 0 | 1 | 2 | 3 | 4 | 5 |

21. I have conversations with myself to clarify what I should do.

| 0 | 1 | 2 | 3 | 4 | 5 |

22. The best boss for me is like a good father who recognizes my achievements.

| 0 | 1 | 2 | 3 | 4 | 5 |

23. I want to feel appreciated.

| 0 | 1 | 2 | 3 | 4 | 5 |

24. I try to keep my options open.

| 0 | 1 | 2 | 3 | 4 | 5 |

25. I compare myself to highly successful people.

| 0 | 1 | 2 | 3 | 4 | 5 |

26. I like to collect things.

| 0 | 1 | 2 | 3 | 4 | 5 |

27. I believe the best decision will result from consensus.

0	1	2	3	4	5

28. I would rather be loved than admired.

0	1	2	3	4	5

29. I like to feel needed by people I care about.

0	1	2	3	4	5

30. What I like about games is the challenge to improve my personal score.

0	1	2	3	4	5

31. I admire creative geniuses.

0	1	2	3	4	5

32. I have difficulty completing projects on time because I want my work to be perfect.

0	1	2	3	4	5

33. Loyalty does not get in my way of doing what is best to succeed.

0	1	2	3	4	5

34. I feel alone and isolated.

0	1	2	3	4	5

35. I am thorough rather than quick.

0	1	2	3	4	5

36. I don't give in when I feel I am in the right.

0	1	2	3	4	5

37. I trust people.

0	1	2	3	4	5

38. I use organizations as instruments to achieve my goals.

0	1	2	3	4	5

39. I keep up with the latest trends.

0	1	2	3	4	5

40. I follow my ideas despite what people say.

0	1	2	3	4	5

41. My sense of security comes from supportive family and friends.

0	1	2	3	4	5

42. I judge people according to strict moral standards.

0	1	2	3	4	5

43. Before I accept an idea, I check it out with people I respect.

0	1	2	3	4	5

44. The best boss for me makes the work group into a kind of family.

0	1	2	3	4	5

45. I feel I get taken in by people I've trusted.

0	1	2	3	4	5

46. I like to help people.

0	1	2	3	4	5

47. I define quality in terms of what experts value.

0	1	2	3	4	5

48. I don't act until I have fully weighed the alternatives.

0	1	2	3	4	5

49. I evaluate behavior in terms of what is considered appropriate by the people I respect.

0	1	2	3	4	5

50. I create meaning for myself and others at work.

0	1	2	3	4	5

51. I am building a network of others who share my values.

0	1	2	3	4	5

52. I enjoy loving more than being loved.

0	1	2	3	4	5

53. I enjoy being part of a cooperative group.

0	1	2	3	4	5

54. I feel better when I save rather than spend.

0	1	2	3	4	5

55. I would rather be admired than liked.

0	1	2	3	4	5

56. I am very tolerant about what others do.

0	1	2	3	4	5

57. I like bringing people together.

0	1	2	3	4	5

58. I sense when people are working against me.

0	1	2	3	4	5

59. I spend a lot of time on details.

0	1	2	3	4	5

60. I like to associate with the top people.

0	1	2	3	4	5

61. I spend a lot of time chatting with my friends.

0	1	2	3	4	5

62. My creativity depends on maintaining my freedom.

0	1	2	3	4	5

63. I enjoy interactions where I can learn something new.

0	1	2	3	4	5

64. I feel I give in too much.

0	1	2	3	4	5

65. Once I start talking I tend to go on.

0	1	2	3	4	5

66. I approach my work as a means to a self-fulfilling life.

0	1	2	3	4	5

67. I try to know everything about everything that impacts my business.

0	1	2	3	4	5

68. I like to have a schedule and keep to it.

0	1	2	3	4	5

69. The best thing about playing games is having a good time with my friends.

0	1	2	3	4	5

70. I seek out people who can contribute to my plans.

0	1	2	3	4	5

71. I test out my ideas systematically.

0	1	2	3	4	5

72. To be successful, I try to look good.

0	1	2	3	4	5

73. People at work are either with me or against me.

0	1	2	3	4	5

74. I like to keep up with old friends.

0	1	2	3	4	5

75. I rely on certain people who care about me.

0	1	2	3	4	5

76. I put my own spirit into my products and creations.

0	1	2	3	4	5

77. My sense of security is based on my reputation in my field.

0	1	2	3	4	5

78. My self-esteem depends on being seen as successful.

0	1	2	3	4	5

79. I like to develop ways to improve efficiency.

0	1	2	3	4	5

80. I admire people who have helped those in need.

0	1	2	3	4	5

PATTERNS OF PERSONALITY

What Is Narcissism?

The term "narcissism" has a relatively short history. It is derived from the myth of Narcissus—the classic story of a boy named Narcissus who can't stop staring at his reflection in a pond, and as a result, dies—that is found in the *Metamorphoses*, a first-century A.D. epic poem by Ovid. The evolution from the proper noun Narcissus to the kind of word we toss around every day took some time. It wasn't until the beginning of the twentieth century that the narrative of Narcissus was first used by students of human behavior to describe a sexual perversion and a psychological attitude. After a few brief appearances in the academic literature, the word "narcissism" was appropriated by Freud, who initially limited it to a theory explaining male homosexuality. But Freud was rarely content with his theories of human nature, which were under constant revision and adaptation, changing with fresh insights from his ongoing work with patients. This was the case with narcissism, a concept that Freud defined in different ways throughout his life; what he first treated as a perversion or a pathology, he later came to see as one of the three normal personality types—the one, it's worth noting, he thought best described himself.

In less than a hundred years, the word "narcissism" has evolved from a psychological term to a commonly used word with a commonly held meaning. "Narcissism" may have entered the vernacular because of Freud, but it is rarely used, either in its most popular sense or clinically, the way Freud intended it. One reason for this is that Freud's own position on narcissism kept changing throughout his life. But this can scarcely account for the wide misunderstanding of the concept; few people who use the word on a regular basis are familiar with Freud's teachings. A better explanation for the common currency of "narcissism" is the enduring power of the myth of Narcissus. Whenever we say "narcissistic," we usually mean someone who looks and acts a lot like Narcissus. Freud's psychologically precise descriptions, in any of their forms, can't compete with the image of someone whose obsession with himself is so complete it brings about his destruction.

It's no wonder, then, that "narcissism" is one of those words that means a broad assortment of entirely negative characteristics, a synonym for every sort of self-absorbed, self-centered behavior. This was never Freud's intention, but before we look at the genesis of Freud's theories, it's important to understand exactly how we define narcissism today. For example, on July 4, 2001, reporters asked

George W. Bush what Independence Day means to him. His answer—"Well, it's an unimaginable honor to be the president during the Fourth of July of this country"—prompted *The New York Times* editorial columnist Frank Rich to write: "Mr. Bush's response was a perfect summation of the man we've seen in office so far: the Second Boomer President, a narcissist who can't see past himself." Rich went on to describe how Bush is so out of touch that he believes that Vice President Dick Cheney's pacemaker operation would help others with heart disorders get the treatment they need—even if most of the American public can't afford a $30,000 heart device or don't have the health insurance to cover the costly operation.

In this context, we all understand what Frank Rich means when he calls Bush "narcissistic," whether we agree with his political opinion of Bush or not. He means that Bush sees the world through his own prism of privilege and is incapable of empathizing with the average American. And he means that Bush has such a self-centered, "arrogant worldview" that he looks at the Fourth of July as a comment on his own achievements rather than a celebration of the country's history.

Another example appeared in *The New York Times* only a few weeks later. Under the title "Sea of Self-Love, but Who's Drowning?" Jon Pareles gives Madonna's live concert a bad review, maintaining that she performed essentially for herself rather than for the audience that filled Madison Square Garden. But, Pareles writes, "If she's narcissistic, her narcissism is backed up by the fact people have been watching her for all those years." Ever since she first told Dick Clark in 1983 that it was her personal ambition to "rule the world," Madonna has personified the grab bag of negative traits that fall under the broad category of narcissism: vanity, an overwhelming preoccupation with one's own image, and the constant need for the admiration and attention of others.

And a final example: On September 26, 2001, Maureen Dowd wrote, "After all these finicky years of fighting everyday germs and inevitable mortality with fancy products, Americans are now confronted with the specter of terrorists in crop dusters and hazardous-waste trucks spreading really terrifying, deadly toxins like plague, smallpox, blister agents, nerve gas and botulism. . . . Judy Miller, a *Times* reporter who is one of the authors of the surprise new best seller *Germs: Biological Weapons and America's Secret War,* said she had been deluged with calls from people asking how they can protect themselves. 'It's the ultimate freakout,' she said. 'I have to tell them that they cannot do a lot as individuals, that it won't work to take Cipro every time they get the sniffles. This narcissistic, us-me culture is slowly starting to understand that they will have to act as a collective on public health to get the vaccines and trained nurses.'" In this case, narcissism is a stand-in for individualism and selfishness, caring only about one's own interests as opposed to the public good.

The interesting thing about these references is not whether they are right or wrong, or an accurate commentary on George W. Bush's political career, the artistic merits of Madonna's live concert, or how we can protect ourselves from bioterrorism. What's striking is how much we rely on the word "narcissism" to conjure up a picture of self-absorption, someone who is arrogant, haughty, grandiose, thinks he or she is superior and deserving of special treatment, requires excessive admiration, is oblivious to the feelings of others, lacks empathy, has a sense of entitlement, takes advantage of others, overestimates his or her abilities, and acts snobby, disdainful, or patronizing. This is the everyday, colloquial concept of narcissism, but it is also the meaning of the term that has been adopted by the psychiatric profession: Every single one of these descriptive words and phrases is lifted from the DSM-IV under the diagnostic criteria used by psychiatrists, therapists, and insurers for Narcissistic Personality Disorder.

This use permeates our culture. Think of the last few times you either heard or said the term "narcissistic" in conversation. It may have been about the waiter who keeps staring at the mirror behind your head instead of taking your order, or perhaps an egocentric actor you read about in *People* magazine, but more than likely, it was about someone you know or work with who is self-centered, the boss who makes you pick up his laundry, or the coworker who takes credit for the work you do on her behalf, the ones who are the butt of the joke "Enough about me, what do *you* think of my last book, picture, etc?" or who say, "What have you done for me lately?" and "Don't you know who I am?" In whatever instance you said or heard "narcissism," I am sure that it was an insult, a put-down.

As you can see, "narcissism" has become a linguistic garbage pail piled so high with entirely negative characteristics that it has lost its descriptive power, depriving us of Freud's insights and their usefulness in understanding different personalities. It is my aim to liberate the concept of narcissism from the negative, to show that it is not an illness or a description of bad behavior, but a personality type, and like any personality, it can be productive or unproductive, creative or destructive, healthy or sick, generous or selfish. "Narcissism," as a psychological term, should not be used as a stand-in for bad manners or rude, self-centered behavior. Anyone, of any personality type, can be selfish, self-centered, overly ambitious, lacking in empathy, or power hungry; narcissistic personalities have not cornered the market on these qualities.

I think it's useful to go back to the examples from the *Times* and pin down the meaning of the words, to describe them for what they are instead of heaping them all under the rubric of "narcissism." As Bush is described by Frank Rich, he thinks the world revolves around him; this is egocentric. He can't see another point of view; this is lacking in empathy or imagination. He believes he is above certain things; this is arrogant and superior. He has a sense of entitlement; this is presumptuous. In the article on Madonna, she is preoccupied with her own image; this is vain. She has a high opinion of herself; this is conceited. She needs to be the center of attention; this is self-centered. She thinks she can do whatever she wants; this is haughty. She thinks she's worthy of attention; this is grandiose. She wants her life to be recorded; this is image-conscious. And in the case of Judy Miller's comment, an us-me culture is selfish; it is self-serving; it is individualistic; it is small-minded. Add up all these separate descriptions of behavior, and I contend that you still don't have a narcissistic personality. What you have is exactly what is being described, behavior that can be attributed, at one time or another, to any type of personality.

I believe that the concept of narcissism is more precise, in the late Freudian sense of a personality type, than the way it is used today. I want to expand our perception of narcissism, refine our thinking about it, give new shape and definition to a word that has been devalued over time. Why? Freud said it best in the paper that is the basis for my understanding of narcissism. He wrote that descriptions of personality are useful if they (1) are consistent with what we observe about human behavior, and (2) if they help us to understand and explain human behavior. Restoring Freud's framing of narcissism as a personality type satisfies both of these criteria: It is consistent with what I've observed in my work as a psychoanalyst, anthropologist, and business consultant; and it helps explain revolutionary leaders, the personalities who bring about change, and the sudden rise and fall of these personalities in today's most innovative companies.

Freud created a vocabulary, gave us the words to speak about personality, affixing names to the complex and conflicted set of responses that make up human behavior. Freud discovered a universal set of personality types that expands our understanding of ourselves and others, that improves our ability to predict behavior. We may like to believe that we create and control who we are, but Freud recognized that there is a central engine of self, a part of our personality that is shaped by forces that are hard-wired into our unconscious. This core personality plays the role that instinct does in lower animals; cats know to attack mice because they are programmed that way. Similarly, we reflexively react to certain stimuli in the same way, over and over again, rather than respond to everything as if it were a new experience. Why? Because without a core personality, we would be overwhelmed whenever we are faced with the unpredictability of events and other people; our emotions would swamp us in indecision and constant crisis. To this core self we add the attitudes and values that we learn from our parents, peer group, and the people we encounter throughout the life cycle. This is our personality, the typical, habitual way we relate to the world, control and direct our passions, and shape and discipline our talents. To some extent, personality changes and adapts throughout our lives, with maturation, the challenges we face, the friends, family, and work we choose, the decisions to have and raise children, our religious beliefs, and the habits we develop, all of which are influenced by how well we understand ourselves. This is what we mean when we say that every person is unique. Yet even with our various responses to the flux and dynamic changes of the life cycle, there is a pattern of behavior that is set early in life and that we share with many other people.

The first time Freud named these repetitive patterns as a personality type was in his 1908 paper "Character and Anal Eroticism." In his clinical work with patients, Freud observed that three distinct and emotionally charged behaviors—excessive neatness, stinginess, and obstinacy—had a tendency to cluster and cohere into one type of person that he called the "anal character." Today, everyone knows exactly what you mean when you call someone anal; it calls up an entire personality type with the economy of one word.

Freud first treated narcissism as a personality type in his 1910 psychosexual biography of Leonardo da Vinci. At this early stage in his thinking about narcissism, Freud limits the actual use of the term to a theory of homosexuality, drawing a connection between the myth of Narcissus and the same-sex love of the homosexual. Although Freud's initial use of the term "narcissism" was narrowly construed, this portrait of Leonardo is filled with insight into the creative personality, describing the innovative personality, the creative genius, in *opposition* to social and sexual norms, that is, in terms of narcissism. Freud wasn't able to connect his observations about creative genius into a coherent theory of narcissism until much later, but he lays the groundwork in his commentary on the life and work of Leonardo da Vinci, a prototypical visionary.

Freud added to and adapted his theories of narcissism in 1914 in a long, discursive essay called "On Narcissism," in which he moved beyond the idea of narcissism as a sexual perversion and saw a different form of narcissism—primary narcissism—as not only normal but essential to self-preservation. We all need primary narcissism, "a measure of which may justifiably be attributed to every living creature," which saves us from thinking that we're inconsequential or expendable. Some people, however, go on to develop secondary narcissism, moving from healthy self-preservation to infantile feelings of omnipotence, placing their own wishes and desires above other people's, and developing an idealized sense of self that they love and adore. Secondary narcissism, Freud theorized, prevents mature love and healthy interpersonal relationships.

It wasn't until 1931 that Freud described narcissism as one of three normal personality types in a brief paper called "Libidinal Type." This four-page essay is the basis for my human typologies and is one of the rare instances that Freud wrote about the "normal" personality. Earlier in his career, Freud worked almost entirely with people who were disturbed or deranged, whose lives were far from what we call "normal." Although there is a relationship between character disorders and normal personalities, we can't extrapolate theories of normalcy from illness; the "wolfman" or the "ratman" (Freud's case histories) don't teach us about people who are highly functional, whether they're CEOs or farmers. Freud's "normal" personality types, on the other hand, can tell us a great deal about people who are working at the top of their capabilities.

Freud's three normal personality types are: erotic, obsessive, and narcissistic. To these three, Erich Fromm added a fourth type, the marketing personality, for people who adapt their personalities to the demands of the market. The remainder of this chapter is devoted to a description of the types and how to recognize them, both in ourselves and in our colleagues in the business world. The *erotic* (which is not a sexual term) is a person for whom loving and being loved are the most important thing. At best, he is caring; at worst, he is dependent. The *obsessive* is the conservative character who preserves order and maintains moral values. The *narcissist* is the type of person who impresses us as a personality, who disrupts the status quo and brings about change. These are not arbitrary types; they have to do with the broad categories of basic human needs and desires: to be loved and admired, to be productive, to have order and stability, to innovate and change, to adapt and fit into society.

Freud recognized that while there are an infinite variety of personalities, one dominant type explains better than the others a person's approach to work and relationships. I believe a good way to understand these types is as they relate to social control: What are the rules that govern your behavior? Who makes those rules, and which do you choose to follow? How do you internalize those rules? Or do you make your own rules, and why? How do you control your impulses? Do you listen to voices of people you interact with or voices in your head? Are these the voices of your mother, your father, your friends, or your mentors? What about your boss or your coworkers? In other words, what part of society does or does not control your behavior?

The Erotic Personality

The erotic personality, which Freud named after *eros*, one of the Greek words for love, describes the kind of people who are driven by loving and being loved. Productive erotics want to help and care for people, but more than that, they want to be *seen* by others as helpers, to be recognized for their good deeds, to be loved and appreciated more than respected or admired.

Erotics dominate the social services, or what I call the caring fields—teaching, nursing, social work, mental health, and therapy—and service industries, careers that involve personal management, nurturing creativity and growth, encouraging others to make more of their lives, and emotional hand-holding. They're usually not bureaucrats, high-level politicians (although they often serve on community boards or in local government), experts, or business analysts—anything that emphasizes the technical or "cold" aspects of work as opposed to the human or personal. I've never worked with an erotic CEO of an innovative or high-tech company; in my experience, they just don't exist. When erotics run organizations, it's usually in the caring fields. I recently gave a seminar on personality type where I met an erotic CEO, a physician who organizes and leads a team of doctors who provide emergency medical service to local hospitals, a perfect use of this CEO's erotic need to care for people and get the acclaim and affirmation that come with the job. While erotics are usually not in the headlines or high-profile leadership positions, they are all around us, providing the basic services that build communities: schools, hospitals, and human resources. At their most productive, erotics bring people together, making

connections and facilitating interdependence. They keep our services running, on both an organizational and personal level, by teaching our children; caring for the elderly; helping displaced, homeless,
or poor people; and on a smaller scale, setting up this friend with
that one, lending a hand with moving, or coming over to cook dinner for a sick colleague. They never like to say no to a favor or turn
down someone in need; it makes them feel loved and appreciated
when they're asked to help out or give up some of their own time
and energy for someone else. They thrive on mutual cooperation,
trusting and relying on friends and family for a sense of security.

This means that erotics are our biggest schmoozers (with the
exception of some networking marketing personalities). They love to
chat up friends and gossip about what's going on, running up big
phone bills and e-mail hours. They enjoy conviviality for its own sake
rather than for career networking. They're the kind of people we
often call "touchy–feely," always asking you how you're doing, won-
dering if they can lend a hand or help you through a hard time. They
press for the intimate or emotional details of your life, and they want
to be included in your inner circle. At work, they like to turn the
office into a surrogate family where everyone is allowed to be heard
and voice their opinions and feelings. I saw this at Volvo, where an
erotic team leader created a tight-knit family that went so far as to
call her "mother." This "cocooning" attracts other erotics who want
the feeling of familial security on the job, a workplace mafia that pro-
tects their own, keeping them safe from threats and invasion.

Our most well-known erotics are in the media and performing
arts, positions that involve audience reaction and approval: Judy
Garland, Marilyn Monroe, Elizabeth Taylor, and Princess Diana all
fed off the adoration of their fans. Liz Taylor has devoted herself

to her causes just as much as to her many husbands. Once she left an unsatisfying marriage, Princess Diana came into her own with her humanitarian work with AIDS patients and war zones in the Middle East. Television entertainment show hosts, such as Regis Philbin, are almost all erotics; the Television Food Network is filled with erotics who want to entertain you and feed you all at the same time. Some of our most talented and successful musicians are erotic personalities: Bobby McFerrin, Wynton Marsalis, and Yo-Yo Ma share their joy and brilliance with their audience, splitting their time between their own career and their work developing and nurturing young musicians and creative talents. The dancer and choreographer Jacques D'Amboise is an erotic personality whose life's work is to inspire young people through the love and mastery of dance, giving them the confidence to follow their own passion. Eve Ensler, the writer and performer of *The Vagina Monologues,* appears to be an erotic personality who has united other actresses and artists in her mission to end violence against women.

The downside of the erotic personality is dependency, in all its forms: neediness, emotional clinging, an inability to leave a bad relationship, and what is popularly known as "codependency." Erotics are subject to brushfire enthusiasms and instant gratification. This makes them particularly vulnerable to addictions. Many of the erotic women I've used as examples were dependent on drugs and alcohol as well as the people in their lives. Freud writes that erotics are "dominated by the fear of loss of love and are therefore especially dependent on others who may withhold their love from them." The erotic strength of trust can turn into the weakness of unquestioning gullibility that leads to inevitable disillusion; erotics often feel used by people who let them down. In the workplace, this translates into an inability to make tough decisions, to risk being disliked. Erotics want to please and are often afraid to take a stand for fear of losing their popularity, making it hard for them to be effective leaders. I worked with an erotic manager at AT&T who was the cuddly father figure, the permissive parent who wanted to be friends with his team of people instead of demanding discipline and accountability. The result: The manager was loved but not respected; the office environment was "nice" and loving, but the team fell behind and the manager was ultimately fired. I know an erotic who holds a mid-level position as a manager to performing artists—we'll call him the Erotic Manager—who are almost all erotics as well (erotics often work best with other erotics). He told me his biggest fear is that his tombstone will read: "Here lies the Erotic Manager, a nice guy." He knows that his need to be liked, to be the good guy in the office, gets in the way of having the aggressive energy—the "balls"—to go after new clients, negotiate tough deals, and advance himself in his career. It matters more to him that his coworkers and clients think of him as a nice guy, a cutup, the one who makes them laugh and feel good, rather than the hard-nosed "bad cop" who can command higher fees for his client list. This goes to the heart of the erotic personality: They would rather be liked than admired. I have encountered two erotic chief financial officers in technology companies who are both helpers to the CEO. The other executives complained that they were too exclusively focused on caring for the boss.

When I did the *Gamesman* study, I found erotics at lower- and middle-management positions in large companies like AT&T and IBM, the ones who kept communication open, built relationships in the company, and mentored other employees. When these companies downsized, the erotic "helpers" were the first to go. It was only after they were gone that their role was apparent: Without the company communicators, there was an increased sense of isolation and distrust in the company. I'll show later in this chapter how this corporate role has been taken up by the marketing types, who have their own brand of relationship building.

Unproductive erotics, taken to their pathological extreme, can become hysterics, filled with an excess of emotion, throwing out threats like "I'm going to die without you" when faced with the loss of a relationship. Another erotic pathology is childlike seductiveness, the kind of indiscriminate flirting a person employs to make everyone in the room like them. This unproductive kind of erotic type needs to feel you like them or are attracted to them; if they sense that you're not on their side, they will having nothing to do with you, making it impossible to have any kind of relationship with them.

The Obsessive Personality

The obsessive is a person who lives by the rules, and the rules are set by some higher authority—a father figure, a strict conscience, or the "way things have always been done around here." Obsessives are motivated to live up to the high standards and ideals they set for themselves, to show at all times that they are a "good child" to an internalized father figure. Freud describes obsessives as "dominated by fear of their conscience instead of fear of losing love. They exhibit, as it were, an internal instead of an external dependence. They develop a high degree of self-reliance; and from the social standpoint, they are the true, pre-eminently conservative vehicles of civilization." Obsessives maintain order and stability, preserving tradition and our ties to the past, resisting anything new or different unless it comes with a seal of expert authority.

Put a productive obsessive in the workforce and you get our top doctors, engineers, financial experts, scientists, researchers, and technicians; craftsmen like electricians, bricklayers, and carpenters; as well as the majority of middle managers and some top managers, especially CFOs, COOs, and some CEOs. I like to call the most productive of these types systematic rather than obsessive; they systematically break down a task into its components and set out to tackle it, one piece at a time. They like to take a good, hard look at their career, decide dispassionately that they need certain skills and knowledge, and work on acquiring them. They commit their thoughts to paper, making lists, spreadsheets, charts, all of which they rely on rather than trusting their intuition or gut; obsessives trust numbers more than feelings. Obsessives have calculating minds, mentally tabulating costs, time, numbers, estimates. They want good orderly fashion in everything they do, whether it's in their well-kept closets or work space or how they organize their time. They are collectors, hoarding information as well as objects. The experts like to display diplomas and plaques. Obsessives tend to have hobbies, especially detail-oriented ones like sewing or doing crossword puzzles. They pride themselves on their ability to memorize numbers, dates, state capitals, U.S. presidents. The word "precise" is a big part of their vocabulary. They want their work to be of the highest quality, always meeting their exacting standards and values. They are the kind of people who say "If you're going to do anything, you should do it right." Expert obsessives see work as performance, a race that must be won, living up to a standard, not helping anyone or furthering the common good. An obsessive accountant at one of the big companies told me, "'Helping' is a bad, crummy word. . . . You don't go to a doctor to help you. You want him to cure you. People pay thousands of dollars for tax advice, not help." This kind of analytic attitude drives caring erotics crazy.

In the eighteenth and nineteenth centuries, when most people were farmers or craftsmen, the obsessive personality was at the heart of the national character. Benjamin Franklin was the model productive obsessive for the infant republic; his *Poor Richard's Almanac* was a bible for obsessives, filled with self-regulating maxims for systematic living like "Early to bed, early to rise, makes a man healthy, wealthy and wise." George Washington was also an incredibly productive obsessive, a successful farmer and businessman who kept detailed records of his expenses both in his personal life and as the commander-in-chief of the continental army. The most creative productive obsessive I've observed in the business world today is Warren E. Buffett, whose analytic, stick-to-his-guns approach to investing has kept him on top for decades. Buffett acquires and invests in conservative companies like Sees Candies for market value, not groundbreaking innovation. In Berkshire Hathaway's 2000 annual report, Buffett wrote: "We have embraced the 21st century by entering such cutting-edge industries as brick, carpet, insulation and paint. Try to control your excitement." I would expect that every one of the companies that Buffett buys is also run by an obsessive personality.

If you take a look at the business landscape, you'll see there are a lot of essentially conservative companies, both large and small, that are run—and run very well—by obsessives. An obsessive may make it to the top of a corporation and take on a leadership role, but only in a company that is itself obsessive—conservative, value-based, focused on the bottom line, where the goals are to cut costs and improve quality and profits. In his book *Good to Great*, Jim Collins focuses on exactly these kinds of companies—for example, Kroger, the supermarket chain, Walgreens, and Circuit City, all organizations where productive obsessive leaders cut waste and follow a consistent, no-nonsense approach to long-term profitability. The CEOs of these companies are typically men like Gillette's Colman Mockler, who put the company ahead of his personal interests, was down-to-earth, a family man, and enjoyed "puttering around the house, fixing things up." Collins summarizes this leadership approach by saying that "throughout our research we were struck by the continual use of words like *disciplined, rigorous, dogged, determined, diligent, precise, fastidious, systematic, methodical, workmanlike, demanding, consistent, focused, accountable*, and *responsible*." These words are a perfect description of the productive obsessive personality, whether it's a CEO, a physician, a lawyer, or an accountant.

I coached an obsessive CEO, whom we'll call Mr. Integrity, in an international consulting firm. His previous job was COO to a narcissistic visionary, the Sancho role to a Don Quixote, keeping the business grounded in reality while the boss looked for risky new business propositions. When Mr. Integrity became CEO of the company, he knew he wasn't a visionary, so we worked on developing his strengths: affirming the company's quality image; promoting good customer, employee, and owner relations; and encouraging his managers to be on the lookout for new business opportunities. He built on his obsessive strengths, moving the company toward continual learning and improvement rather than rapid change and innovation. I see the same qualities in Paul O'Neill, a superbureaucrat in the Ford administration who demonstrated his concern for improving systems and eliminating petty bureaucracy first as CEO of companies such as International Paper and Alcoa, and then for two years as treasury secretary in George W. Bush's cabinet. Glenn Kessler wrote in the *Washington Post* that "one of the contradictions of O'Neill is that while he loves to focus on the big picture—staffers say he is constantly pushing them to generate 'Big Ideas'—he is fascinated by the minute details of bureaucracy." O'Neill is aware that he can bring order to an organization, all the while demanding excellence and innovation from the people around him. Another productive obsessive in the Bush administration is Colin Powell, who is both praised and criticized for his cautious, step-by-step approach to strategy.

I don't know any obsessives running innovative companies in fast-moving, innovative industries where a productive narcissist is needed to create a new vision to change the world. In these instances, an obsessive may not be in the number-one position, but often holds the number-two position, the chief operating officer or chief financial officer who works hand in hand with a narcissistic CEO. This can be an unbeatable business combination of narcissistic vision and obsessive implementation, which we see in successful companies such as Southwest Airlines. While Herb Kelleher was running around in his high-profile position, his COO, Colleen Barrett, was running the company. Barrett described the symbiotic obsessive/narcissistic relationship in *Fortune*: "Herb could have a dream in the middle of the night and say, 'Okay, this is what I want to do.' But he wouldn't have a clue, God love him, what steps have to be taken. I'm not the most brilliant person in the whole world, but I can see systematically from A to Z, and I know what has to be done." (There it is: systematic, the best skill of the productive obsessive.) Or as Glenn Engel of Goldman Sachs put it: "[Barrett] built the infrastructure on which Southwest's culture is based." Almost every productive narcissist CEO today has an obsessive COO (and if they don't, they probably should). Some other well-known examples are Ray Lane, COO of Oracle (before he quit), Steve Ballmer of Microsoft, Craig Barrett of Intel, Bob Pittman of AOL (before he was pushed out), and Daphne Kis of Esther Dyson's EDventure Holdings.

With rare exceptions (perhaps Babe Ruth is the most notable), all of our great sports stars are obsessives. Most professional athletes are born with natural physical skills, but these skills have to be reinforced with hours of rote practice, the habitual repetition of the same movement over and over again. Other personality types would get bored with this kind of practice—but not an obsessive. This is the only way you ever get a Tiger Woods, an extremely productive obsessive who spent thousands of hours practicing his golf stroke before he even reached puberty. Same for Michael Jordan. Or Roger Clemens. Or Cal Ripken, Jr. Or Marion Jones. Or Bill Bradley, whose autobiography details the hours he spent practicing his foul shot. This attention to detail is not limited to the sports arena or golf green; in *Sports Illustrated*, Steve Rushin observes that Woods travels to tournaments with ten suitcases, all filled with carefully chosen clothing: "Woods demands order and routine at the majors. For four days he is afflicted with a kind of tournament Tourette's, exhibiting countless obsessive compulsions. In practice he sometimes requires himself to hole 100 six-foot putts. Consecutively. Using only his right hand . . . He's a neat freak who picks lint off greens with the fastidiousness of Felix Unger." In an interview with Oprah Winfrey, Woods called himself anal, obsessively making his bed every morning, whether he's at home or in a hotel, before the maid arrives. He also irons, or rather re-irons, every shirt that comes back from the dry cleaner. You can see this trait in other athletes' obsessive rituals and game good-luck charms, like wearing a favorite shirt over and over again, or not shaving during a winning streak (and this from someone who would ordinarily require absolute cleanliness). An obsessive sports star like Woods obviously likes to succeed, but it isn't just winning and setting records that motivate him. His competitive drive is also turned against himself, trying to better his last score and beat his own personal best. Self-improvement, on the playing field or in business, characterizes the productive obsessive.

So far I've shown how productive obsessives can use their personality type to be successful, how they can be assets in the right profession or workplace. What about their unproductive traits? There's a well-known checklist of obsessive pitfalls: They can become mired in details and rules, losing sight of the overall goals of the company; they are more concerned with doing things in the right way than doing the right thing; they turn into control freaks, paper-pushing, bean-counting bureaucrats; they resist change to the point of obsolescence; they are rigid, judgmental, stubborn, cheap. In short, they are "anal" in exactly the way Freud described the character. A little psychoanalytic humor makes this point: Jung once described Freud's anal character to a meeting of Zurich doctors, prompting one of them to say, "But, Dr. Jung, why do you call it the anal character? It's just human nature." He meant that he was surrounded by "anal" types; the Swiss-German character is known for its extreme order, cleanliness, and careful handling of money.

What may be the obsessives' most annoying and damaging work habit is that they always want to be right. They are know-it-alls. Given the choice between being right and being liked, they usually choose being right, leaving you sometimes with obnoxious, pompous blowhards. We saw this at the 2000 presidential debates, where Al Gore tried to impress everyone with his statistics, lock-boxes, percentages, and even his correct pronunciation of the names of foreign leaders, causing him to lose votes to the more affable and eager-to-be-liked Bush. Gore may have been coached by a team of advisers, but personality type always wins out; he couldn't suppress his true nature in the heat of the moment, his obsessive qualities apparent in his rigid, robotic strides, sharp finger-pointing, and aggressive body language.

The obsessive belief in self-improvement is behind most of today's business literature. It speaks directly to a market of middle managers who are snapping up copies of *The 7 Habits of Highly Effective People* and *The One Minute Manager,* a consistent best seller since it was first published in 1982 that tells managers to delegate more instead of micromanaging the work of subordinates. Obsessives want structure, guidelines on how to organize their time, formulas to follow; they make to-do lists and then cross off entries as the day goes on. Most of the business how-to books on the market today are aimed at obsessives who need to learn how to be less hardheaded in their approach to work, more open and receptive to change.

The obsessive pathology is well known: compulsive chattering, hand washing or grooming, stinginess or hoarding, and overwhelming doubt about whether they're performing well or up to their standards. Obsessives tend to become either passive-aggressive or just out-and-out aggressive, rebellious, or angry when they feel they're being treated badly or oppressed, or when you can't see their point of view.

The Marketing Personality

Describing the marketing personality is like trying to describe the color of a chameleon: It changes all the time. The best word for a marketing personality is "adaptable"; a marketing personality operates by radar, sensing what the market wants and needs and then conforming to it. Their self-esteem or self-valuation comes from what could be called a personal stock market that goes up and down depending on what they're selling: their accomplishments, how well they align themselves with key people, a client or account base, good looks and style, new skills and expertise—or "whatever," as they are fond of saying. Everything they do is relative: It needs to meet the approval of other people. They almost never use the words "right" or "wrong" (as do obsessives); they want to be "appropriate." They intuitively know how to adapt to changes in the marketplace, and they are not as unsettled by upheaval in the corporate or economic climate as obsessives are. In fact, they thrive on change because they adapt quickly. They have little use for self-help books like *Who Moved My Cheese?* and *The One Minute Manager*, but if the book is a best seller, they want to make sure they know what's in it, so they may flip through it at the bookstore so that they're up-to-date on what people are talking about, either at the office or a cocktail party. It's not just that they like to be "in the know"; they think they *have* to be up on the latest trends and information or they will lose ground in the marketplace.

Obsessives used to be the most common personality type. Today, the marketing personality outnumbers all the others, and most of us share aspects of this type in order to survive in today's volatile workplace. This shift began in the 1950s, predicted with accuracy in *The Lonely Crowd* (1950) by David Riesman, who coined the phrases "inner-" and "other-directed personalities." Two decades later, Daniel Bell, in *The Coming of the Post-Industrial Society* (1973), saw the rise of information technologies and service industries forcing people to market themselves, to compete with each other rather than tame the industrial world. Seen in this way, post-industrial society isn't a contest so much of people against nature but rather of people against other people—a competition in which self-promoters, quick-change artists, and networkers rise to the top. In the past thirty years, a few trends have contributed to the rise of the marketing personality: Vast numbers of women have entered the workforce, meaning that children have been and are raised more and more by their peers rather than their parents, peer pressure becoming central to enforcing a code of conduct rather than an ancillary factor. Service and knowledge jobs—which require people to use brain rather than brawn to solve problems, give advice, provide reports, and manage other people—continue to grow, making up more than 75 percent of all employment in the United States. Add to this the constant changes within corporate America, and you have a workforce that, for the most part, no longer believes in loyalty and lifelong commitment to one organization. Constant marketing of one's skills and self-promoting have been the norm for many people.

The most productive marketing personalities are what I call self-developers. They think of their life and career as continuing education, a chance to pick up new skills, continually learn and grow, intellectually and emotionally. They are the types who want to do well, feel and look good. They exercise, diet, talk to therapists, organize reading and study groups, and take classes. Unlike the obsessives, they don't think that saving money is a virtue for its own sake. They like to spend it not only on appearance and intellectual development but on new experiences: gourmet food, wine, travel, museum hopping. They are some of the most productive freelancers, setting their own goals and working well on their own; they are a big part of the current trend toward self-employment, and are tireless self-promoters. Marketing types do well in all manner of sales professions—real estate, public relations, advertising, publicity, events planning, venture capital, money raising. They like talking to clients and customers and learn from these encounters. They are effective in consulting, technical design, acting, the arts, publishing, and entertainment. They increasingly play a part in the legal and medical professions because of their ability to bring people together and facilitate meetings. They are often chosen as school principals and college presidents because they make the different interest groups feel understood and supported; they build coalitions that don't insult anyone. They are often CEOs of companies or divisions that are expanding into new markets. Productive marketing types use their superior networking skills to their advantage to build organizations, invigorating, and in some cases replacing, the erotic skills of caring and relationship building. They are interactive rather than bureaucratic. A colleague of mine worked with a productive marketing manager for a technology services company and showed me his in-house reports; I would like to excerpt from one of them because it's a perfect example of the marketing game plan of building a business with connections and networking, selling skills rather than products:

> First I got an idea because I had a relationship with [a partner] in the past. . . . A few years ago we did a small thing with [the partner], a local outsourcing effort. I kept the business card of the guy we worked with—keeping business cards is almost a religion with me. So when I had this idea I first put together a communication praising the local team with [the partner] on their good work and forwarded it to higher levels. Then I said to the senior manager: We should look at how to advance these opportunities. I got a response from him saying great, here's my E-Business head from LA, talk to him.
>
> Then I sat down in my office and made a war map on the wall about who I needed to get involved within the company. I outlined under each of them what the alliance would bring to them. . . . Then I hit the phone and talked to each of these main contacts, chitchatted a bit, then introduced this idea—sold it to them. I forwarded them documentation and presentations. Then I called back to talk to them again a week after. That's how I started my "war."

Notice how important contacts are to this marketing manager—almost a "religion"—and that his business strategy involves a detailed, mapped-out flowchart of how he can connect people to

create business. It's chatting on the phone taken to its most productive business application.

Marketing personalities hold up other successful people as
models, then go about acquiring the skills and characteristics of that
person. I saw an interview with Sean Combs, the artist previously
known as Puff Daddy and, more recently, P. Diddy (only a marketing personality would change his name to change his image), who
said that he has fashioned his entire career after Russell Simmons.
Whatever Simmons did, Combs copied; Simmons was the first hip-
hop impresario; Combs created his own hip-hop label, Bad Boy
Entertainment; Simmons made a fortune marketing his Phat Farm
clothing line; Combs created the Sean John line. Combs is a perfect
example of the marketing personality who adapts to the latest trend,
watching what works for other people and adding it to his repertoire
of skills: His girl group Dream followed the success of the Spice
Girls and Destiny's Child as well as the boy group explosion; his best
songs are based on classics—"Mo' Money, Mo' Problems" samples
"I'm Coming Out," and "I'll Be Missing You" samples Sting's "Every
Breath You Take." Without much in the way of innovation, Combs
has created an empire with a net worth of $231 million (2001 *Jet*
magazine figure), showing just how far a marketing personality with
the right radar can take a carefully constructed image.

I believe this is the case with Carly Fiorina, the CEO of
Hewlett-Packard, who has successfully modeled herself after
another marketing personality, John Chambers of Cisco. In Eric
Nee's July 2001 *Fortune* magazine article, Fiorina is described as
"outgoing, photogenic, and articulate, someone who, as Cisco Chief
Executive John Chambers still says, 'has the skills to be one of the
top CEOs in America.'" Note the qualities that Nee attributes to

Fiorina: She is attractive, has a great personality, talks a good game, and appeals to the public. In other words, she looks and acts the part of a CEO, much like Chambers. Fiorina's career makes perfect sense when it is seen as a case study of the marketing personality, the kind of person who can make it to the top of a company like HP, one that is run essentially the same way it was when Bill Hewlett and Dave Packard were at the helm. If we focus on profitability, HP is more like an old-fashioned product company where the goal is to ship more units, particularly computer printers, while keeping costs down, than it is like more revolutionary high-tech companies. The fact is that the most profitable part of the company is not even the printer division: It is the straightforward sale of ink and ink cartridges, which generates $9 billion annually. HP does not rely on innovation to build its business; it missed out on the Internet revolution and is in the difficult, if not impossible, position of playing catch-up within the computer industry. Fiorina's merger of HP with Compaq is a high-profile and extremely costly maneuver that does little more than increase the combined company's market share and cut redundant staff. The merger is not based on what each company brings to the table and how they complement each other; it's the kind of move that is orchestrated by a marketing personality who plays to the press. This has always been Fiorina's strength. When she first arrived at HP, she decided to star in the company commercials, positioning herself in front of HP's birthplace, a garage in Palo Alto, vowing to make the company great again. She may not have a carefully thought-out strategy for the future, but Fiorina was ranked number one on *Fortune* magazine's Most Powerful Women in Business for two years running (1999 and 2000), again showing how successful marketing personalities can be at selling *themselves* as opposed to their products or companies.

The media may well call Madonna and George W. Bush narcissistic, but I see them as two of our most successful marketing personalities. Madonna is a master of continual reinvention and self-marketing. In her 2001 concert tour (the very same one that a *New York Times* critic called a "sea of self-love" and narcissism), she flashed successive images of herself over her twenty-year career, a slide show of her marketing savvy and ever-evolving styles: club kid, boy toy, virgin, naïf, Monroe-esque goddess, Harlem vogue-dancer, Hispanic street singer, peep-show player, S&M artist, Eastern-inspired chanter, cowgirl, techno musician, and guitar-strumming balladeer. At the same concert, Madonna introduced one of her songs in a country twang, a voice that she seemed to get stuck in, saying, in essence, to the audience, "I don't know how to speak like myself." She actually has no self to speak from, no real persona, no voice of her own. Despite the fact that Madonna renews her audience all the time, appealing to younger fans, her music lacks the deeper meaning of popular artists such as Bruce Springsteen and Bob Dylan, whose audiences evolve and grow with them, rather than the other way around.

George W. Bush is our first president with a marketing personality combined with elements of the erotic. His political positions change according to his constituency and advisers; he relies on key members of his staff, especially Vice President Cheney and Karl Rove, to dictate his policies, responding with an acute sense of how and when to change directions. His career pattern also shows his marketing personality—he partied a lot in college, giving in to peer pressure, and later jumped from career to career, never making much of a commitment to a job until he was in his forties. When he's addressing an audience, you get the sense that he's not speaking from the heart, that his words are scripted or rehearsed. The only time he seems "real" is when he's reaching out and asking that we all get along, talking about how we need to love all our children or support our armed forces after September 11 (that's his erotic side speaking). One of Bush's key advisers in his campaign was Governor William J. Janklow of South Dakota, who said about Bush: "There's nothing worse than having all your friends tell you when to smile, what to say, how to act—all at the same time. It's insanity. My job was to tell him just be himself. I'd tell him, 'George, don't listen to people.'" It's interesting that Bush needed someone to tell him not to listen to others, to be himself. The problem is, how do you be yourself when that sense of self is always shifting?

This is the biggest danger for the unproductive marketing types: They lack a center. Since marketing types are constantly checking their own personal stock value, they may suffer a continual feeling of anxiety, fed by the nagging questions "Is this the appropriate answer?" "Am I doing OK?" "Is this working?" They can end up chasing the new thing so often that they make no lasting commitments to their work or to people. They can be superficial, caring more about how they look than what they have to offer. For example, when they hear about an upcoming event that could help their career, they might think, "Do I have the right outfit? Do I look successful?" instead of asking if they're mentally prepared or have done their homework. They favor style over substance. They spend so much time selling themselves that they're oblivious to what others can teach them. This was the case with John Walter, a marketing personality who was chosen in 1996 by Bob Allen to succeed him as CEO at AT&T. After only a year, he was let go by management because he couldn't come up with an overarching strategy. An anecdote from one of my colleagues, a longtime AT&T consultant, makes my point: He scheduled a meeting with Walter right after he arrived at Basking Ridge to talk about what was going on at the company. Instead of asking my colleague about the key decisions he was involved in, Walter spent the entire time ticking off his own qualifications, proving how he was the right man for the job. By the time he was done selling himself, the hour was up, and Walter had wasted the chance to find out more about the company and prepare for the hard job ahead of him.

Taken to their most unproductive, the marketing types that my colleagues and I have seen in psychotherapy complain of pervasive anxiety and depression, a sense that each new project or relationship will disappear, leaving them incapable of fully committing themselves to anything or anyone. Much like the lead character of Woody Allen's *Zelig*, they complain that they have no sense of self, a lack of an inner core that characterizes the inaction and ennui of the Prozac nation.

The Narcissistic Personality

All of the three types that I've just described—the erotic, obsessive, and marketing—are controlled by different psychic forces that differ for each type; it can be a parent, a boyfriend, a strict conscience, market research polls, the year-end review, or even the *Vanity Fair* In and Out List. The narcissist is the personality type that has few social control mechanisms built into the psyche, making narcissists entirely different from the other types. Unlike the obsessives, they're not troubled by a stern father figure or superego; unlike the erotics, they're not worried about losing love; and unlike the marketing type, they don't bend to peer pressure.

I want to move away from psychoanalytic terms in order to make the distinction between social control mechanisms in a way that makes sense when you look at yourself and the people around you. As opposed to the narcissist, the other three types are driven to do the right thing. It's how they define "the right thing" that differs. For an obsessive, it's doing things the way his father did, or his teachers told him to, or how his conscience dictates. He tries to live up to and preserve a time when things worked, when the family or the country or the company ran well, making it worth protecting and preserving. For an erotic, doing the right thing means holding on to the love and interest of significant others and keeping that love at any cost. And for the marketing person, right is whatever friends, colleagues, and peers indicate in a multitude of ways is "appropriate" (there is no right and wrong in the marketing person's vocabulary). All three use emotionally mnemonic devices, repeating and imitating the behavior and ideals of people who have either gone before them or are their peers.

The narcissist has very little or no psychic demands to do the right thing. Freed from these internal constraints, the narcissist is forced to answer for himself what is right, to decide what he values—what, in effect, gives him a sense of meaning. Unlike the other personality types, there is a long list of things that do *not* necessarily provide meaning for the narcissist: He does not look for approval from others, does not hear the chorus of voices that say "You're a good boy, keep it up" or "This job/spouse/accomplishment will make you happy," doesn't try particularly hard to be liked or even to have many friends, doesn't care about getting good grades, impressing the teacher or the best-looking girl in the class, doesn't necessarily want to follow in his father's footsteps or take over the family business. The list goes on, leaving the narcissist without the usual social barometers of how to conduct himself—how, in essence, to lead a productive life.

Another important way of distinguishing among the types is how they each create a sense of security: Everyone needs to feel able to survive economically and emotionally, without fear of being abandoned without any protection from isolation or vulnerability. For the obsessives, a sense of security may come from shoring up skills, becoming an expert, or building a reputation in a field. Or it can be institutional—obsessives may seek a secure position in a stable company, or gain the protection of a father-figure boss. For erotics, security comes in the form of someone who loves them or, better yet, a supportive family or familylike group, and knowing that they can depend on the love and protection of their team. For the marketing types, security depends on marketable skills, appearance, and networking. All these types are deeply motivated to do whatever it takes to maintain their sense of security. Narcissists stand out from the other types in this respect; they do not gain a sense of security from these kinds of relationships or skills. It is only by recruiting people to join them in their worldview, their vision, that narcissists can feel a sense of security and overcome isolation. For this reason, narcissists are driven to be captivating, inspirational, charming, and seductive.

These feelings of isolation also force the narcissist, more so than any other personality type, to find his own answer to the existential question of the meaning of life. Instead of asking "How do I do the right thing?" the narcissist asks "Why do anything, and is it worth it?" In the absence of any set of psychic guidelines, the narcissist must create his own sense of meaning; if he does not, or cannot create his own way of seeing the world, of deciding what he thinks is right in a way that can connect him with other people, he is left with meaninglessness and isolation. I was discussing this with a British CEO I was counseling, and he said that he remembers the exact moment when he realized he had to decide for himself what was meaningful. He was standing on the banks of the Thames and it hit him: It was up to him to create meaning. This is the kind of big, philosophical statement that may be hard to swallow, but look at the existential questioning found in Napoleon's youthful diaries, written before he found a sense of purpose in his military and polit- ical reforms: "Alone in the midst of mankind, I return to my room to muse and to succumb to all the force of my melancholy. Wither does it turn today? It turns to death. . . . Because I have to die any- way, should I not kill myself?" This hardly seems like the private musings of an empire builder; it sounds much more like the inter- nal dialogue of another narcissist, Hamlet, or, for that matter, Steve Jobs, whose close friend Mike Murray was worried that Jobs would commit suicide, never finding anything in midlife that would ignite his interest or passion.

Needless to say, rather than retreat into isolation or a suicidal slide into psychic paralysis, Napoleon and Jobs were able to create their own sense of purpose, a mission that first engaged their pas- sions and then engaged others. This is the key to understanding the productive narcissist, and it is the focus of the next chapter, on the strengths of the productive narcissist in the business world. But for my purposes here in drawing a psychoanalytic portrait of the narcissist, I want to use both Napoleon and Jobs as examples of the narcissistic *need* to get others to buy in to their vision, to create a world that they populate with their devoted followers. The ability to inspire others is described perfectly by Napoleon's biographer, Robert Asprey: "No commander in history has so inspired his troops to march, often without adequate food or wine, on occasion without shoes, frequently with meager clothing in dreadful weather. Time and again . . . he asked his men to do what appeared impossible—and they did it." In terms of Jobs, think of how he recruited young programmers to join him in creating something "insanely great." There's a possibility that some of them thought they might get rich, but they had to be motivated by something more than money. Imagine a time when there was no PC to speak of, no company that called itself Apple, and no real monetary meaning for the phrase "stock options." The programmers who signed on with Jobs, the ones who spent countless hours of the day and night creating what would become the Macintosh, believed in Steve Jobs and his vision. They thought they were creating something that would change the world, and they were right. They are the modern-day equivalent of the soldiers who fought for Napoleon.

This kind of wildly creative act, in which the narcissist envisions an entire world and then draws others into it, starts with a rejection of what Freud calls the "established state of affairs," a turning away from social norms. Since narcissists don't buy in to the meaning offered by parents or peer groups, they feel little pressure to fit in or conform to the other kids. This can show up in small ways, like deciding not to wear what everyone else is wearing, or in bigger ways, like refusing to take part in school and social activities. Many of today's well-known CEOs were considered outcasts and oddballs back in grammar and high school. We all know the familiar story line of the technically advanced kid who holes himself up in his room, only to emerge later in life as the head of a computer company, putting all the popular kids to shame. But this is only one narrative version of a story that's common to narcissists throughout history, in different settings and disciplines. Jan Carlzon told me he was thrown out of business school, bodily, when he barged into a meeting and argued for an unpopular disarmament policy. Oprah Winfrey says that she was harassed by the other kids in her schoolyard, and instead of running away or getting weepy, she defended herself by preaching to them, a response they thought was slightly nuts. Esther Dyson told me that she felt no pressure to go out on Saturday night at Harvard; she preferred to do her own thing. Stephen King was holed up in his basement, printing his own fiction on a jerry-rigged press and selling it to his fellow students before the school shut him down.

Almost everyone passes through a period of adolescent rebellion when you experience a burst of infinite possibility, a taste of freedom, a brief flash when your parents no longer seem to control your every move, high school is about to end, college or work hasn't yet begun, and the "boss" seems like something that will never happen to you. This is what I call the "narcissistic moment." Look back on your own life, and recall your teens and early twenties. (Or if you are now at that age, reflect on your feelings.) Was it a time when you felt as if the whole world was open to you, that you could do anything you put your mind to, that you were going to accomplish great things? Do you sometimes think that this was the best time of your life? This "narcissistic moment" is celebrated in our popular culture and explains, in part, the emotional draw of teen movies. The best of the bunch is *Risky Business*, a cinematic ode to the power of the narcissistic moment. The parents (both of whom are portrayed as obsessives—the mother is obsessively status-conscious and neat, the father obsessively controlling) go out of town, leaving Joel, the Tom Cruise character, to turn up the music, dance in his underwear, and adopt a new credo: "Sometimes you got to say, 'What the fuck!'" The big house in the suburbs becomes a brothel, a business that turns Joel into the best "future enter-priser" his school has ever seen, his own boss, and an instant success story. The end of the movie is triumphant, but you have to wonder what happens to Joel's narcissistic moment and how long it lasts at Princeton, his father's alma mater. That may be the reason there's no sequel, no *Risky Business II*—it's a pretty good bet that the postcollege Joel abandons his narcissistic moment, returning to the demands and expectations of his suburban role models. The moment has passed.

You might want to think about your own narcissistic moment, and what happened to it. Looking back, you probably dreamed of working for yourself or coming up with a new way of doing things or rejecting your father's ideas about what you should do for a living or rebelling against the tyranny of your peer group. It's a time when you probably weren't so afraid to talk about your ambitions, or worried about being told you were crazy, that you were aiming too high. When teenagers imagine their adult life, they often think in narcissistic terms, turning essentially obsessive jobs that require years of rote study and training, such as doctor or lawyer, into heroic, high-wire acts: A doctor is a brilliant, cutting-edge surgeon

who is world-famous for his skill and nerve, or a lawyer is a litiga-
tor who stuns the courtroom with his verbal gamesmanship. In
other words, who wants to be an obsessive when they grow up?
Maybe one of the first people to interview you for a job said:
"Someday I'm going to be working for you." Maybe you were told
you were a real go-getter, the one who was most likely to succeed
or make their first million. Maybe you, like Stephen King, got into
trouble at school for charging kids for what you love to do. But if
you're not a narcissistic personality, you more than likely left that
moment behind you. Narcissistic personalities, on the other hand,
never leave that moment; they live their entire lives in a state of
questioning their relation to society and trying to create their own
sense of meaning.

A crucial difference between narcissists and other types is that
from an early age they do not internalize their parents or peer
group, and therefore don't need to rebel against an inner voice. Is
there a family history that we can point to that fosters the narcissistic personality? In general, I'm wary of overly mechanistic expla-
nations of how the narcissistic personality is formed in early
childhood, since there are any number of reasons that a gifted and
endlessly creative child doesn't identify with parents or peers. That
said, there are a few clear patterns and parallels in the family history of narcissists that are impossible to ignore. The most common
family dynamic shared by narcissistic personalities is the Stephen
King scenario: a strong, supportive mother and an absent or failed
father who "piled up all sorts of bills and then did a runout." This
fits with Freud's "social control" model of personality type. Without an admired father figure, or without a father who is a strong
and positive presence, a narcissistic child, especially a boy, is free

from paternal domination, someone to measure himself against or live up to. But everyone, even a narcissist, needs encouragement and affirmation, which he usually finds in a supportive mother. The similarities are striking, and to show you just how common this family dynamic is among narcissists, I want to give a brief biographical rundown of some narcissists throughout history, in different fields. It's worth asking yourself if they are in line with the family background of any narcissists you know personally:

Jim Clark's father abandoned his family when Jim was a child, leaving him in the care of his mother, who worked hard to keep the family afloat, never going on welfare. *John D. Rockefeller's* father was, quite literally, a snake-oil salesman who was on the road most of the time, peddling his products in different towns, until he finally left his family for another woman, becoming a bigamist who died and was buried under the assumed name of Dr. William Levingston. *Leonardo da Vinci* was an illegitimate child who was later adopted by his birth father at age five, most likely because his stepmother was unable to bear children. Leonardo remained close to his natural mother throughout his life. The mother of *William Durant*, the founder of General Motors, was a divorced, single parent, something unusual at the turn of the century, who doted on Willie and supported him in everything that he did. To quote one of his mother's letters to Durant when he was forty: "You have been a good boy, thoughtful, kind and patient, doing always for my comfort. It is a joy to have such a thankful son. . . . I know—and feel the strong tie of affection that binds our love." Durant's father was a hard-drinking get-rich-quick schemer who was shunned by his family. *Duke Ellington's* elegant and strong-willed mother supported and encouraged his musical genius, while Ellington's father

worked as a servant in the White House. *Bill Clinton*'s step-
father was an alcoholic, and his relationship with his mother is legendary. James Carville says "anytime he was asked who was the
most influential person in his life, he would say, without a doubt,
'My mother.'" *Richard Nixon*'s father was an unsuccessful lemon
farmer and gas station owner, but Nixon was encouraged in his
career by his mother. Nixon carried in his wallet a note that she
gave him on the night of his vice presidential inauguration, keeping it with him at all times. *Ronald Reagan*'s father was an alcoholic
shoe salesman, his mother another legendary figure; Lou Cannon
said that you would never have heard of Ronald Reagan if it hadn't
been for his mother (it's interesting to note that Reagan's nickname
for his wife was "Mommy"). *Richard Branson*'s father was unsuccessful as a barrister; his mother was a daredevil glider pilot and
air hostess who encouraged Richard to take risks. I've seen this
pattern in my own work with narcissistic leaders: *Sidney Harman*'s
father was a brilliant but failed businessman whose compulsive
gambling and abusive behavior alienated his son. His mother was
totally caring and supportive. *Goran Collert*'s father was critical,
and his love was conditional on his son's success—Goran "felt like
a stock, valued accordingly"—whereas his mother was uncondi-
tionally loving and generous. *Robert Johnson* was the ninth of ten
children born to a strong mother and a womanizing father who
abandoned the family.

There's another family scenario that's described by Heinz
Kohut, the leading post-Freudian theorist on narcissism, in which
the mother's own ambitions and dreams are frustrated and trans-
ferred to her son, whom she pushes to excel and succeed in ways
that she couldn't—similar to Alexander the Great's mother

Olympias, who told him he was the son of a god, not his mortal father, Philip of Macedonia. The following are a few notable examples of this dynamic: *Jack Welch's* mother totally supported him, but also molded him into a tough competitor. She used to play cards with him, goading him to keep up and try to beat her. After she won, she'd tell him that he wasn't good enough, that losing just wouldn't do, and make him play again. Welch writes admiringly of his mother's reaction when he was a sore loser in a hockey game. She walked right into the locker room and grabbed him by the shirt, shouting in his face: "You punk! If you don't know how to lose, you'll never know how to win." *Douglas MacArthur's* mother encouraged and promoted his military career, sticking close by him throughout his career to make sure he was measuring up to her standards. When he was at West Point, she lived in a nearby apartment; she even followed him when he was shipped out to the Philippines, renting out a room in a hotel. *Frank Lloyd Wright's* mother Anna decided, before he was born, that he would be the greatest architect in the world. She wanted the first images he saw as an infant to inspire him, so she placed engravings of great cathedrals around his crib. His toys were wooden building blocks, all to encourage his architectural talents.

Recently, I've noticed a different kind of family pattern take shape in which the narcissistic personality has gone so far beyond his father in terms of his knowledge and skills in a highly technological society that he looks for outside mentoring and affirmation. This seems to be the case with Bill Gates. He was raised in a well-to-do and apparently loving nuclear family; his mother, Mary, was strong, intelligent, supportive, and involved in his business, even going with Bill on his business trips. She played a key role in his career by suggesting that he speak to Sony executives about when he should take his company public. Gates's father is a successful lawyer with a knack for business, but he has no particular talent for technology. Rather than rejecting his father or family values, Gates looked outside for other technologically advanced peers and older mentors, such as his good friend Warren Buffett, who could teach him things that his father simply could not.

When you have some sort of idea, even at an early age, that won't let you accept the world as it is, you have a very hard time identifying with your peers and finding any kind of role model, or even someone to talk to about your ideas. You are the odd man out. One way that narcissists deal with this is to compare themselves to historical figures as a way of reinforcing their idealized image of themselves and how they fit into the world. As a child, Camille Paglia, a narcissist who in *Sexual Personae* created an entirely new way of interpreting Western history, looked forward to Halloween, when she could become one of her heroes for the day: "At four, I was Alice [in Wonderland] . . . at five, Robin Hood; at six, the toreador from *Carmen*; at seven, a Roman soldier; at eight, Napoleon; at nine, Hamlet. Long before the women's movement, I was making eccentric nonconformist gestures." Freud was fascinated by the life of Hannibal and also identified with Moses. At the height of Michael Saylor's career, he thought he was similar to Caesar. John D. Rockefeller made a comparison between his corporate role and Napoleon's military command, saying he needed his business colleagues the way Napoleon relied on his marshals. Richard Nixon identified with Charles de Gaulle, even underlining this passage in his personal copy of de Gaulle's memoir *The Edge of the Sword*: "Great men of action have without exception possessed to a very high degree the faculty of withdrawing into themselves."

Another way that narcissists try to solve the problem of isolation is by talking to themselves, by holding conversations in which
they are both the speaker and the listener. It's through this internal dialogue, a mental back-and-forth, that a narcissist can reinforce his view of things, can, in effect, "talk himself" into his own
vision. A narcissist is so often alone, dreaming up alternate worlds;
his vision needs protection from the attacks and criticism of the
outside world, with its pressure to do things the way they have
always been done. Narcissists train themselves from an early age to
block out other voices, other opinions, so one of the few voices they
trust is their own. They are accustomed to listening to themselves
talk, debating different sides of the same issue, finally reaching a
decision about what to do and the best way to do it. John D. Rockefeller held intimate conversations with himself, counseling himself, repeating homilies, and warning himself to be aware of moral
as well as practical pitfalls before he went to sleep at night: "Look
out or you will lose your head—go steady. Are you going to let this
money puff you up? Keep your eyes open. Don't lose your balance." This is the routine that Joe Klein noticed in Bill Clinton; in
order to reinforce his position on an issue, he would argue the exact
opposite of whatever position he had taken, making cases against
himself, until he finally returned to his original position, strength-
ened and more sure of himself than ever. Clinton communicated
this surety when he spoke to the country. A lot has been made of
Clinton's skill at public speaking; I think Clinton's genius is engaging his audience in his own inner dialogue, drawing in listeners and
turning them into believers, getting them to identify with him and
his views.

The best description of narcissistic dialoguing can't be found
in any business literature; it's in a popular novel. In *Timeline*,

Michael Crichton says more about the narcissistic leader in this one paragraph than most business books I've ever read. To set it up, he creates a relationship between Kramer, playing the female lawyer and loyal sidekick to Doniger, the brilliant billionaire, a thirty-nine-year-old who made it big in high tech. When I read this, I immediately recognized it as a dead-on description of what I had experienced with narcissistic leaders.

> Over the years, Kramer had fallen into the habit of repeating whatsoever Doniger said when he was in one of his "pacing moods." To an outsider, it looked like sycophancy, but Doniger found it useful. Frequently, when Doniger heard her say it back, he would disagree. Kramer understood that in this process, she was just a bystander. It might look like a conversation between two people, but it wasn't. Doniger was talking only to himself.

What I like about this nuanced description is that it goes beyond the caricature of the egoistic "boss" who doesn't listen, doesn't care what you say, doesn't want to hear anyone contradict him. The most successful narcissistic business leaders aren't interested in talking to their employees because they're not interested in talking to *anyone*. They talk almost exclusively to themselves. Shakespeare recognized this when he created literature's greatest monologuist, Hamlet. To quote Harold Bloom: "Hamlet, in his seven soliloquies, teaches us what imaginative literature *can* teach, which is how to talk to oneself, and not how to talk to others. Hamlet is not interested in listening to anyone, except perhaps the Ghost."

Without the support of others, it's easy to see how narcissists have a highly developed "me against the world" way of looking at things. Freud saw this as self-preservation, the need for narcissists to shore themselves against the rest of the world. This often comes out as paranoia, a heightened awareness of danger that may be realistic, given narcissistic ambition, competitiveness, and unbridled aggressive energy. Andy Grove gave the high-tech world a slogan that resonated with the Silicon Valley culture of narcisissism: "Only the paranoid survive." There's not a lot of gray area in the narcissistic view of the world—you are either a friend or a foe, for or against the vision. This is exactly what David Dorman, then CEO of Pacific Bell, claims that Steve Ballmer said, or rather screamed, at him: "You're either a friend or a foe, and you're an enemy now," the competitive mantra of Microsoft that comes directly from the top, from the productive narcissist Bill Gates.

Earlier in this chapter, I showed how the other personality types have a tendency to cluster in certain fields—obsessives are exceedingly good managers, professionals, and bureaucrats, erotics gravitate toward the caring fields. But productive narcissists are not limited to any particular field; you can find them in any and every area of human endeavor. They may not change the entire world (although some notable narcissists have done so), but others do reinvent the world that *they* inhabit. They can found a school of thought (Ayn Rand, Gertrude Stein, Sigmund Freud); a completely new aesthetic or way of looking at architecture or design (Frank Lloyd Wright, Frank Gehry, Philippe Starck); social services that engage groups of followers (Dorothy Day of the Catholic Worker movement, Mother Teresa); artistic breakthroughs (Michelangelo, Leonardo da Vinci, Pablo Picasso); fashion (Coco Chanel); cosmetics

(Helena Rubenstein and Mary Kay); the organic food move-
ment (Alice Waters); films and film schools (Orson Welles, Francis
Ford Coppola, Stanley Kubrick); acting styles (Stella Adler, Marlon
Brando); musical revolutions (Richard Wagner, Miles Davis, Duke
Ellington, Louis Armstrong); new religious schools (St. Augustine,
St. Francis); political leadership (Churchill, de Gaulle, Stalin, Mao,
FDR, LBJ, Reagan, Nixon, Clinton); literary movements (Marcel
Proust, August Strindberg, James Joyce, Ernest Hemingway). You
can find narcissists changing any world that they inhabit (perhaps
even your own), and remaking our world along with them.

The next chapter is devoted to the productive narcissists who
are remaking our world through business and economic reform,
and how their strengths can often give way to their weaknesses, the
set of traits that either work together to further their vision or bring
about its collapse.

THREE

THE PRODUCTIVE NARCISSIST

A sk yourself this series of questions: Do you look forward to your work? Do you jump into your job every day, eager for new challenges to put your mind to? Does your work engage all of your faculties? Are you energized and enthusiastic, even fully alive at your job? And finally, do you think that your work uses all of your talents, or, as it's usually phrased, your potential? Look around you at your boss, coworkers, subordinates, your spouse or partner, and ask the same questions about them. If you're like most people, you answered these questions right away and the answers were no— you're not fully engaged by your work. Don't despair; you're not alone. In my experience, only about 10 to 15 percent of all people can honestly answer these questions in the affirmative. But even though this is a common situation, you can do something about it.

Although you can't change the circumstances of your childhood, rewrite your personal history, or alter your genetic makeup, you can, by sharpening and focusing your abilities, become more passionate and engaged by your work. In short, you can become more productive.

In the first chapter, I used the terms "productive" and "unproductive" to indicate the best and worst expressions of each personality type in the workplace. This chapter offers a more complete understanding of the concept of "productiveness" and how you can apply it to your own development, no matter what your personality type.

Over the past forty years of work with individuals and corporations, I have come to believe that "productiveness" is the best descriptive noun for every person's potential and the degree to which they're able to realize and employ this potential. Anyone who has ever read a self-help book or talked to a therapist or taken a class of continuing education is engaged in a process of trying to become more productive—that is, more than what they presently are. In both my private practice and as a business coach, I have helped people in their journey to become better versions of themselves, to search, uncover, focus, sharpen, and use their powers—and bring those powers to bear in their work. In other words, I have made productiveness the central study of my life's work, the intersection of a person's abilities and how he or she chooses to use them in the workplace.

Many of my theories of human nature have come to me slowly, circuitously, influenced by both study and clinical work. This is the case with my understanding of "productiveness," which has evolved over time. I was first drawn to the concept after reading Aristotle's *Ethics*, which describes the development of human potential in terms of "activeness," or consciously pushing your skills and talents to their limit in order to find continued renewal and happiness. Benedict de Spinoza builds on Aristotle's theories in his seventeenth-century treatise of the same name—*Ethics*—in which activeness, or being free to fulfill your potential, is contrasted with the limitations of oppression, fear, and dependency on imprisoning appetites. Without freedom from constraints, whether they are psychic or circumstantial, man is incapable of acting in a reasoned way, frustrating his creativity and thwarting his human purpose.

It was under Erich Fromm's tutelage that I began to see that the philosophical teachings of "activeness" were limited. Plenty of people are active, busy, and constantly "doing," filling their day with errands, social encounters, meetings, and other career obligations. They may hold a high position, an influential job, or make a lot of money; but all of this "doing" doesn't necessarily mean that they're doing their best work, using all of their abilities in a way that engages their passions. Seen in this way, activeness is only one component of "productiveness," and a small one at that. Fromm impressed upon me that "productiveness" is a more complete and encompassing term that can be used to describe everything that human potential entails. What exactly does "productiveness" mean, and how do I use the term in my work as a psychoanalyst and business consultant? Fromm's *Man for Himself* offers this definition:

Productiveness is man's ability to use his powers and to realize the potentialities inherent in him. If we say he *must* use his powers we imply that he must be free and not dependent on someone who controls his powers. We imply, furthermore, that he is guided by reason, since he can make use of his powers only if he knows what they are, how to use them, and what to use them for. Productiveness means that he experiences himself as the embodiment of his powers and as the "actor."

A close reading of this paragraph reveals five essential elements of productiveness. Those who live up to their potential, who are productive, possess (1) freedom ("free and not dependent"); (2) reason ("guided by reason"); (3) activeness ("experiences himself . . . as the 'actor'"); (4) understanding ("knows what [his powers] are"), and (5) purpose ("what to use [his powers] for").

I first put my understanding of "productiveness" to practical use in my work with Fromm in the Mexican village. I worked with volunteers to found a club for teenage boys that made farm animals—cows, chickens, pigs—available to them, giving them the chance to learn how to care for and eventually sell the animals. Our goal was to raise their aspirations and teach business skills. When I first got together with the boys, I found that these otherwise energetic kids didn't accept their task well, didn't see the point. For the most part, they didn't think much about a profession or making money; they expected that their lives would be roughly the same as their parents', and their parents' before them, with little hope of change. I tried to draw them out by asking them what interested them, using the Spanish *interesarse*, which implies being engaged, a word, it turns out, that was not part of the boys' vocabulary. My question was met with silence. I had my work cut out for me.

At the next meeting, we got down to the real issues that prevented the boys from taking charge of this business opportunity: fear of authority, passive acceptance of whatever the boss or patron said, an inability to make their own decisions and act on them.

Once the boys were guided through the elements of productiveness, they were able to break away from some of their psychic constraints, freeing them up to take charge of the animals, but also to talk in new ways about their futures, what appealed to them. The most important lesson that the boys took away from our sessions was the idea that they could turn their interests into vocational passions—they could make a living by doing what they loved to do, what stirred them and excited them. Years later, when I visited the village, I found out that many of the same boys went on to satisfying careers that they never would have aspired to before our work together: One became a doctor, another a professional soccer player, another an army officer, another a prosperous businessman.

This experience with the Mexican boys taught me that there is an essential element missing from Fromm's concept of "productiveness," and that element is *passion*. Or perhaps a better word for it is "enthusiasm," from the Greek word *entheos*, meaning "the god within." People with enthusiasm seem possessed by an inner god, a drive, that enlivens and elevates the everyday to the extraordinary. We often speak of the creative "spark," attributing it to inventors and artists, but all productive people retain this passionate spark, a lively energy, a sense of freshness that energizes their work. I see passion as the juice that brings the other elements of productiveness to life, catalyzing them; passion makes a person more than the sum of the productive parts. Without enthusiasm and passion, even the most skillful, focused, reasoned, and talented person can just go through the motions at work, passively accepting tasks as if they were assignments. Passion is what makes the difference between a talented actor who just "phones in the role," and a highly productive one such as John Gielgud, who brought all of his talents to bear in his work, remaking each performance with fresh insight. Throughout his career, Gielgud played Hamlet six times, more than any other actor of the twentieth century, and directed it four times. But Gielgud never played Hamlet the same way twice; we marvel at Gielgud's ability to approach the play with a searching mind, experimenting and uncovering new interpretations, stretching his own abilities as he grew in experience and wisdom. Gielgud himself wrote about the role of Hamlet that "it is a great *adventure* every time one plays it." How many of us can say that each time we go to work it is a great adventure? The most productive among us see our lives and work as discovery, constantly unfolding our own skills and expressing them in our work.

This brings me to the final element of productiveness that I also found lacking in Fromm's definition: perseverance. Productive people simply do not give up, even when faced with defeat or failure. They are resilient. Gielgud, for example, had a disastrous stage

We can contrast the elements of the productive and unproductive personalities:

PRODUCTIVE	VS.	UNPRODUCTIVE
Freedom	*vs.*	Constraint/aversion to risk
Reason	*vs.*	Irrationality
Activeness with passion/ enthusiasm	*vs.*	Reactiveness with busyness
Understanding	*vs.*	Superficial knowledge
Purpose	*vs.*	Aimlessness
Perseverance	*vs.*	Quitting

debut, saying, "I'm surprised the audience didn't throw things at me." But he went right back to the stage.

Productiveness is what pushes any personality type to live up to its potential. I don't want you to come away from the last chapter with the belief that only narcissists can be leaders, whereas the other types are destined to be followers. Although some types are more suited to certain roles than others, and have different strengths and weaknesses, there is no type that is "good" or "bad," or better or worse than the others. Don't judge yourself by your type, thinking, "Well, I'll never be a leader or be able to make the hard decisions because I'm an erotic personality." Judge yourself instead on the degree to which you are productive. It's up to each person to find the most productive expression of their type, to use all of their faculties, and find ways to overcome their limitations. To return to John Gielgud, he was essentially an erotic personality who brought out the best his type had to offer. We can see that not only in his extraordinary acting career, but also in his role as a director of more than eighty productions; his leadership style was based not on fierce reproach or intimidation, but on humble, self-effacing example. He knew how to develop and nurture the talent of other actors, an erotic skill that he put to its most productive use. Dirk Bogarde told Gielgud's biographer: "Everybody adored him, so the book might make rather flat reading." The same may be said of another extremely productive erotic personality, the jazz musician Wynton Marsalis, whose passion for music breathes life into his own ensemble, radiating outward into the audience. Both Marsalis and Gielgud push their personality type to the limit, animating all they do with the spark, the inner drive, that elevates the work of all productive personalities.

The labels "productive" and "unproductive" are not fixed throughout our lives. A personality who has been productive can, with enough stress and inner conflict, tip over into an unproductive state, turning a strength into a weakness. This happens when people become complacent, lazy, pompous, puffed-up, grandiose, dependent, afraid, or addicted to anything—food, drugs, spending, you name it—that weakens them. When unconscious or irrational needs become the driving force, the ability to make rational decisions and move toward a healthy purpose is thwarted. Let me give you a hypothetical example using one of our most productive obsessive personalities: Tiger Woods. In my description of him in the last chapter, I mentioned that he calls himself "anal," a neat freak who makes his own bed every day, even in a hotel room, and likes to iron (or rather, re-iron) shirts that have come back from the dry cleaner. Imagine if he woke up one day and became consumed with making his bed or ironing his shirts, so obsessed that he couldn't practice or play golf. The entire day would be devoted to getting just the right crease on his shirt cuff, the perfect collar point. Now, in his productive state, Tiger's purpose, his aim, is to beat Jack Nicklaus's record of eighteen major golf titles and continually improve his game. But if getting the perfect wrinkle-free shirt took over his life, he would tip over into irrational, unproductive behavior. His sense of purpose would be thwarted.

The same thing can happen in the business world. An obsessive COO can be extremely successful—think of Steve Ballmer, Ray Lane, and Colleen Barrett—in building the company infrastructure, watching the bottom line, and managing people. They are passionate about how things work—and making them work better. But the very same passion can be turned into unproductive behavior. An obsession with the bottom line can turn a COO into a petty bureaucrat who cares more about the cost of a pencil than the human who uses the pencil. The unproductive obsessive floods employees with paperwork and memos, becoming a prisoner of rules and regulations. I saw a perfect example of this at AT&T's Cleveland office, where a computerized system decided in 1980 that telephone operators should take a break between 8:00 and 8:15. The operators who punched in at 8:00 asked if they could forgo the imposed break and come in at 8:15, a reasonable request that was rejected by the bureaucratic management. So the operators came in at 8:00, clocked in, and then took their fifteen-minute break. The concern for absolute efficiency replaced reason and understanding, ruining the morale of the workers, making them less productive, victims of an obsessive vision.

This process can also happen in the reverse; someone who was hopelessly stuck in unproductive, self-defeating behaviors can, with positive and active effort, turn productive. I saw this in a brilliant marketing type at an international banking firm—the Marketing Manager—a woman who had a tendency to wear short skirts and seductive outfits. While her outfits spoke up, she didn't; she sounded like a scared mouse in meetings. No one valued her ideas and strategy, even though she was more knowledgeable and better prepared than her colleagues. When she came to me and asked what she could do to move up in the company, I asked her what her goals were. She said she wanted the other managers to embrace her ideas and put them into action. I told her that she was getting the attention of the men but not their respect. She was unconsciously seeking male attention by looking sexy, unaware that this made her appear less serious. And she was waiting for them to seek her viewpoint rather than insisting on being heard. To get them to listen to her, she was going to have to speak up and lower her hemline. She did, and today she is an executive vice president who could become a CEO. The Marketing Manager became more productive, was able to realize her potential. Her purpose is being fulfilled.

I've seen the same kind of transformation in another client, an obsessive CEO who kept coming to me with long lists and pro forma notes on the company goals. I asked him if this was what he liked to talk about, did he really want to lecture his workers on a boring litany of company inner workings and processes? (Notice how I had to lead him with questions, rather than instructions. Obsessives want to get the right answer, but usually rebel when they're told what to do.) His response, which I expected, was no, he would much rather share in his workers' learning, brainstorming about new business directions, creating new opportunities. (Since *he* came up with the answer himself, he beamed when I congratulated him on it.) All of a sudden, his company talks came to life, and so did his workers. Seems so simple, doesn't it? If he had thought, on his own, about what he enjoyed and passed it along to his team, he would have arrived at the same result. But, as an obsessive, he needed to be guided, given the permission to do what *he* wanted, and liked, to do. He said that for the first time in his life, he's having fun at work.

Take another example: Goran Collert, the CEO of Swedbank, walked into a meeting of his vice presidents, sat down, and announced that I was psychoanalyzing him. What did they think of that? After a moment of nervous shuffling, one executive piped up: "Well, whatever Michael's doing, he should keep doing it, because it's working. You're a lot less impossible to be around." Before we started psychoanalysis, Collert's constant outbursts and ruthless put-downs got in the way of his ability to lead the company toward his goals, undermining his strategic purpose. By asking for psychoanalysis, he made a conscious decision to become more productive, to be more reasoned, to be free of irrational emotions, and to achieve his purpose. And it worked.

Stimulating a client to move from unproductiveness to productiveness is what most motivates me. Once I was able to grasp the holistic concept of productiveness, I saw how it could be applied to anyone, of any personality type, in any culture, in any work environment, in any job. What if I could work with people in boring and repetitive jobs, people who thought they were stuck, and give them the same sense of hope for change as the Mexican boys? The concept of "productiveness" directed my work with Sidney Harman when we tried to revolutionize factory work. I applied it when I led a companywide program at AT&T with the Communications Workers Union to improve the quality of the work life of frontline employees and middle managers. It was at the heart of the research in the early 1970s when I interviewed engineers and managers at innovative high-tech companies like HP, IBM, Intel, and Texas Instruments. I was astonished to find that even though they were some of the most highly educated professionals around, only 22 percent were highly productive, or, as I saw it, were engaged in their work with a passionate purpose in creating something that would improve people's lives as opposed to doing a job that was formatted for them by someone else. But in every one of these instances—the auto factory, the big corporate bureaucracy, the high-tech companies—I watched people who had been complacent, stuck, ready to quit, and bored become more productive when they were encouraged to think for themselves, free up their situation, and try out ways of doing things that engaged their passion.

I would even go so far as to say that productiveness is what most self-help books are trying to get at, just with different names and catch phrases. Take, for example, *Who Moved My Cheese?* and *The 7 Habits of Highly Effective People*. If you distilled the advice that you find in each book and tried to unite it in one approach that applies to anyone's career, you would be hard pressed to come up with a coherent theory. The two separate approaches don't offer an overall philosophy that works together. But if you think of both of these books in terms of the concept of productiveness, they make sense. *Cheese* is about adapting to change (grasping freedom as opposed to being held by past expectations, understanding, purpose), and *7 Habits* is about pushing your skills in the workplace and keeping up your knowledge (active rather than just busy, reason, purpose), while also teaching obsessives to be more cooperative and less self-centered (again, activeness, purpose, reason). I believe a thorough examination of the different criteria of productiveness and how they play out in your work can do more for you than any specifically focused self-help book. I explained this to one CEO, outlining the different components of productiveness, and when I was done, he said, "Well, Dr. Maccoby, that's pretty simple. That makes perfect sense," as if I were telling him something that he, and everyone else, already knew. Of course, it is simple, but when you try to apply these concepts to your own life, it becomes much more complicated. It's not so easy to know what to do, to make the right choices, to know what limits your freedom, to have the guts and courage not to take the passive, easy way out, but to kindle the spark that creates passionate purpose and leads to a more productive work life.

Now that you have a better understanding of the terms "productive" and "unproductive," I would like to apply them to the narcissistic personality. The first point I need to make is that every narcissist that I've mentioned in this book is, to a large extent, productive. But a productive narcissist doesn't equal success and an unproductive narcissist failure. It doesn't work that way. A productive narcissist can be either a success or a failure; for example, Vincent Van Gogh was an extremely productive narcissist who never sold one painting in his lifetime. I once interviewed Barbara McClintock, a biologist who worked in isolation for fifteen years without any recognition, focusing on scientific discovery, before she was "discovered" and awarded the Nobel Prize for her pioneering work in genetics. McClintock is an example of a highly productive personality whose work was both ignored and appreciated in her lifetime, but her outward success and failure had no effect on her productivity.

The distinction I want to make is that an unproductive narcissist doesn't even make it onto the economic playing field, can't even participate in creating a business at a high level. We don't know the names of the unproductive narcissists of yesterday and today (unless they happen to be our friends or colleagues); they are not on the covers of magazines, they are not CEOs of global companies, they are not getting the attention of investors and VCs. To run a company, or even to run it into the ground, a narcissist must be, to some degree, productive. Or, to put it in terms of failure, all of the narcissists who have become high-profile failures *are still productive,* or at least were so in leading their companies—men like Bernie Ebbers, Michael Saylor, Michael Armstrong, Joe Nacchio, Percy Barnevik, Jean-Marie Messier, and Thomas Middlehoff.

But what we *can* say is that his strengths are the productive side of a narcissist and his weaknesses are the unproductive side. We can look, then, at the productive narcissist's strengths and weaknesses in terms of *degree* of productiveness. Those on the furthermost trajectory of productiveness are using their abilities at their highest level. Those who are on the lower end may be letting their weaknesses undermine them. Or, in practical terms, Bill Gates is more productive than Steve Jobs, Jack Welch is more productive than Jürgen Schrempp, and Henry Ford was, in his early years, more productive than William Durant.

In the rest of this chapter, I'll highlight a number of different productive narcissists and give real-life examples of their strengths and weaknesses. What will emerge from this composite is a clear portrait of the productive narcissist, a personality that is often fuzzy or indistinct in the context of the business press and literature. It's my aim to bring the personality type into sharp focus, highlighting the similarities between leaders such as Gates and Welch, men who seem so different on the surface but who share the narrowly defined strengths of the productive narcissist. To give a fuller composite, I'll focus on a few narcissists from the last century, another revolutionary time that favored the narcissistic personality—Rockefeller, Ford, and Durant; a few from today's global economy—Jack Welch, Bill Gates, Steve Jobs, Robert Shapiro, Jim Clark, Craig Venter; and several of my own clients—including Goran Collert, a health care CEO, and Robert Johnson, the CEO of Black Entertainment Television (BET). Some of these people succeeded, and some did not.

But no matter their level of success, they are all productive narcissists. And I can sum up in one paragraph exactly what strengths, in varying degrees, they share: They are independent thinkers who act out of freedom, even when it means taking big risks. They are all motivated by a vision of changing the world, creating something that shapes not only their own future but that of their followers. They live in reality—while their dreams may be a stretch, they zero in on what is possible, "doable." They use everything they can, including people, to implement their vision, learning as much as possible along the way. They are passionate, energized by their vision, charismatically drawing others into their internal dialogue. They know exactly who is with them and who is against them, and are alert to threats. And finally, they are emotionally connected to the real world and have some awareness of how their colleagues and coworkers see them; they can even

---

STRENGTHS OF THE PRODUCTIVE NARCISSIST

- Visioning to change the world and create meaning
- Independent thinking/Risk taking
- Passion
- Charisma
- Voracious learning
- Perseverance
- Alertness to threats
- Sense of humor

---

make a joke or two, often at their own expense. To sum up, they are highly productive narcissists and use all of their strengths to accomplish their purpose.

Now let's break that description of productive narcissists down into their specific strengths before examining their weaknesses.

Visioning to Change the World and Create Meaning

Freud wrote that narcissists do not find meaning in the existing norms; they are the ones who change the world, but more than that, they see their world as a place that *needs* changing. Vision, therefore, is the key to understanding the productive narcissist and his strengths; once a narcissist's vision falls into place, he is able to mobilize his strengths in order to accomplish his goals. Consider the crucial importance of visioning to these productive narcissists:

John D. Rockefeller consistently maintained that Standard Oil was more than a multinational corporation or a moneymaking concern; rather, it "rendered a missionary service to the whole world. Strong as this statement is, it is the Gospel truth." Historian Ron Chernow reminds us that this belief was not just a public relations ploy; it was evident in Rockefeller's public statements and private correspondence. In a letter to his colleague Henry C. Folger, Rockefeller wrote, "Let the good work go on. We must ever remember we are refining oil for the poor man and he must have it cheap and good."

Historians have often viewed Rockefeller's religiosity, his habit of saying "God gave me money," as a ploy to blunt the popular opinion that he was, in H. L. Mencken's words, a "money-grubbing theologian." In more recent years, historians such as Ron Chernow and Paul Johnson have recast Rockefeller's image, recognizing his brilliance as a business leader and his contribution to the modern industrial complex. It's not my aim to enter the debate over whether Rockefeller was in truth a religious man, or whether he was "good" or bad" in his business dealings; what I would like to do is offer a new way of looking at Rockefeller in terms of his personality type: He was a productive narcissist whose vision of Standard Oil as "missionaries of light" engaged his own considerable talents and passions, and that of his followers.

In light of what we've learned about the productive narcissist, consider this quote from a journalist's interview with Rockefeller: "I believe that the power to make money is a gift from God—just as are the instincts for art, music, literature, the doctor's talent, the nurse's, yours—to be developed and used to the best of our ability for the good of mankind. Having been endowed with the gift I possess, I believe it is my duty to make money and still more money, and to use the money I make for the good of my fellow man according to the dictates of my conscience." Remove the religiosity and what you have is an almost pitch-perfect definition of productiveness: Everyone has certain skills, and as human beings we are obligated to use these skills to the best of our ability for some greater purpose. This comment, as well as many others, has often been misunderstood as more "money-grubbing," or as proof that Rockefeller did it all for the money. But look again—the money is only a means to an end, only as good as what it was used for: low-priced oil for the masses, the direct result of the Standard Oil economy of scale, and the first systematic philanthropic foundation in the world, the ability to make and then, in turn, give away more money ·than the world had ever seen.

Goran Collert was running Swedbank when it was merely the bank that serviced the Swedish savings banks. He told me that he wanted to do more than just increase the company's size and profits; he wanted to re-create the Hanseatic League of the fourteenth century with a twofold strategy: building an international banking community that would protect Scandinavian and Baltic banks from foreign invasions by larger, more powerful countries, while strengthening Sweden's banking system and broadening the global reach of the local communities.

When *Robert Johnson* hired me as a business coach, he had invested every cent he had in BET, then a small cable start-up that catered exclusively to a black audience. He was in debt, living in a small house, scraping by on his wife's salary as a music teacher. When I asked him his goal, he told me that he wanted to be the king of an African-American media empire. Although there was no reason to think he was the guy who could pull it off, he mobilized a team of employees, persuaded John Malone to sign on as a shareholder, and convinced me that I had something to learn from his vision.

I coached a *health care CEO* whose vision was to revolutionize the entire American health care system, doing away with the old model of the single, independently run hospital and replacing it with centrally organized hospital units and satellite clinics that could pool their resources, providing teams of roaming doctors, wider availability of services, and lower costs. He convinced six major hospitals and 1,500 physicians to buy in to his vision before it was shot down by the doctors who were threatened by the massive reorganization of the existing system.

Robert Shapiro, formerly CEO of Monsanto, has been known to say that genetically modified crops are the single most important agricultural discovery since the plow. In an interview with the journalist Michael Specter in *The New Yorker*, he said that "there now exists an opportunity to create a genuine science of nutrition, something that has never existed in human history. . . . When you go home at night and you talk to your family about what you're working on, it isn't like 'Gee, I designed a really cool paper clip today.' It's about the earth, it's about the environment, it's about food. It's about health and nutrition. Those are deep, ancient things for civilization, and they are for the people." Even though Shapiro was fired before he could implement his ideas, he energized his staff with his vision; a former executive at Monsanto said that "there was a real sense of a noble purpose, a sense of Camelot."

J. Craig Venter, formerly CEO of Celera Genomics, the private company that mapped the human genome, believes that genomics will change not only the life sciences industry but the fundamental meaning of life and its basic forms. And for what end? "To turn knowledge into new treatments for diseases . . . to explain to the larger public what genetic discoveries mean, how they change who we are." Venter, who told me that he has been called the Henry Ford of biotechnology, sees himself "working for the greater good and larger purpose." The comparison to Ford is not mere grandiosity on Venter's part: Both he and Ford made it their mission to turn specific scientific discoveries into broader social movements with the power to change people's lives.

Jack Welch not only wanted to "change GE from one of the great companies to absolutely the greatest company in world business," he wanted to transform the entire structure of bureaucratic silos into a dynamic, evolving dynasty of highly competitive professional teams in separate businesses that all work toward the same goal: embracing the GE value system and moving the company to greatness.

What can we make of these examples? On the surface, it seems that these business leaders have a lot in common—they are all pompous big shots, always letting everyone know their big plans. There *is* a lot of big talk in these anecdotes, but that's not how I look at these stories. Beyond the overblown statements, what I find isn't the usual self-aggrandizing; what I see is that they all sound like men on a mission. All of the CEOs I've cited have a unique kind of vision that we don't see in the other personality types. In the last chapter, I showed how the other types are motivated by internalized controls that differ from those of the narcissist; that is, they have a different sense of purpose. An *erotic* nurse wants to take care of people, or a teacher wants to motivate kids to learn. An *obsessive* wants to make things work better—the company, the family, the government, the restaurant, the cast and crew, the personnel, the team, the golf game—and to be the best there is. The *marketing* personality wants to feel he is continuously improving himself, to see his stock rise in the personality market in order to provide value to others. But narcissists must create their own sense of meaning, and it has to be attractive enough to engage their own abilities as well as those of other people.

You may know some people who think that they, too, should be the ones who change the world with their invention, their great idea, their company. G. K. Chesterton pointed out how misleading it is to think that supreme self-confidence in one's vision guarantees success: "I know of men who believe in themselves more colossally than Napoleon or Caesar. . . . The men who really believe in themselves are all in lunatic asylums." What distinguishes a productive narcissist from these idle dreamers and big talkers is that their vision engages others, provides them with meaning. This may seem counterintuitive, especially when you take an even glancing look at the business pages or read the words I've quoted from the CEOs above—they certainly sound like they are out for themselves, or in some cases, full of themselves. But take another look—they are all passionately engaged in a mission, and in turn, engage others. The most productive narcissists, the ones who do actually change our world, provide meaning not only for themselves but also for the people who work for them, who believe in them, who follow them.

Vision, therefore, is the key to understanding the productive narcissist. Once a productive narcissist has found his purpose, his vision, it crystallizes his strengths. His passion flames up, bringing his talents and skills to life. This became clear to me when I was talking to Craig Venter; he said that it is impossible to separate his vision from the passion it takes to make his vision a reality: "Passion is purpose." He went on to say that "there are many people with wonderful skill sets, but they lack a broader vision. I've provided the context for them. Everyone wants to believe in something greater than themselves."

It is conventional business wisdom that our visionaries were born with their big plan, that they knew from a young age what they wanted to do, that they would be a successful CEO, engineer, artist, and so on. This is a myth, and not a particularly useful one. Some like Frank Lloyd Wright had a sense of destiny, but more often than not I've found that narcissists don't find their purpose until later in life. Some stumble upon it, some search for it, while others may never find it and end up isolated. Take, for example, Jim Clark. He told Michael Lewis that he felt like an absolute failure when he was approaching middle age: "All those years you thought you were achieving something. And you achieved nothing. I was thirty-eight years old. I'd just been fired. My second wife had just left me, I had somehow fucked up. I developed this maniacal passion for wanting to achieve *something*." He didn't know what it was at the time, but it wasn't long before he created Silicon Graphics, a company that did change the world by revolutionizing computer graphics and their use in design, film, games, and other media. Clark then went on to create Netscape, the company that ushered in the Internet revolution. His latest creation is Healtheon, and it remains to be seen if it or his next company will engage Clark's sense of purpose, or if his narcissistic weaknesses have gotten the best of him.

The point I'm trying to make is that Clark—and many other narcissists—*become* productive narcissists only when they develop a passion to "achieve *something*," in Clark's words. Achieving something doesn't mean designing buildings that no one will construct, or cooking up plans that never see the light of day; it means engaging others. Clark became energized, came out of his deep funk, only when he saw that people were starting to follow his lead: "I don't know how many people around me noticed. But my God I noticed. The first manifestation was when all of these people started coming up and wanting to be part of my project."

Clark's story is similar to that of Henry Ford, who was forty when he started his own car company; or Craig Venter, who was about forty when he broke open the field of genomics by recognizing the possibilities of rapid sequencing; or Sigmund Freud, who discovered psychoanalysis and wrote *The Interpretation of Dreams* in his forties, after failures in other fields; or Goran Collert, who was fifty when he predicted the collapse of the Swedish savings bank system and created Swedbank; or Sidney Harman, who left a secure job in a loudspeaker company in his thirties and bet everything he had on his first hi-fi company; or Robert Shapiro, who was general counsel at his father's company, General Instrument Corporation, a rather humdrum office products company, before he started working at the pharmaceutical company G. D. Searle, where he found his passion: "We were doing something important for people. It wasn't just making a handheld calculator, as we had in my previous incarnation. This thing actually mattered."

The move from office products to pharmaceuticals isn't a natural one, and Shapiro probably had no idea that it would take a job heading up the NutraSweet division of Searle to jump-start his creativity. But as soon as Shapiro started to receive grateful letters from diabetic kids who could finally eat Jell-O and other artificially sweetened foods, he knew he could change people's lives through food. This is a common thread in the careers of productive narcissists: They don't know what they want to do until they find it. All of the CEOs that I've quoted are in different fields—oil, a traditional product company, banking, bioengineering, health care, genomics—yet they sound surprisingly similar in their passion to change the world via their own vehicles.

This is the case with the productive narcissist Henry Ford. Before he started his own company, the forty-year-old Ford had always worked for someone else, first for Westinghouse as a traction engine operator, and after that as an engineer at the

Detroit Edison Illuminating Company. It was only when he started playing around with internal combustion engines in his own home that he knew, all of sudden, what he wanted to do: build the "universal car" for the "great multitude" (notice how similar, even in terminology, his vision is to that of Rockefeller). Once Ford discovered his purpose, he pursued it with nothing short of absolute clarity; he was not about to subordinate his vision to any other company or person. Along with several investors, Ford opened the Detroit Automobile Company in 1899, and promptly left two years later over design disputes with his backers. He then partnered with new backers to form the Henry Ford Company. Once again, Ford felt constrained by his partners and their opposing ideas about how to build a car company. In less than a year, Ford jumped ship and started his third—and last—car company, the Ford Motor Company. Why? "I found that the company was not a vehicle for realizing my ideas but merely a money-making concern."

This is a wonderful comment, one that says a great deal about Ford in particular and the narcissistic personality in general. Ford was completely uninterested in turning the Henry Ford Company into a better version of itself. This middle-aged man, who had always been satisfied enough with his life as a midlevel employee, all of a sudden wouldn't settle for anything less than running a company that was an extension of himself and his belief system—and his belief system was simple: changing the world with the car. The companies that productive narcissists create embody *all* of their personality, their strengths and weaknesses, so that the company is the leader's personality writ large. As Marc Andreeson, the programmer who created Netscape with Jim Clark, currently CEO of Opsware, says: "These companies are like organisms. It's as if you took a DNA sample from the chief executive and blew it up to monstrous size." This is a fundamental point about the relationship of a narcissistic personality to his company: *Productive narcissists see the company as a means to their own ends; other types, even the most productive ones, see themselves as a means to their company's end.* The latter case, the CEOs who see themselves as serving the organization, are usually heading up companies that are based on continual improvement, becoming the best versions of themselves, winning within the game of making and selling products to more customers, rather than creating a new game.

Narcissistic leaders, on the other hand, "damage the established state of affairs"—or, to put it in terms of business, smash the old economic rules and create an entirely new game with their own rules. They use their corporations as vehicles for their own vision. A contemporary example of this is Southwest under legendary former CEO Herb Kelleher, who created a social system that both supports his business strategy and reflects his personality and did it better and more profitably than most CEOs. In an astute article, Michael Porter, the Harvard Business School professor and noted theorist of business strategy, asks: "What is Southwest's core competence? . . . The correct answer is that everything matters. . . . Its competitive advantage comes from the way its activities fit and reinforce one another." Kelleher's company embodies his own belief system and guiding principles, the first of which he learned from his mother: "She taught me that every person and every job is worth just as much as any other person and any other job." How, in practical terms, does this philosophy play out at Southwest? The company does very few things but does them all well. The customers know what to expect from a Southwest flight, ensuring a high percentage of repeat business. There are regular flights that almost always leave on time. There are no frills—no seat assignments, no food, no drinks, no baggage service to connecting flights. High-volume airports are avoided. Electronic tickets are favored over ticket agents. Employees are treated with respect regardless of their place in the corporate hierarchy. Wages are high within the industry. Union contracts are weighted in favor of the employees; stock ownership is encouraged, as is keeping employment within the family with one or more members working together at Southwest. To hire team players, Southwest asks job candidates to prepare a skit or routine, to sing a song or recite a poem. Some perform while the other candidates watch. Little do they know that the candidates who are hired are the observers who cheer and applaud others and not the ones thinking about what they'll do when it's their turn to perform.

This basic business model is reinforced with an environment that is known throughout the business world as a place where the employees have a good time, where fun is institutionalized in the culture. At a time when it has become deeply uncool and even immoral in corporate America to drink and smoke, Kelleher makes excess acceptable again, and encourages it in his employees. When Jim Parker, the new CEO of Southwest, was asked last year how he and Colleen Barrett (the current president of Southwest and Kelleher's former secretary) plan on replacing Kelleher when he retires, he replied: "Well, Colleen is going to handle the smoking, and I'm going to handle the drinking." This all may sound like good fun, but in the worst industry in the world in terms of turning a profit, Southwest has not lost money since 1973, a record that is unmatched in the airline industry.

Narcissistic leaders are obviously not limited to corporations. A productive narcissist can convert any organization into a vehicle for his vision, even in the world of professional sports. Picture this: You are a white, middle-aged coach and a bit of a has-been, an ex-jock whose athletic career could be described only as below average. You have been asked to coach a group of players who are young, make much more money than you, are more famous than you, and are almost all black. One of them is the best athlete on the planet. As you see it, there are a few ways you can handle this situation: (1) Take total control—do what I say or else; (2) cater to your star player and hope the rest of the team follows; (3) let them do whatever they want—they made it this far, so they must be doing something right. If you are like most coaches, you pick one of these options and hope that it works long enough to win a few games. If you are Phil Jackson, however, you choose an entirely different approach: You provide your team with a way of life.

When Phil Jackson was hired to be part of the coaching staff of the Chicago Bulls in 1987, he had already spent years studying Zen and Christian spirituality, and he wanted to put into practice his "grand scheme" for coaching: "My goal was to find a structure that would empower *everybody* on the team, not just the stars, and allow the players to grow as individuals as they surrendered themselves to the group effort." This sounds like Leadership 101: give everyone a chance, get them to act as a group. But it is a lot more complicated than it sounds. NBA players, when they reach that level, have been valued their whole lives for their physical strength, their ability to play hard, their singular achievements and individual records, and their willingness to win at any cost and never back down. And this is only on the court; off the court, everybody has always told them how great they are and let them get away with all sorts of self-centered behavior. Surrender—to any one person or to a group—does not come easily to a twenty-three-year-old athlete who earns a few million dollars a year. As Jackson saw it, any attempt to cater to the players, to talk to them in their own language, would fail. He had seen other coaches try, and "unless they're incredibly gifted psychologists, these coaches inevitably end up feeling as if they're being held hostage by the players they're supposed to be leading." So what did Jackson do? He made the Bulls speak *his* language, surrender their own assumptions about basketball, and buy in to his belief system.

Jackson's revolutionary way of working with the Bulls began with breaking down their usual "me-first" playing attitude—essentially, pass the ball to the best players and let them run with it—and developing an offensive system that gives everybody on the floor a chance. Along with "basketball professor" Tex Winters, Jackson created the now-famous triangle offensive, what he calls a continuous-motion dance that requires the players to work as a coherent whole. At first, the players didn't have much confidence in the triangle. It took a big investment of both faith (it went against everything the team had learned up to that point) and time (months of repetitive drills and practice to get it down). But then it started to click, and they began winning game after game. When the Bulls won the 1991 NBA championship, the team rapped about their conversion: "We believe, yeah, we believe in that triangle. It's the show for those in the know."

The playing strategy was just the beginning: Jackson asked his players for full commitment, at least while they were on his time, to his moral system. He began the early team meetings with a dis-

cussion of ethics, passing out a modernized version of the Ten
Commandments for the players to discuss and relate to their lives.
They practiced group meditation, an exercise that was harder for
some players than others: "The first time we practiced meditation,
Michael [Jordan] thought I was joking. Midway though the session,
he cocked one eye open and took a glance around the room to see
if any of his teammates were actually doing it. To his surprise, many
of them were." Rather than watching the usual game films, Jackson spliced clips of Hollywood films into the game tapes, mixing in
The Wizard of Oz or *Pulp Fiction* to break up the criticism with
comedy. Jackson's reasoning? Humor is the reality principle, and
he wanted to bring the mighty down to earth. He gave homework
in the form of reading assignments: *Ways of the White Folks,* by
Langston Hughes, for Scottie Pippen; *All the Pretty Horses,* by
Cormac McCarthy, for Steve Kerr; *Zen and the Art of Motorcycle
Maintenance,* by Robert M. Pirsig, for John Paxson; *On the Road,*
by Jack Kerouac, for Will Purdue; and *Fever: Twelve Stories,* by
John Wideman, for Michael Jordan.

Jackson got the Bulls to read, something that they probably
had never valued in their lives, a hard task requiring concentration
and no visible reward. The reward was in participating in Jackson's
ethos, a show of faith that's impressive for any group—and remarkable for a group of NBA basketball players. In describing his strategy, Jackson said that it "embodied the Zen Christian attitude of
selfless awareness. In essence, the system was a *vehicle* for integrating mind and body, sport and spirit. . . ." The italics on the word
"vehicle" are mine. I've added them to make the point that Jackson sounds similar to Ford here; his triangle, the machinery of the
team, is a vehicle for his ideas in the way that Ford's assembly line

was a vehicle for his. When you look at Jackson's strategy in this way, he has a lot more in common with Ford than he does with Pat Riley. Riley's style is the leader as motivational speaker, delivering constant, pumping pep talks and encouraging winning at any cost. Riley wants to make the team a better version of itself, rather than create a new team based on his vision. Jackson can take his show on the road, to any team he coaches—a theory that has now been tested and proven: The Bulls are no longer the championship Bulls; the Lakers have become the vehicle for Jackson's way of life. Brian Shaw, one of the Lakers, says about Jackson: "He has this way of getting you to give yourself to something you never thought of before. We do Tai Chi and yoga and meditate. I never did those things before, never thought of them. And maybe there's no direct correlation between these things and basketball. But it broadens our horizons. It challenges us."

Independence and Risk Taking

This leads directly to the next strengths of the productive narcissist—independence and risk taking. Productive narcissists are relatively free from both internal and external constraints, and are willing to take risks in order to realize their vision.

Let me address internal independence first. As a personality type, narcissists are more free than the other types; they don't listen to the usual social pressures to conform. From childhood, they resist the herd mentality, any kind of conformity in thinking. A good word to describe them is "wary": They are wary of a moralistic father figure, teachers, the "in" crowd. Rockefeller told his children: "Never mind the crowd. Keep away from it. Attend to your own business." And be wary of everyone, including him. I noted that Esther Dyson was wary of the popular kids in college and felt no pressure to go out on Saturday night. This may seem like a small, insignificant example, but think about most of the people you know: They usually try to fit in by wearing the right clothes, going to the most highly ranked school, showing up at the popular places, or taking the job that looks great. Obsessives may stubbornly resist fashion and stick to traditional conservative habits, but narcissists like Dyson are not resisting; they are *ignoring* what is popular and doing their own thing. This is what I mean by internal independence—freedom from psychological constraints, the ability to do what you think is best for you, not just what others do or think you should do. According to Goran Collert, "A free person is not just autonomous. It means there are no borders—you are free to think."

What exactly does external independence mean in today's workplace? This question has become more relevant with the rise of the "free agent" and the freelancer, groups of people who are no longer tied to one company throughout the life span of their careers. But don't confuse being a free agent with being free, either internally or externally. You are not independent if you have flexible hours but are caught up in trying to impress the boss. You aren't free if you are a freelancer who obsessively worries about making money, living from paycheck to paycheck. And you haven't created circumstances that allow you to create in your own image if you are always looking over your shoulder at who's coming up behind you. How many people can say that they never wake up in the morning afraid that they are going to be fired, that today is the day they'll get a pink slip? Or are never troubled by the thought that their business will go belly-up? Or think that their résumé doesn't show enough experience or depth in their chosen field? Most people can't say that these thoughts never play a part in their actions; they are not free. Productive narcissists, on the other hand, may have these thoughts, but they don't *act* on them. They are free to be fired. They are free to fail. And they are free to start over again. They are not tied to one job or even one profession. They have external independence.

Let me give you a straightforward example. When he was interviewed for *Black Enterprise* magazine, Robert Johnson was asked about his business philosophy. He answered: "I chart my own course." This is the sort of business advice that, on first reading, seems completely useless. Who wouldn't want to chart their own course? It's kind of like asking who wouldn't want to win the lottery. But on second glance, it turns out that it is an instructive way of looking at Johnson's career. At the time that he said it, he was a billionaire, so it makes sense that he would be able to chart his own course. When you're a winner, you get to call the shots. But this is exactly the same philosophy that Johnson embraced when I met him in 1985 and he was barely making ends meet. He was in debt, having invested everything he had in BET. But he was already creating the external circumstances that allowed him to pursue his vision and start his own business, something he never could have done in his previous job as a congressional aide. It was a risk that Johnson, his wife, and his staff decided to take, all betting solely on Johnson's vision.

This is a philosophy that Johnson trumpets whenever he can. Years later, in the early '90s, I introduced Johnson to a senator who was trying to pass a bill on a program that provided jobs for African-Americans. Johnson was absolutely opposed to the program, believing that it turned blacks into employees, killing any of their entrepreneurial vision and spirit. Where were the programs that gave African-Americans the freedom to pursue their own vision and the financial support to get it off the ground? The senator's program, in Johnson's opinion, ensured that its participants could never chart their own course, as he did. Productive narcissists believe that freedom allows them to create. The cosmetics entrepreneur Mary Kay built an entire door-to-door empire with women "reserves" as her sales force, giving housewives financial freedom at a time when they weren't even expected to work outside the home. Esther Dyson's goal is to empower people, give them more work options; she told me that "people behave badly because they lack power over their lives. I know it sounds simplistic, but people without control over their lives have stress."

You may wonder who wouldn't want freedom, or rather, who wouldn't want to chart his own course? As it turns out, plenty of people would rather have the security of a job, even a bad job, than have to come up with their own plan; they stay in mind-numbing and painful work situations rather than take the risk of leaving. Narcissists can't stand situations that contain them and their ideas, and have the guts to go out on their own, risking security and failure in favor of their vision. A colleague of Sidney Harman's said that you could drop him in the middle of Times Square naked, without a penny, and he would become a millionaire again in no time. Jim Clark created and walked away from two companies that generated two separate industries, and has gone on to start a third, all the while making, and risking, billions of dollars. The health care CEO left a professorship to create his first clinic. Henry Ford left his steady paycheck as an engineer to start not one but two car companies that he left before starting his third and last—the Ford Motor Company. Jack Welch actually quit his job at GE when he saw he wasn't advancing fast enough, before being lured back and put on the fast track to the CEO position.

When I interviewed Craig Venter, he told me that freedom was "essential! I couldn't stand rules and confinement. I wanted freedom and left home at age seventeen." After doing service in Vietnam as a medic, Venter kept on the same career path, attending medical school. He then decided that he could help more people with scientific study than by practicing medicine; his influence and impact, for the general good, would be greater in the research field. After working in academia and at the National Institutes of Health, Venter started his own nonprofit research company to realize his vision of genetic mapping. At the time, he had only $2,000 in the bank and was going into the decidedly low-paying nonprofit sector. He started several nonprofits before founding Celera, the for-profit company that mapped the human genome. At every stage of his career, Venter decided against the easy route, the safe one, in favor of the riskier path that offered the most freedom from constraint. Failing wasn't an option; Venter says: "Maybe I'm so egotistical I'm not afraid of failing."

There are some interesting parallels between the scientific career of Craig Venter and the literary career of Michael Crichton, one of our few contemporary productive narcissists in the multimedia field of books, film, television, and video games. He was trained as a medical doctor and wrote his early, pseudonymous medical potboilers while in med school. But he, like Venter, left medicine, choosing to have a greater impact on people by *writing* about medicine and science than practicing it. Crichton has created entire multimedia worlds where dinosaurs come back to life (*Jurassic Park*) and virtual reality is an everyday office reality (*Disclosure*). He is the rare literary productive narcissist who is always one step ahead of the public's concerns and fears—whether it's genetic manipulation, sexual harassment, airline safety, or computer imaging and nano-technology—and has turned his abilities into a multibillion-dollar industry. Stephen King, another literary productive narcissist, worked at a laundry and taught English while he wrote his early short stories and novels. Benedict de Spinoza held a steady job as a lens grinder throughout his entire working life, a profession that gave him the freedom to write his philosophical treatises on the side without worrying about whether they appealed to the commercial concerns of publishers.

Passion

Once productive narcissists find their purpose, it ignites their passion; they go after their vision with an overabundance of energy and determination. Nothing seems to stand in their way. Let me repeat Venter's "Passion is purpose," a personal credo that could be the mission statement of so many productive narcissists.

We need to differentiate between the all-consuming nature of a productive narcissist's work and run-of-the-mill workaholism. People like Welch, Gates, and Jobs may keep going around the clock, but it is not the same as other personality types who are chained to their desks, writing another memo, trying to finish everything on their to-do list, or taking that last phone call. This kind of workaholism can undermine the efforts of the other personality types—an obsessive can worry into the middle of the night about the accounts that don't add up; or a marketing personality may replay over and over again a conversation or event that he could have handled better; or an erotic can get caught up in so much client hand-holding that he has no personal life. But for the productive narcissist, passion is a restless curiosity that never stops or settles. Garry Wills writes that "genius is . . . the ability to keep asking the same questions and a dissatisfaction with all former answers." Replace "genius" with "productive narcissism," and you have an accurate description of the working habits of a productive narcissist—a constant bubbling up of new ideas that need to be tested and tried out, no matter what time of the day or night.

For the passionate productive narcissist, there is no such thing as a personal life, because their work *is* their life; changing the world is not something that happens during office hours. Venter told me that "it's difficult to separate your ego from your work." Other personality types think they can replicate a productive narcissist's success by mimicking their work habits—having flexible hours, working from home—without realizing that the all-consuming nature of the productive narcissist's work is a reflection of what is going on in his endlessly questioning mind. I overheard a conversation between a productive narcissist who is known for his tremendous work output and a colleague; the narcissist was ticking off the many projects he had undertaken recently, to which the colleague said, "Wow, no rest for the weary." The narcissist looked at him and said, absolutely straight-faced, "Why would you ever rest from what you love?"

This kind of constant and passionate devotion is what brings about change, but it can be brutal on the colleagues, sidekicks, and advisers of productive narcissists, who are almost always on call. Steve Jobs is famously known for his endless barrage of questions, calls, impromptu meetings. Alan Deutschman reports that "he tormented Heidi Roizen [a top executive] with constant calls to her office phone, home phone, cell phone, and pager, starting at 7 A.M. almost every day." There was simply no avoiding Jobs. When Ford was working on the design of what would eventually become the Model T, he and his team worked until ten or eleven o'clock at night, every night, with Ford watching over every detail. One of the engineers on the job recalled that "there was a rocking chair in the room in which he used to sit for hours and hours at a time, discussing and following out the development of the design." (It's interesting to note that the rocking chair had been Ford's mother's before she died.) Ford's round-the-clock devotion prompted one of his suppliers to comment: "We often wondered when Henry Ford slept."

Bill Gates and Jim Clark are both known for working around the clock, sending off e-mails in the middle of the night. When Jim Clark was cooking up Netscape, one of the venture capitalists who backed the company assigned a kid just out of Harvard Business School to follow Clark around and take notes on whatever he was doing. It just happened that Clark was *doing* all the time; the kid was even told to "sleep under Jim's bed if he had to" so that he would be there, ready, whenever Clark's next idea hit him. William Durant would call meetings any time inspiration struck, even if it was one-thirty in the morning, but like so many other productive narcissists, he was the first one into the office the next morning, never showing any wear and tear. For Durant it was fun, not work, so why would he be worn out?

Some of the productive narcissists I've worked with—Harman, Collert, health care CEO—called me at all hours, trying out new ideas, asking me, "What do you think of this?" and then hung up before I even had a chance to answer. The phone is a technological way of having an inner dialogue with a captive audience. Most narcissists aren't interested in the give-and-take of a real conversation; they want to test and put into action their ideas, even if it means waking me or their other advisers in the middle of the night. They are, in a sense, addicted to the phone. It brings them out of their isolation, if only for a few minutes. Sometimes it's an efficient way of pumping people for information. Jürgen Schrempp calls ten to fifteen people on weekends to bounce ideas off them. Some productive narcissists want someone around them at all times—not to keep them company, but to be there when a new idea hits. Harry Bennett, Ford's sidekick, received a phone call from Ford first thing in the morning, usually every day, before Ford drove to his home, picked him up, and drove him to work.

Charisma

Productive narcissists have an undeniable emotional pull on others. Freud compared our attraction to them to our fascination with felines; we're curious about any creature that seems so self-contained, appearing not to need anyone or anything. Narcissists may appear cool, emotionally detached, but as soon as they need anything from you, the most productive ones can turn on an enormous amount of charm and charisma. They are aware that they need to draw others into their internal dialogue, to engage followers, all of which requires a seductive dance with the people they recruit.

Almost all productive narcissists, at one time or another, are thought of as big charmers. Rockefeller was said to have a "magnetic power over workers." Durant was legendary for his ability to talk his way into anything. Walter Chrysler wrote about Durant in his memoirs: "I cannot hope to find words to express the charm of the man. He has the most winning personality of anyone I've ever known. He could coax a bird right down out of the tree, I think." Steve Jobs is a perfect example of a narcissist who runs hot and cold, turning on the charm when he wants something from you, becoming indifferent and even angry when he doesn't. Narcissists need their followers much the same way politicians need their audience, their constituency. Some of our narcissistic presidents—Lincoln, FDR, Reagan, Clinton—have been extraordinary communicators and charmers. Clinton is famous for his ability to "feel your pain," and equally well-known for dropping those who have been close to him.

To be sure, charisma has to do with a productive narcissist's dual attraction, the combination of catlike distance and certain charm. But charisma can also be seen as the result of an interaction, a relationship between the productive narcissist and the people who are charmed and motivated by him. A narcissist feeds off of the admiration of others, becoming more spontaneous and sure of his message. I thought of this when I read that Jürgen Schrempp said that the "long applause gave me strength" after he gave a talk to an audience that was previously critical of him—the Social

Democratic work counsels in December 1996. When the public's admiration seems to drop, so too does a narcissist's magnetism. You can almost see them deflate. This happened to Ross Perot in the 1992 election campaign. Once Perot's paranoia emerged, his audience drifted from him, draining him of his charm and charisma.

Perseverance

Anyone who has big dreams and the daring to go after them is bound to fail at one time or another. It's how a person reacts to failure that differentiates the productive personality from the unproductive one; productive people are not discouraged by failure. They are resilient. They learn from it, rebound, don't give up.

I see this quality in infants who crawl around any obstacle you put in their path—it's almost as if they don't *see* the obstacle; they just see where they're going, and try to get there any way they can. Some of these children lose that quality as they get older; once life starts to hand them a string of obstacles, many will start to heed the voices of "That's not possible" and "You can't do that." They no longer have the childlike ability to persevere. Productive narcissists retain the ability to ignore any and all obstacles throughout their lives. Like the infants, they don't seem to see the things that stand in their way. Productive narcissists have to be like that, or they would never believe that they, out of all the people in the world, are the ones who are going to change the existing order. It goes beyond the usual persistence that we hear from sports coaches and inspirational teachers; the perseverance of the productive narcissist is a kind of childlike, blinkered way of seeing the world as a place where he will always prevail. Churchill, who knew a thing or two about perseverance, said it best: "Success is going from failure to failure without loss of enthusiasm."

It's one thing to show persistence and hard work when things are going your way; it's quite another when you're faced with huge losses or utter economic failure. Many productive narcissists suffer the kind of defeat that would leave other personality types cowering under their covers for years but refuse to acknowledge or even register their defeats. Take William Durant. Throughout his career, Durant went from one public loss and business humiliation to another: He lost control of his own company twice, and was always teetering on the edge of personal and corporate financial disaster. When a reporter asked him about another one of his financial fiascos in 1921, he said: "Forget mistakes. Forget failures. Forget everything except what you're going to do now and do it." Durant never gave up, even after he had a small heart attack at the end of his life. Here he was, reduced to managing a bowling alley, with all his auto industry years behind him, and he still boasted that the "plan of winning the bowling championship of the State of Michigan is being postponed from day to day." John DeLorean is Durant's modern-day counterpart. Despite his highly public business and personal defeats (he was arrested twice, once accused of trying to sell cocaine, the second of money laundering, and beat the charges each time), he is *still* trying, at the age of seventy-eight, to launch a new car company.

Steve Jobs's career is a case study of perseverance. After getting kicked out of Apple, the company he founded, he started Next, which promptly and very publicly failed, then went back to Apple, where it is unclear what the future holds for him. Susan Barnes, a former employee, said that no matter what happened to Jobs, "he kept getting off the mat." The health care CEO's dismissal was a humiliating blow; other personality types probably would have switched careers entirely, but he is back in the same field, still trying to change the world with his own plan for a nationwide health care system designed for the poor and uninsured. Goran Collert's plans for a merger with SEB, the Wallenberg Bank, the culmination of years of planning and strategizing, was squashed by the EU, a major setback for Collert's vision to re-create the Hanseatic League. But no matter. Collert is right back in the game, plotting new mergers within Sweden and the Nordic area. In the political or military arena, we use the word "undaunted" to describe leaders who persevere, and when we do, it almost always is used in connection with a productive narcissist: Winston Churchill and Charles de Gaulle went on to write best sellers in exile; Nixon and now Clinton have had second careers as high-priced authors after their involvement in political scandals.

Even business leaders who have had great success, a long, uninterrupted winning streak, still face obstacles that require perseverance, the ability to go around whatever is blocking their business. Early in Rockefeller's career, the oil industry faced a crisis that threatened its survival—the East Coast wells had dried up, and price fluctuations forced drillers and refiners out of business. The Standard Oil executives urged Rockefeller to get out, to do something more stable. Rockefeller's response to his anxious colleagues was to point solemnly upward and say, "The Lord will provide." You can interpret this as spirituality; but you can also look at it as simple perseverance, Rockefeller's passion for his purpose, no matter what the obstacles.

When Rockefeller and Gates were the objects of the formidable force of the U.S. government in their antitrust suits, both hunkered down, refusing to back down or give in on either the witness stand or in their business dealings. In Rockefeller's case, this lasted for years; he was essentially a wanted man in a number of states, and he never capitulated. In Gates's case, he has pursued a business strategy of growth and expansion rather than lying low, a clear message to the government that he remains—here's that word again—undaunted. Just look at this statistic from Ken Auletta's account of the Microsoft case: "Despite the government lawsuit, between January 12, 1998, and November 11, 1999, Microsoft acquired or invested in a total of sixty-three companies, an average of more than one deal every twelve days."

Voracious Learning

Freud said about himself that he left behind his original career plan of law for medicine, preferring to study the physiological aspects of the mind and write about their impact on human behavior. Freud's motivation? His "greed for knowledge." This is a terrific phrase that I find descriptive of many of the productive narcissists I've known or observed, especially in the business world. We're used to hearing the word "greed" applied to captains of industry, men like Rockefeller or Ford or Gates; but I've found that most of them don't do it for the money. They, like Freud, have a voracious appetite, not for mere money but for information and understanding. They seek out and acquire knowledge, learning everything they possibly can about whatever subject they happen to be interested in. To quote Freud's description of Leonardo da Vinci, they have "an insatiable and indefatigable thirst for knowledge."

As we've seen, this doesn't necessarily mean that productive narcissists are good students; on the contrary, they're usually uninterested in formal schooling, bored with classes and the required curriculum. They have no desire to please the teacher or prove that they can get good grades or show up the other students. They excel only when they think classes are interesting or useful to them. Craig Venter said that he thought Phi Beta Kappas worked for C students—that is, that the good students are the employees, whereas the so-called bad student is often the boss. Daniel Goleman explains this with his theory of emotional intelligence; the most successful businessmen weren't necessarily the smartest kids in the class, but they do know how to treat other people. But if you look at some of the most successful productive narcissists, the ones who are often insensitive to others, it's not their intelligence that limited their academic careers, it's their independence. They usually don't do well in school because they are not interested in grades (and are therefore termed "underachievers" in high school and college); their passion is ignited independently, only by what *they* decide they care about, leaving them free to succeed on their own terms, outside the formal structures of school and study programs.

Craig Venter would have flunked out of high school, but he squeaked by with a D– rather than an F in a government class because he cared about the topic, an anti–Vietnam War paper, saying that "I felt passionately about it, so the teacher passed me." Sidney Harman told me that "as a kid, I read voraciously, under the covers with a flashlight. I read everything I could get my hands on."

He thought the classes at Brooklyn College were boring, but he found a study group at NYU and "I read again with great appetite." Esther Dyson almost never went to class; instead, she read on her own and went to as many movies as she could. Bill Gates read constantly in high school, shifting his appetite to computers once he discovered them, sneaking out of his room at night and breaking into his high school computer department. When he turned his foundation to curing AIDS in Africa, he read every book written on the subject. He even takes a week off every year to spend his time just reading.

We can see the same characteristic in productive narcissists throughout history. Napoleon was never a star pupil or even that noticeable as a military cadet, but he pored over history books, refining his political and military philosophy with Rousseau, James Boswell, and Abbé de Raynal. Lincoln, of course, is known for reading everything he could get his hands on; given his farming background, there wasn't much around, but what he had, he read over and over again and could quote from memory. Rockefeller was nicknamed "the Sponge" as a kid (it's interesting to note that Bud Tribble said the same thing about Steve Jobs: "The guy's a sponge once he zeroes in"). Bill Clinton's childhood friends used to say "Let's go over to Bill's and watch him read." A narcissist's appetite for knowledge, for learning, is not limited to reading. Henry Ford learned by doing. As a kid, he took apart windup dolls and watches and then put them back together to figure out exactly how they worked. His first hands-on experience with an internal combustion engine was in his own kitchen sink on Christmas Eve; he asked his wife, Clara, to put aside the holiday meal to help get it started.

The way I describe this is that productive narcissists *use* books, computers, machines, movies, rather than just read, operate, see them. Knowledge is a means to their end—their purpose, their passion. For example, David Gergen writes that "when [Clinton was] elected, he was barely functional on a computer but learned all about Silicon Valley and how technologies were changing the economy. By the end of his presidency, he was giving the best speeches on science and technology of anyone on the public stage." Clinton didn't necessarily care about computer technology, but he knew it was a key element to his financial policies, a way to make lasting changes in the economy.

Alertness to Threats

According to Freud, the narcissist's main interest is self-preservation. Think about this for a minute: How do you view the outside world? In general, do you try to befriend, seduce, ignore, keep your distance, embrace the people who surround you? Narcissists have a very clearly defined position vis-à-vis the people around them: You are either a friend or a foe; you can either help them or you are a threat to their survival. In business, this translates into a keen awareness of any competitive threats. Jack Welch may well say that "business is a game," but it is a very serious game in which he will do everything he possibly can to either use you to the company's advantage, beat you, or get rid of you, whether you're a colleague or a competitor. We can see this in Rockefeller, who never let anyone sneak up on him when he was young; he always knew who was around him, and he watched what we now call his "personal space" closely. As he grew in the business world, this translated into an acute sense of who was going to help or harm him, a trait that served him well in the ruthlessly competitive early days of the oil industry, where you either killed your business rivals or were extinguished yourself. Rockefeller himself defended his questionable business practices as the only way to survive: "It was forced upon us. . . . We had to do it in self-defense." His words could have been lifted directly from Freud's description of the narcissist.

Andy Grove famously put his finger on this narcissistic trait in his book *Only the Paranoid Survive*. An awareness of threats from competitors is the only way to see what he calls market "inflections," subtle changes that tell a company to either change strategies or market new products. Jim Clark has his own spin on this; he believes that any successful company must continually look to put itself out of business, to improve on its own products so much that earlier versions become obsolete. This is the awareness of threats taken to the extreme—you must kill your own business or be killed by someone else. This is the ethos that Bill Gates has instilled in Microsoft; while the lawyers who represented the government's case against Microsoft may not have been able to find any memo or e-mail in which Gates threatened to kill Netscape (or any other competitor, for that matter), no one doubts for a moment that it is Gates's intention to do just that.

Goran Collert almost always speaks to his staff in terms that are reminiscent of military maneuvers, rallying his troops with the threat of extinction in the event of foreign financial invasions. Venter thinks that his competitors are trying to destroy his credibility by accusing him of doing it all for the money rather than scientific advances, a claim he counters by calling them envious hypocrites and pointing out how they hustle for grants and patents, pretending that they're uninterested in money and fame.

Humor

O ne of the most underrated and most important positive characteristics of productive narcissists is a sense of humor, especially about themselves. In fact, I would go so far as to say that humorless narcissists have little chance of succeeding. Why? Because it means that they're not grounded in reality and have no idea of how other people see them. To give an extreme example, Camille Paglia can joke that she dressed up as Napoleon for Halloween because she knows she's *not* Napoleon; she just has a Napoleonic *concept* of herself and her achievements. I've found in my psychoanalytic practice that the patients who are humorless have the worst prognosis; those who can't laugh at themselves, see life's absurdity as well as its pain, are the hardest to treat.

Productive narcissists aren't big joke tellers or class clowns; their humor is usually self-effacing. For example, Rockefeller almost never used the word "I"—Standard Oil and the company was always referred to as "we"—unless he was telling a joke. Herb Kelleher was featured in a series of commercials for Southwest in which his employees took turns making fun of him, a self-effacing style he used in public and private. He once arrived at a dance for airline executives wearing a tutu and smoking a cigar. Martha Stewart appeared as herself on David Letterman with Martha Stewart's Worst Tips for Living. Number eight? "Add glitter to every damn thing you own." At the end of my interview with Craig Venter, he said, "I've talked a lot about myself." To which I said, "That was the point." Venter shot back: "As my PR guy says, 'It's always just about you, isn't it?'" Sidney Harman did a brief stint as a part-time president of an experimental college before he was let go, quipping: "I left as I came, fired with enthusiasm." David Gergen noted that "humor was the one place where [Ronald] Reagan might easily talk about himself." Reagan was able to joke about his age, the assassination attempt (telling the press "I forgot to duck"), his movie background. In a way, he was pointing out his weaknesses before anyone else could, a tactic that defused criticism.

This is one of the reasons to use self-effacing humor—it is an offensive tactic rather than a defensive one. When Phil Jackson got his team together to watch the game tapes, he spliced in movie scenes that poked fun at players' mistakes as a way of teaching them to lighten up about themselves. He knew that humor was one of the only ways he could get a bunch of superstars to acknowledge their vulnerabilities, to puncture their overblown egos and bring them down to earth.

The strengths of any personality type can, when taken to an extreme, become the very thing that weakens them. The most obvious example of this in business is the obsessive bureaucrat who becomes compulsively concerned with details, facts, money, and overall perfectionism. But it is just as true of the other types. An erotic can care too much about clients, colleagues, customers, becoming overly dependent on them, incapable of making any kind of tough or honest call for fear of offending them and losing their business. The marketing personality can adapt so much that he is rootless, lacking any commitment to sustained projects and career choices. So it is with even the most productive narcissists—their weaknesses are intimately tied to their strengths; the very things that got them to the top are the qualities that can bring them down. In order to be productive, every personality type needs to stay grounded in reason; narcissists, more so than the other personality types, run the greatest risk of losing their reason, a sense of reality, especially when they start to succeed. Or, to put it in terms of a specific case of a strength turning into a weakness, Steve Case said of Microsoft: "Their greatest vulnerability is themselves."

Also, just as the strengths work together, holistically, so do the weaknesses. They are usually a *syndrome* of weaknesses. For example, look at this four-year drama in the life span of a narcissist who was overcome by his weaknesses: The narcissist has a vision that he pursues with great aggression, passion, and intensity. He has a highly developed us-vs.-them mentality that allows him to ignore any dissent or moderating voices. He is persuasive and charismatic. He makes it to the top of a huge global technology company. On his way up, I work with him, and he tells people that he would not have become CEO without me. But once he is CEO, he doesn't want anyone to think he needs help, and tells me that he has learned enough from me. He becomes more isolated. As he begins to restructure the company, he boasts to me that all his top executives support his moves. I hear from a key vice president that he doesn't listen when they disagree with him. He becomes cramped with paranoia. He tries desperately to control everything because no one can be trusted. He starts to see enemies everywhere. He can't slow down or stop, continuing on his path of expansion and debt even though his colleagues counsel against it. No one can talk to him. He thinks his critics are just protecting themselves or jealous and out to get him. This vice president starts to negotiate for a position as CEO of a smaller company, a danger that I report to the CEO. He becomes angry, telling me that he would have already heard about it if it were true. The vice president leaves. So do others. No one can reach him, and he is fired three years after he took the position.

With a few variations on the basic plot, it resembles the syndrome of weaknesses that have crippled the health care CEO, Mike Armstrong, Jürgen Schrempp, Robert Shapiro, Pehr Gyllenhammar, Jean-Marie Messier, Thomas Middlehoff, and so many other of our innovative business leaders. Bear this in mind when you read this rundown of each specific weakness, the set of traits that are not the flip side but rather the amplification or exaggeration of the very traits that make narcissists such compelling leaders. In my work with CEOs, I have observed all the weaknesses presented here. Some of the CEOs have accepted help in overcoming them, while others have not. In Chapter 5, I'll give more detailed advice on how to spot when this syndrome of weaknesses starts to act on a productive narcissist and what you can do about it.

Not Listening and Oversensitivity to Criticism

Often, the very quality that makes it possible for productive narcissists to climb to the top of the business world is the quality that brings them down. This is the case with not listening;

WEAKNESSES OF THE PRODUCTIVE NARCISSIST
- Not listening
- Oversensitivity to criticism
- Paranoia
- Anger and put-downs
- Overcompetitiveness and overcontrol
- Isolation
- Exaggeration and lying
- Lack of self-knowledge
- Grandiosity

---

narcissists never listen to anyone, throughout their lives. I opened the introduction of the book with a story of a productive narcissist who told me that he didn't get to be CEO by listening to people. Not listening is exactly what got him to the top; it's also what got him fired. Now, you have to remember that he hired me specifically to tell him what he needed to work on, to change, in order to be more productive. In order to be an effective business coach, he had to listen to me. The problem was that he had spent his entire life shutting out other voices, especially dissenting or critical ones, to protect his vision. He couldn't just turn on a dime, change a characteristic that was so essential to his personality and become someone who listens. When I questioned him about the need to listen to some of his critics, he told me that they were just a bunch of whiners and complainers who resisted leaving their comfort zone.

Consider this example: Another client of mine, a CEO, took me aside and asked me exactly what his staff thought of him. I told him that they thought he was very creative, a smart guy, but they were frustrated by the fact that he never listened to anyone, that they couldn't talk to him about the business or make suggestions. His immediate response was "What did you say?" This story almost sounds like he was making a joke at his own expense, but this CEO had no idea that his complete inability to hear any kind of criticism bordered on the comical.

Almost every productive narcissist, even the most successful ones, are hard of hearing when it comes to criticism, whether it comes from their staff, the market, the press, or their adversaries. When Henry Ford started losing market share in the mid-1920s, he refused to listen to his staff, who told him that, in order to keep up with the competition, the Model T needed mechanical revisions, an automatic starter, a better transmission. I sat in a meeting with Mike Armstrong where he didn't let a VP finish a sentence, much less listen; he knew everything. In the midst of huge losses at Chrysler, management turnover, and an onslaught of bad press, Jürgen Schrempp boasted: "What I want people to understand is that the operational issues have nothing to do with what I term an absolutely perfect strategy."

This pitfall sometimes degenerates into name-calling. Craig Venter calls his critics "hypocrites." Rockefeller called his critics "blackmailers, sharpsters, and crooks," names that many historians think are an accurate description of Rockefeller himself. Gates calls his critics liars. In fact, both Rockefeller and Gates ignored their biggest critic—the United States government—and went into lengthy, costly, and damaging lawsuits without the proper preparation. They simply didn't believe, against all evidence to the contrary, that they could lose.

Robert Shapiro never took his critics seriously, a very damaging and public mistake that undermined Monsanto's position in the field of seed technology and bioengineered food. Despite public protests against "Frankenfood" and a lack of trust in Monsanto's policies, Shapiro ignored the outcry and pursued his own strategy without any regard for the fears of the market. After he was fired, Shapiro conceded: "Our confidence in this technology and our enthusiasm for it has, I think, widely been seen, and understandably so, as condescension or indeed arrogance. Because we thought it was our job to persuade, too often we forgot to listen." The former vice president Michael Winkel commented: "We bought too many companies, paid too much money, and we didn't pay attention to the grassroots [opposition]."

The new CEO of Monsanto, Hendrik A. Verfaillie, seems to be a marketing personality, someone who listens to the public and will placate them at the expense of visionary leadership. This is one of the dangers of narcissistic weakness—it can stall a company—and, by extension, an entire industry—when it is allowed to go unchecked. If Shapiro had partnered from the start with someone like Verfaillie, who understands the broader social issues surrounding bioengineered food, he might still be at Monsanto. Shapiro's vision may ultimately prevail and prove an effective way of fighting global starvation, but the simple fact that Shapiro was incapable of listening to any of his critics may well have delayed an enormous amount of progress in the life sciences field.

Paranoia

Paranoia can show up in any personality, but it plays out differently in each type. The erotic can become extremely jealous;

the obsessive may see disease and dirt everywhere; the marketing personality can worry that someone won't return his calls. Because of the narcissistic focus on survival, and the narcissist's aggressive impulses that stimulate rational wariness, irrational paranoia can become a very real danger.

A dose of paranoia can be useful, an awareness of the market or personal threats to the business base. After all, many visionary CEOs are under constant attack from competitors—or, in the case of Gates, the government; or, in the case of Clinton, his political enemies and rivals. Ron Chernow notes that "Rockefeller made a fetish of secrecy, flavored with paranoia," and recounts a story of a friend of a Standard Oil employee dropping by the office; when Rockefeller caught sight of the "outsider," he promptly took the worker he was visiting aside and questioned him about the friend's visit. Just saying "hello" seemed out of the question to Rockefeller—he must want something—so he warned his worker to be "be careful, be very careful." Gates complains of being discriminated against by his enemies. Joe Klein points out that one of Clinton's most annoying qualities was his self-centered whining, a kind of narcissistic mantra of "Why is everyone being mean to me?" Nixon's well-documented paranoia turned the White House into a fortress that was run on fear. Lyndon Johnson's tapes reveal a deep paranoia about his supposed enemies—especially Robert Kennedy—who he thought were plotting against him even as he went on to a landslide victory.

Despite the idea that a paranoiac can be well informed, paranoia starts to be a liability whenever a CEO's thinking becomes focused on possibilities—anything and everything that *could* happen—as opposed to probabilities—what it's reasonable to expect *will* happen. The extreme example of paranoia is the Mel Gibson character in *Conspiracy Theory*, whose entire life is a routine of locks and bolts and security measures that keep everything, including his coffee grounds, safe from outside invasion. There are strains of this kind of nutty paranoia in the most productive narcissists, who can be so isolated, so cushioned from the rest of the world, that any intrusion is seen as a potential threat. Henry Ford built elaborate tunnels—or, rather, escape routes—throughout his home in case he was invaded or attacked. His paranoia also fueled his virulent anti-Semitism, including his theory that the Jews were conspiring to take over the economy. Rockefeller installed a series of tricky locks and doors in the Standard Oil offices that required you to know the "secret" way of turning the knob or you would wind up trapped. The Standard Oil conference rooms were protected from any intrusive eyes with custom-made opaque glass partitions.

Anger and Put-Downs

Freud wrote that a narcissist's "ego has a large amount of aggressiveness at its disposal, which also manifests itself in readiness for activity." I thought of this description when I heard Martha Stewart tell Larry King the key to her success: "I have an urge to get things done." Stewart effectively channels her aggressive energy into her hyperhomemaker image, preaching to women everywhere that they, too, can cook, clean, and create basically everything from scratch, all with a hot-glue gun and her do-it-yourself inspiration. Stewart's aggressive energy is both a strength and, at times, a weakness; her empire is based, to a large extent, on the value of her own industriousness. Yet sometimes this aggressive energy is aimed at those around her, including her staff. She's known for her outbursts and eruptions over the smallest of mistakes and a lack of attention to detail by her underlings.

Anger and personal put-downs are certainly not limited to narcissists. Any personality type can get angry or yell at their staff. But the other personality types usually don't have as much free-floating aggressive energy. Erotics can become aggressive when their dependent ties are threatened or those close to them are attacked; obsessives can become aggressive when they think that they are right and you are wrong, or feel self-righteous (remember Al Gore looking furious when he said he was "fighting for you"?); I find that marketing types are so detached and uncomfortable with aggression that they're more likely to turn it inward, to blame themselves or get depressed. The narcissist's aggression is always on the surface, readily available; in a sense, it *must* be used, and it can either further his or her purpose or undermine it. Sometimes this aggressiveness is used to protect the vision or to motivate people. Other times, it is used to silence dissent.

We can see this in a comparison of Bill Gates and Steve Jobs. Both are known for fits of anger and incredibly rude, even sadistic insults, almost always aimed at the stupidity of other people in relation to their own brilliance. For example, when a PR team was pitching Jobs for a Pixar account, the youngest and most junior member of the team spoke up, telling him what she thought they could bring to the job, to which Jobs responded: "Nothing you say means anything to me. Why do you keep opening your mouth?" reducing the woman to tears. Gates is famous for blurting out

"That's the stupidest thing I've ever heard" to a person who just said something, often humiliating them publicly. However, Gates also seems to be able to *use* his anger to provoke a response, to get people to try harder, to squeeze out ideas, especially ones that are presented with force and quick clarity.

This is the key point: Narcissists need to know how to channel their anger into a tool for getting the best out of people. A CEO I analyzed saw himself as a destructive force. He said, "I put a barrier between me and people because I am afraid I'll kill them." He recognized that he must learn to control and focus this energy productively. One of the major achievements of my analysis with Goran Collert was that he learned to *use* his anger, to stop letting it erupt uncontrollably and instead shape it into an almost theatrical display that motivated his staff. Faced with competitive threats, he accused executives of "a bunker mentality," hiding rather than fighting. His anger and passion fired up the best of his vice presidents.

Overcompetitiveness and Overcontrol

Because of their paranoid tendencies, narcissists may try to maintain total control over an organization, making it impossible for their best people to make any kind of contribution or further the narcissist's vision. It's worth quoting this passage on Henry Ford from David Halberstam to make my point:

> While [Henry Ford] was off on a trip to Europe, his top engineers made a few changes intended to improve the car. Their version of the T was lower and some twelve inches longer. It was

a better, smoother-riding vehicle, and his associates hoped to surprise and please him. When he returned, they showed it to him. He walked around it several times. Finally he approached the left-hand door and ripped it off. Then he ripped off the other door. Then he bashed the windshield. Then he threw out the backseat and bashed the roof of the car with his shoe. During all this he said nothing. There was no doubt whose car the T was and no doubt who was the only man permitted to change it.

Ford couldn't bear it when anyone else in his company got any press. The same thing can be said of Larry Ellison, who couldn't stand it when a former COO, Ray Lane, generated an enormous amount of publicity, much of it favorable to Lane and critical of Ellison.

One CEO I've worked with doesn't want his vice presidents to work as a team. He rationalizes that there will be greater creativity if they compete against each other. But he admitted to me that he doesn't want them plotting together and undermining his authority. The source of this productive narcissist's paranoia is his own aggressive competitiveness, and he is quick to see it in others. Speaking about a dynamic vice president, the CEO asked me, "Can I trust him? Does he want my job?" Of course, the most ambitious and competent vice presidents do want to be CEOs. But a weakness of some productive narcissists is to surround themselves with yes-men who are no threat but also not much good. Ford's sidekick, Harry Bennett, said that he lasted so many years with Ford because he did everything he was told to do. This was an accusation Ray Lane, on leaving Oracle, made about Larry Ellison. This distrust of competent lieutenants who might challenge them is one reason that narcissists are particularly vulnerable to Iagos who flatter them but play on their fears.

The extreme need to control also plays out in a narcissist's intimate relationships. A CEO in analysis complains that his sexual encounters are never fully satisfactory. He can't let go: "I need to stay in control to the extent that I feel detached from myself, watching myself perform." This kind of overcontrol is very difficult to overcome by talking to oneself; it usually requires psychoanalysis.

Isolation

The narcissistic CEOs I've analyzed suffer from loneliness. This has to do with their attitude toward people. One divorced CEO had a series of conquests, but he didn't trust the women he seduced and had paranoid fantasies that they were cheating on him. When I asked him what he wanted in a woman, he said: "Beautiful, bright, accomplished, feels I'm the most remarkable man ever in this century and the next twelve. Thoroughly devoted to me and no other man could conceivably interest her." But he drew the line at an equal partner.

It seems to me that as long as narcissists see people of any gender as objects to seduce, they will never overcome their feelings of isolation and loneliness. They will either become disillusioned with the precious object or distrustful when they discover that the person has a mind of his or her own. Only when they realize that they need a partner, not an object, do they overcome the loneliness. This is the case with Bill Gates, who chased a lot of women until he found a partner in Melinda. Same with Craig Venter and Claire Fraser. But other productive narcissists, like Larry Ellison and Steve Jobs, are like Picasso, leaving a trail of resentful women, as well as male colleagues, who feel they have been used. Michael Eisner used Mike Ovitz when he was at the top of his game, recruiting him for Disney and then, almost immediately after, discarding him. I've been used in a similar fashion by some narcissistic CEOs, who lauded me as the greatest psychologist in the world while they were getting something from me, and then abruptly stopped speaking to me after they accomplished their goal.

Exaggeration and Lying

A narcissistic CEO I once counseled said: "The definition of an entrepreneur is somebody who lies but gets other people to make his lies true." Narcissists tend to ignore, to the point of lying, any obstacles they may experience or anything that stands in the way of their vision. They treat the vision as though it already has become reality. This accounts for the high-tech phenomenon known as "vaporware," whereby CEOs such as Gates and Jobs claim to have products that don't exist and may never materialize, or Ronald Reagan's claims that he fought in World War II when in fact he never left the movie studio. Ray Lane, who must be a real thorn in the side of Larry Ellison, told the press about Ellison's tendency to tell customers what they wanted to hear, rather than the truth, which wasn't nearly as appealing.

This tendency can become out-and-out illegal when a narcissist manipulates the company's finances. One of the most public examples of this is Michael Saylor's padding of MicroStrategy's year-end balance sheet to live up to his extravagant promises to shareholders, or the inflated results trumpeted by Al Dunlap, who presented himself as the shareowner's champion. Joe Nacchio, the CEO of Qwest, was accused by Morgan Stanley of misleading accounting practices. Nacchio complained to institutional investors, "Anything I tell you, you're not going to believe anyhow. We're obviously under a cloud. You all think we lie, cheat, and steal." At AT&T, Mike Armstrong continued to maintain that he had not abandoned his grand strategy of one-stop shopping for telephone, wireless, cable, and Internet shopping even when it was clear to everyone that the company was splintering off its various business concerns.

Lack of Self-Knowledge

In general, CEOs are not introspective. They can't afford to be. They have to make decisions that affect hundreds and thousands of people and their livelihood. They can't allow anxieties, self-doubt, or any hint of guilt get in the way of their decision making. That said, narcissists are particularly unreflective; they justify all of their behavior as necessary to their vision. Rockefeller tells us that he was forced into all of his questionable business tactics by the market and his competitors—it was all merely self-defense. Even at the very end, when Napoleon was trying to mobilize a desperate losing battle with no chance of success, he maintained that he was doing it all to protect France. Bill Gates rationalizes his exclusionary practices and financial favoring as essential to his customers, a way of delivering the most compatible and least expensive products, saying things like: "The notion that somebody could misconstrue those negotiations with Apple! We did something incredibly valuable to them." This is common. Narcissistic CEOs often explain self-interested acts as beneficial to customers or employees without any awareness that they are the main beneficiaries.

Grandiosity

Narcissists don't have a monopoly on the seven deadly sins, but they do run a greater risk of grandiosity, going too far, and the simple sin of pride than the other types. One Oracle vice president told me that the saying around the company is that the only difference between Larry and God is that God doesn't think he's Larry. Once productive narcissists start to succeed, fame and adulation start to chip away at their already tenuous hold on reality. They enjoy being known by employees, customers, waiters in restaurants. Fame lets them experience a sense of relatedness for the first time in their lives. In contrast to successful obsessives like Sam Walton, founder of Wal-Mart, who tend to maintain a modest style of living, narcissists feel entitled to live in a grand manner. They build palaces and buy large yachts. They begin to put themselves before the interest of the company, expanding their empires, making the company bigger rather than making strategic sense. After Miramax Films announced the biggest cutbacks in their history in March 2002, the result of taking on too much too fast, Harvey Weinstein told *The New York Times* that "for a few years there, it just got away from me. The success of the company was intoxicating. You start to think, 'Yeah, I can do anything.'" Pehr

Gyllenhammar seemed to believe that Sweden was too small a canvas for his overblown vision. He already had purchased an apartment in Paris before his merger with Renault fell through, a move that was not lost on one of his executives, who told me that Gyllenhammar was letting his own interests dictate his business decisions.

The danger of grandiosity is well-known. I think it's worth citing *Beowulf*, the eighth-century epic poem, that warns Beowulf, the Scandinavian hero, not to succumb to the universal temptation of pride:

> *Here find your lesson*
> *of virtue . . .*
> *Wondrous seems*
> *how to sons of men Almighty God . . .*
> *sends wisdom,*
> *estate, high station*
> *[to] the hero . . .*
> *puts in his power great parts of the earth . . .*
> *until all within him obstinate pride*
> *waxes and wakes while the warden slumbers,*
> *the spirit's sentry; and the murderer nears,*
> *stealthily shooting the shafts from his bow . . .*
> *His heart then is hit*
> *by sharpest shafts;*
> *greedy and grim, . . . for his pride; he spurns,*
> *forgets the promised future, with all God has sent him.*
> *Ban, then, such thoughts, Beowulf, dearest,*
> *best of men, and choose the better part,*
> *eternal profit; and temper your pride.*

What can we take away from this excerpt? When successful people are overcome with their success and the "spirit's sentry"—reason—sleeps, they allow pride and grandiosity to sneak in under their radar and do the deadly work of undermining them and all their efforts. Some narcissists, such as Rockefeller, realized this, warning themselves at night against the dangers of pride and becoming puffed up with success. Other narcissists aren't so smart; they are usually lacking in what I have come to call strategic intelligence, the interrelated set of skills that allows productive narcissists to stay on top once they've reached success, to act in a reasoned way to keep the company on track. The next chapter is devoted to this set of skills.

FOUR

STRATEGIC INTELLIGENCE

I f you were asked to make a list of the qualities that a business leader needs in order to build a solid and sustained business, what traits would be on your list? With the confusing and conflicting leadership theories that are found in today's business literature, how do you determine if your boss, colleagues, or potential employees have what it takes to get to the top and stay there?

Here's an actual report from human resources about a guy who is up for a promotion to run a $400-million division of a large corporation. (For our purposes here, I've replaced the person's name with The Candidate and the real company with The Corporation.) Imagine that you are a member of top management of The Corporation. Based on this review, ask yourself if you would put The Candidate in charge of a key division of your business, one that

is crucial to your overall strategy for growing the company. Furthermore, do you think that this type of personality is worth grooming for the future, perhaps even for the CEO position—that he has
the right combination of traits that can lead The Corporation to
sustained and measurable success? The promotion

> carries with it more than the usual degree of risk. Despite his
> many strengths, [The Candidate] has a number of significant
> limitations. On the plus side, he has a driving motivation to
> grow a business, natural entrepreneurial instincts, creativeness
> and aggressiveness, is a natural leader and organizer, and has a
> high degree of technical competence. On the other hand, he is
> somewhat arrogant, reacts (or overreacts) emotionally—par-
> ticularly to criticism—gets too personally involved in the
> details of his business, tends to overrely on his quick mind and
> intuition rather than on the solid homework and staff assis-
> tance in getting into and out of complex situations, and has
> something of an "anti-establishment" attitude toward [The
> Corporation's] activities outside his own sphere.

What is your impression of The Candidate, and how would you rate
his potential? Would you give him the promotion?

As it turns out, in spite of the "risk," The Corporation decided to
promote The Candidate, not only for this specific job but many times
over, until he finally became CEO. The Candidate is Jack Welch, and
this report was prepared by human resources when Welch was up for
VP of the chemical and metallurgical division of GE in 1971.

If you read and practice the formulas for effective leadership
in some of the most popular business literature today—Jim Collins,

Stephen Covey, or Daniel Goleman—it's not likely that you would have promoted Welch, someone who is "arrogant," has a lot of "aggressiveness," "overreacts" to criticism, and is not seen as a company man. Welch has few of the traits that Collins attributes to "great" company CEOs, doesn't practice a number of Covey's seven habits of highly effective leadership, doesn't have the hallmarks of Goleman's "emotional intelligence." In fact, Welch's entire career flies in the face of some of the most prevalent beliefs about what makes a great business leader. But by all accounts, he *is* a great business leader, steering General Electric to clear and measurable success; in a study reported by *The Economist* of companies that have created the most wealth for their shareholders between 1996 and 2001, GE came in first.

When GE's human resources department prepared its report on Jack Welch, the term "emotional intelligence" hadn't yet been coined; but even without the phraseology, it's clear that the HR manager thought that Welch's set of skills was at odds with success, that someone who is arrogant, who overreacts emotionally, is a corporate risk. This leadership theory was in the air throughout the 1970s and '80s, but it wasn't until Daniel Goleman attached the name "emotional intelligence" to this thinking, contrasting it with intellectual intelligence, or IQ, that it really caught hold in business circles. In Goleman's best seller of the same name, he explains that emotional intelligence includes qualities such as empathy, sensitivity to other's feelings, and an understanding of one's own emotions. Managers with emotional intelligence are self-aware; they control their impatience and anger, leading to an open environment where everyone is free to dialogue. If they need to discipline or criticize members of their team, they do it privately, in ways that are constructive. Goleman offers this advice to managers who need to deliver critiques: "*Be sensitive.* This is a call for empathy, for being attuned to the impact of what you say and how you say it on the person at the receiving end. Managers who have little empathy . . . are most prone to giving feedback in a hurtful fashion, such as the withering put-down." This is very similar to the advice you will find in Stephen Covey's fifth habit for success: "When I say empathic listening, I mean listening with the intent to *understand.* I mean *seeking first* to understand, to really understand. . . . Empathic (from *empathy*) listening gets inside another person's frame of reference. You look out through it, you see the world the way they see the world, you understand their paradigm, you understand how they feel."

There is a sense in which everyone needs some degree of emotional intelligence, to learn how to react to the world in ways that befit the circumstances, or, as Aristotle says, "to be angry with the right person, to the right degree, at the right time, for the right purpose." Goleman contrasts someone who is emotionally intelligent with a person who goes berserk and starts gunning down people. There's no question that it would be better for all concerned if the gunman had some emotional awareness and self-control—that there is a minimum of emotional intelligence required to participate in society.

In my own work with productive narcissists, I've found that most of them are insensitive to feelings and have almost no awareness of how their emotional outbursts affect other people. Some may have empathy, but this does not mean they are careful about the feelings of subordinates. Bill Clinton is a notable example of a narcissist who uses empathy to seduce and manipulate people, but disregards the feelings of those who work for him. Empathy is a skill that has different uses for different personality types. The erotic is more likely to use empathy in caring for another person; the marketing type to avoid friction and sense where people are coming from; obsessives tend to be the least empathic because they are driven by the parental voice that insists on sticking to what is right rather than other people's demands.

If you look at some of our most productive narcissists, the ones who have built highly successful and sustained businesses, you'll find that they score very low on emotional intelligence. Just a few examples make the point in a dramatic way: Anne Jardim, a Ford biographer, wrote that Henry Ford's "attitude to the men around him at times bordered on the sadistic." Craig Venter's wife and business partner told me that he is "not as diplomatic as he might be. He's always pissing people off." Bill Gates is known for his put-downs in meetings. Steve Jobs has brought subordinates to tears during business meetings. And compare the qualities of emotional intelligence with Welch's description of his own managerial style: "I was blunt and candid and, some thought, rude. My language could be coarse and impolitic. I didn't like sitting and listening to canned presentations or reading reports. . . . And I never hid my thoughts or feelings. During a business discussion, I could get so emotionally involved that I'd stammer out what others might consider outrageous things, [such as] 'My six-year-old kid could do better than that!'"

Jim Collins picks up where emotional intelligence leaves off in fashioning the myth of the good business leader as modest and self-effacing. In *Good to Great*, Collins and his team of researchers summarize the type of leadership required to turn a good company into a great one. The eleven "great" companies were chosen mainly for offering a high cumulative stock return to shareholders over a fifteen-year period. After conducting interviews and gathering data on the companies for five years, Collins asked: What do the great companies have in common? While Collins and his team identify a number of factors that contribute to "greatness," the most crucial and provocative thread is what they call "Level 5" leadership. The Level 5 executives, Collins claims, are not celebrity CEOs, larger-than-life personalities who are ambitious about their own careers; instead, they are *"quiet, humble, modest, reserved, shy, gracious, mild-mannered, self-effacing, understated,* [do] *not believe* [their] *own clippings."* One such Level 5 leader that Collins singles out in the political field is Abraham Lincoln, "who never let his ego get in the way of his primary ambition for the larger cause of an enduring great nation." How is it that I've termed Lincoln a productive narcissist, whereas Collins has such a different understanding of Lincoln's personality? Collins's view of Lincoln seems to come directly from his eagerness to fit a fairy-tale model of Lincoln's "personal modesty, shy nature, and awkward manner" into the results of his research and his overall leadership theory. But in doing so, Collins ignores history. Lincoln's contemporaries never considered him shy or humble; they thought he was extremely ambitious at an early age, a big personality and presence, outspoken, a charismatic speaker and performer, and aggressive when it came to his career. According to Lincoln's law partner, William Herndon, "His ambition was a little engine that knew no rest." Lincoln even pushed the limit of legality during the 1858 senatorial race against Stephen Douglas by suggesting that his campaign sway voters at the polls with "a true man, of the 'detective' class . . . among them in disguise, who could, at the nick of time, control their votes," hardly the act of a shy and retiring personality. The only trait that Collins gets right is "awkward." But Lincoln wasn't emotionally awkward; he was physically awkward and thought of as ugly, a face-to-face impression that he overcame with wit and charm.

Despite the claim to be scientific, to let the empirical evidence speak for itself, Collins has a clear ideological agenda that was apparent to me when I met him. I was on a panel on leadership with Collins in the spring of 2000, and before the debate got under way, I asked him what he thought of a few CEOs, including Jack Welch. The answer? Not much; he was put off by Welch's lifestyle, publicity seeking, and seemingly self-centered behavior. Even if Collins had the results of his so-called scientific research that proved that a headline-grabbing CEO is not as "great" or effective as one that shows humility and reserve, it seemed to me that his personal bias leaned toward a softer, self-effacing leadership style.

Collins and the other critics of Welch, including the GE human resources evaluator, see the qualities of aggression and drive as negatives, traits that are antithetical to the emotionally intelligent manager or Level 5 executive. In his review of *Jack: Straight from the Gut,* Joseph Nocera writes that Welch "is a great CEO who plainly likes to be told how great he is. He cares far too much about his press clips. . . . His egocentrism is everywhere on display; there is a sense throughout that everyone and everything are supposed to orbit around his sun." These business theorists are making a judgment, a *moral* judgment, in labeling these qualities as bad, and the qualities of humility and self-effacement as good. There is only one area of Jack Welch's leadership that I find morally troubling, and that is his treatment of GE's pollution of the Hudson River. Other than this ethical lapse, I see no reason to attack him for his personality, his huge salary, his egocentrism. Why do we care if a leader is self-promoting if that goes together with effective leadership and shareholder rewards? There appears to be a communal need to believe that successful people are modest and caring, that the people who make it to the top are the good guys and are rewarded in kind for their goodness. This is a willful disregard for the lessons of history. There is no such thing, for example, as an American president who is humble and shy; it takes drive and tough resolve in order to succeed in both business and politics.

Leadership can't be considered separately from its context—whether it's the overall business and economic climate, the type of company, or the role within the company. I have argued that Collins's "great" CEOs are great only in businesses that are not innovative, that follow the basic business model of moving more product, lowering costs, and improving shareholder value. Collins writes: "Throughout our research, we were struck by the continual use of words like *disciplined, rigorous, dogged, determined, . . . consistent, focused, accountable,* and *responsible.*" This is a description of the productive obsessive, the kind of person you may also want as a middle manager, a team player, or even a COO or CFO to a narcissistic visionary. But it is by no means a complete description of a visionary, whether he is a technology CEO or a political leader such as Abraham Lincoln who must create a unified vision for the country during wartime. Furthermore, there's no indication that an aggressive, big personality like Jack Welch is any less disciplined, determined, demanding, or accountable than the CEOs who are held up as leadership models by Collins. The critics are so put off by Welch's extravagant, narcissistic self-promotion and sense of entitlement that they miss out on the important lessons of his tenure at GE and perpetuate leadership myths. Even Welch himself wrote that he's glad that he didn't see the cited human resources report on him until later in his career or he just might have listened to it, changed his behavior, and "done something stupid."

As I admitted in the preface, I had to revise the view of leadership I held throughout the 1980s and early '90s. I summed up my own leadership theories in my 1981 book *The Leader:* "Leadership with values of caring and integrity and a vision of self-development must facilitate the trust that no one will be penalized for cooperation and that sacrifice as well as rewards will be equitable." What I overlooked in my case studies of managers who fostered cooperation and caring is that not one of these leaders created great wealth or innovation. It wasn't until I ran a series of workshops in 1995 with the CEO and executive team of Swedbank that I realized that the model of an empathetic, understanding, humble leader is not necessarily suited to head up a competitive, change-oriented industry. My experience with Swedbank was a defining moment for my ideas about leadership, a clear example of the importance of developing theories that actually work in a business setting. To give you some background, I was first hired as a coach by Goran Collert, the CEO of Swedbank, in 1988 to advise him on implementing his strategy—an ambitious plan to create an international banking empire—and develop his team of VPs. Within five years, Collert took the central savings bank (Sparbankarnasbank—or, literally, the savings banks' bank) and turned it into Swedbank with the merger of eleven savings banks (more than 700 branches), many of which were in danger of going under during the Swedish savings-and-loan crisis. Next, he merged the savings bank with the farmers' bank, thereby minimizing competition and significantly reducing costs. Once he orchestrated these mergers, Collert took over as executive chairman of the organization.

Collert's immediate challenge: Who could succeed him as CEO? To deal with his succession, we gathered together top management and asked them to describe the qualities of an ideal leader, ranking them in order of importance. Along with the usual skills of intelligence, judgment, energy, and competence, the team made a list of fourteen essential traits that included: "listening and learning, 'humbleness'" (number seven), "self-awareness, knowing oneself" (number eight), "enabling others to succeed, supportive and cooperative" (number nine), and "generosity and openness" (number ten). Once we had the list, we matched up the qualities with an executive who possessed every single one of them. This executive—the ombudsman, what the Swedes call an employee representative—was voted CEO and accepted the job. After just a few years, he was kicked out. Although the ombudsman represented all the qualities that his coworkers valued—likability, empathy, supportiveness—it became clear that he was not an effective leader. He had no core convictions of his own, and was incapable of dealing with the inevitable conflicts among executives over strategy. I then thought about the qualities on the list and how they applied to Collert, the executive chairman, and it struck me: Collert possesses an entirely different set of skills than the ombudsman. Besides intelligence, good judgment, energy, and competence, Collert does not have any of the other qualities that his team thought were essential for successful leadership. He never listens to anyone unless he needs something from them, and he has unexpected bouts of rage, an arrogant contempt for people less intelligent than he, and an annoying tendency to lecture instead of having a conversation, traits that he is known for inside and outside the company: The Swedish press regularly refers to him as a "dictator." But he is a visionary, a brilliant strategist, and an effective leader. In other words, he is a narcissist who is highly productive. This story shows the importance of revising our understanding of leaders, replacing old or overly idealistic models with ones that have practical application in the workplace.

What should Swedbank's leadership wish list—or, for that matter, your own from the start of this chapter—look like? If emotional intelligence is not the answer for effective leadership, what is? I've observed a kind of intelligence that has not been described by psychologists. I call it *strategic intelligence,* and I think it's the missing link of current business theory. Based on my experience with successful leaders, I've observed five interrelated elements or competencies that make up strategic intelligence: foresight, systems thinking, visioning, motivating, and partnering. Some leaders score well on different elements; a few notable leaders like Bill Gates and Jack Welch seem to score highly on all five.

Any personality type may have strategic intelligence, and I believe that any type who wants to succeed in business can benefit from developing strategic intelligence. Warren Buffett, for example, is a productive obsessive who seems to have all the elements of strategic intelligence; if he were lacking in any area, I doubt that he would have been able to build a solid business that continues to perform no matter what's going on in the market. Another person with an acute sense of strategic intelligence is Louis V. Gerstner, a combination productive marketing/obsessive who revitalized IBM, transforming what was an old-fashioned product company into a solutions company that offers products and services in concert.

While strategic intelligence may help any type, it is essential for productive narcissists to work on their strategic intelligence. A narcissist who is productive can make it to the top of a company or have an impact in the business world; but I believe that only a productive narcissist with developed strategic intelligence can *stay* on top, can sustain success. This is because the narcissist, more so than any other type, is susceptible to a quick rise and a precipitous fall; if the stories of Michael Armstrong, Jean-Marie Messier, and Bernie Ebbers teach us anything, it's the importance of connecting vision to implementation with strategic intelligence.

Before I break strategic intelligence down into its specific elements, I want to provide an overview by picking up where we left off with the story of Goran Collert's ascendancy to the executive chairmanship of Swedbank and his leadership techniques. In the fall of 1998, Goran Collert asked me to gather together his top fifteen vice presidents and teach them how to think strategically— basically, how to think like the boss. In order to do this, *I* needed

---

THE FIVE ELEMENTS OF STRATEGIC INTELLIGENCE
- **Foresight**
- **Systems thinking**
- **Visioning**
- **Motivating**
- **Partnering**

---

to understand how Collert thinks, how he develops his own strategy. I started out by sending Collert questions: What forces does he look for in the broader business culture and society, whom does he talk to, what influences on the banking culture are important to him? He came back to me with: "Strategy is a puzzle, systematically understanding and then acting on how Sweden, the banking community, and the surrounding world forces will interact. I start out thinking about society. Banking is a mirror image of society. What changes can we predict? We're moving from an industrial society where wealth is created by products to a knowledge society that builds wealth through partnering and strategic solutions. We need to establish our legitimacy and place in the knowledge society by adding value to *all* our stakeholders: customers, owners, employees, and the culture at large. This is not a linear, if . . . then process. It is based on pieces of a puzzle that are constantly shifting, and our strategy has to reflect these societal changes."

In our next meeting, Collert laid out his views of what was happening in Sweden, and in turn the broader banking world, and how it shapes his strategy. Collert saw the collapse of Sweden's collectivism and trust in government, and the growing economic disparity between the rich and poor. He responded to these trends by expanding the customer base, appealing to different needs and creating banking solutions—the use of the Internet, new technology, and a greater reliance on banks for financial answers and advice on investments. The bank had to be local and global at the same time, or *glocal*. An increase in the domestic customer base must be coupled with acquisitions and partnering with other Nordic banks. Collert saw threats from neighboring European countries—invasions, so to speak—that needed to be factored in before they happened; the weaknesses of other countries cleared the way for takeover opportunities. Sweden, more so than the United States, is dependent on fluctuations in international trade. Collert predicted two major market shifts: the 20 percent fall of the U.S. stock market (which didn't happen for another two and half years) and the Japanese banking crisis that stalled development in Asia.

After six months of intensive discussions, brainstorming, and batting around ideas, we came up with a clear blueprint of Collert's strategy, how he adjusts and reorients his thinking to each shift in the global economy. Some of the scenarios we discussed have come to pass over the years, foretold by Collert with great accuracy; some were wishful thinking on his part; and some were as inspiring as they were outlandish. Collert sees the financial world much the way a skilled chess player imagines how each single move restructures the board: Move one element, and the entire game changes. In this sense, strategy is not a set playbook but an evolving, never-ending process.

Armed with an understanding of how the boss thinks, Collert and I gathered together the VPs for three two-day seminars. Their assignment? Prepare a discussion on these elements of strategy and why they are important: legitimacy, independence, sustainable risk, broad customer base, and glocal. We asked these specific questions:

Why are these elements important parts of our strategy?

What do we have to do, operationally, to implement these strategies?

Where do we see important holes or gaps in our competence?

How are these five elements related to one another?

These are the answers the VPs came up with:

We need to sell more products.

We need to increase business and productivity.

We are too bureaucratic.

We need to cut costs.

Needless to say, these results were disappointing: We came to
the conclusion that the VPs always turned strategic discussions into
implementation and operations, breaking down every scenario into
parts, laboriously analyzing each one, and then solving each element,
ticking it off the list. After a few frustrating sessions, we decided that
the VPs needed more feedback, more guidance. Collert and I tried
again with a seminar on the different Nordic and Baltic banking cultures, and presented scenarios on partnering and alliances, trying to
steer the VPs away from the specific microsolutions to a more holistic view. But it was useless. Collert threw up his hands, and started
lecturing them on their "bunker mentality," acting, or rather, *react-
ing,* to events defensively instead of taking a look at the global situation and offering a systemic vision to build a banking empire. The
seminar reminded me of Sidney Harman's complaint about *his* managers; he told me that most of them came to him with the equivalent
of to-do lists, the kind of *One Minute Manager* thinking that appeals
to obsessives who don't think systematically.

What emerged from our sessions was the early stages of my
theories of strategic intelligence: Collert starts with foresight, then
plays around with different systemic models, turning them into
visions, strategies of what to do, goals, actions he needs to take.
Through my observation of this process I was able to break down
the five elements of strategic intelligence. Before I explain each
specific element, I want to show how they work together in

Collert's career: In 1992, Collert foresaw the coming savings-and-loan collapse in Sweden and developed a vision for the integration of all the banks with his central bank. His VPs said it would be impossible, but he made it happen (foresight). When envisioning his strategy, he looks at the economic landscape as a puzzle; what forces could play out in society that the banking system can fit into (systems thinking). Collert's vision isn't limited to Sweden. He has a grand scheme to re-create and exploit the Hanseatic League of the fourteenth century, the trading network including Scandanavia, the Baltic countries, and northern Germany, strengthening his bank with the support of the international banking community (visioning). Rather than just using economic incentives to get his team to work harder, Collert gets his staff worked up with the threat of foreign invasion, describing competition as a life-and-death war for survival (motivating). And perhaps his greatest skill is making strategic alliances. He recently orchestrated a merger with the farmers' bank and was set up for a merger with SEB, the Wallenberg bank, until the European Union demanded that he sell off important parts of the bank. Now he's looking for new partners in Scandinavia and the Baltic region (partnering).

Let's look more closely at each element.

Foresight

Any business guru will tell you that a clear sense of strategy is essential to a company's overall success. It's hard to argue with this view; but how do you craft a strategy, especially when there are so many different definitions of strategy and advice about how to apply it to your own workplace? Most of the business literature relies on catchphrases and trends to give shape and weight to their theories: You need to get into the "flow" or avoid the "innovator's dilemma" or imagine you're crafting a clay pot or discover your core competencies or build a business ecosystem. If you strip away these terms and trends, however, you'll find that any coherent view of strategy involves thinking about the future. A strategist anticipates how current movements, ideas, forces will play out in the future, driving changes in technology, products, the global market, competitors, and customer needs and values. This is the first element of strategic intelligence: foresight.

Foresight is the ability to think in terms of unprovable forces that are shaping the future. In business, foresight means sensing a coming wave so that you can ride it. I want to make the distinction between *foresight*, which is imagining how events will play out in the future, and *extrapolation*, simply transferring the rules of today into the rules of tomorrow. Most of the dot-comers were guilty of extrapolation, thinking that any particular e-business could be extrapolated from its retail counterpart. This was clear to me when I saw *startup.com*, a documentary of the genesis and failure of govworks.com, a business that was based on improving the mechanisms of municipal government, starting with paying parking tickets online and expanding into other Internet services that would ease the quotidian burden of running a city. In a scene from the film, one of the founders tells the employees how he and his business partner came up with the idea for the company: They just kept throwing out different ways of capitalizing on the Internet, including virtual tombstones and online wedding registries, until they finally arrived at parking tickets (eureka!). You can imagine versions of this happening all over the country at exactly the same time: aspiring entrepreneurs coming up with different ways to make it big on the Internet, bringing about such ill-conceived ideas as Hardware.com, Kozmo.com, Boo.com, and Pets.com. This scene is a perfect illustration of the difference between foresight and extrapolation. People with foresight do not ask "How do I capitalize on what already exists?" but rather "How do I capitalize on what doesn't exist now but will in the future?" It's the difference between seeing the lightbulb as an invention that was complete unto itself and Edison envisioning the power-generation system crisscrossing the country. It's the difference between Microsoft understanding the social implications of e-mail and AT&T viewing it as just another service that it could offer customers. And it is the difference between Henry Ford, who took the *idea* of the car and turned it into an everyday reality for consumers around the world, and the entrepreneurs who believed that cars would remain luxuries for the rich. Ford envisioned the car of the future, creating a need for what didn't yet exist: an affordable, mass-produced machine in one size, one make, one color.

A CEO with foresight has a gut sense of exactly what trends are important to his company and its position in the market, and how to determine which interactions and relationships will create value. I want to emphasize the word "gut" in the last sentence. People with foresight know when to follow a hunch, to trust their instincts, even when it goes against quantifiable facts and figures or market research. They are prepared for opportunities, and can take advantage of them when it "feels" right. Craig Venter talks passionately about his awareness of the "wind," "forces," "where things are going," the almost imperceptible shifts that signal change, a business skill that I think explains why he and so many other narcissists love sailing and flying—think of Larry Ellison, Jim Clark, and Richard Branson. The HR report on Jack Welch said that he relied on his intuitions rather than the research of his colleagues, an implied negative in their opinion.

The HR report, once again, points to a commonly held misunderstanding in the business world: the belief that "gut" is another way of saying that you don't have solid information. This isn't the case: A good sense of "gut" instinct almost always grows out of a deep and thorough knowledge of a subject. The position that Welch was up for was head of the chemical and metallurgical division, a field in which he had received a doctoral degree; he didn't need to trust the reports of other people. He had already done *his* homework, and had the knowledge and freedom to sense where things were leading him rather than relying on secondhand reports from staff members. When he went into a new business, Welch took "deep dives" into the material, learning as much as he could, equipping himself with the intellectual tools to let intuition take over. Welch himself says: "More often than not, business is smell, feel, and touch as much as or more than numbers." You can see this in some of our most productive narcissists: Gates has a deep knowledge of every aspect of computers; Jim Clark has a Ph.D. in computer science; Craig Venter has a Ph.D. in microbiology and did advanced research for years; Sidney Harman was a sound engineer who worked with PA systems; Goran Collert has an extensive knowledge of international finance. Go back in history and you'll find that Napoleon studied military history and was recognized for his understanding of artillery. Henry Ford knew what every single car part did and where it went, as seen in this astute comment from

Richard Tedlow: "Henry Ford had done what not one top automobile executive in the world could do today. He had built a complete car with his bare hands."

This kind of gut feeling can be contrasted with Stephen Covey's second habit for success: Begin with the end in mind. Working toward a goal can be an important part of a business; it has its purpose, but only if you already have a holistic idea of where your business is going. There are times when it's impossible to know the result, to predict what it is that you're moving toward. This was the case with the late physicist Leo Szilard, who once told me that he applied for grants for research that he had already completed so that he could finance the kinds of fuzzy hypotheses that would never receive funding. This worked until the grant committee of the National Science Foundation rejected one of his proposals, saying it was impossible, forcing Szilard to confess that he had already successfully completed the research. Backward planning can shortcut creativity and innovation, can be a stand-in for strategic intelligence. It is often busywork rather than brainwork; the list-making quality of this rule for success appeals to obsessives. Rather than formulas and techniques, people with strategic intelligence want information they can transform into knowledge about the forces determining the future.

Foresight does not mean that all your bets about the future are correct. But it does mean that you are more right than wrong. Many productive narcissists have been off track at times, but they are often correct about some of their large, overarching visions. Time Warner sunk $30 million into Jim Clark's vision for interactive television before Clark changed his mind, switched visions (in what Michael Lewis calls "one of the great unintentional head fakes in the history of technology"), and went on to develop the Internet browser. Sidney Harman tried to convince everyone that quadraphonic sound would become a home stereo staple, an idea that didn't take hold right away; he now says that "the discrete, multiple channel surround sound that music and movie lovers covet and increasingly buy is today's quadraphonic sound." Edison's technological history is riddled with errors and missteps. He may have invented the record player, but not for listening to music; he thought it was a great way to store and replay phone conversations, but he was on the money about electricity.

Clearly, anticipating new technology is one example of foresight. But there are other, less obvious ways to lead through foresight. Foresight is often the ability to predict how social and economic forces will interact in ways that can change the business climate. For example, when GE acquired RCA in 1985, it was the biggest non-oil deal ever. At first, Jack Welch's colleagues were skeptical about the deal—RCA was considered a bit of a corporate dog back then—so Welch said: "Now, just think: Ten years from now, as we're sitting there out in the middle of the 1990s, do you think you'd rather be in the network business, or the lightbulb business or the circuit breaker business or something like that? Where do you think you'll be more in touch with where the world's going to be?" Or consider how Robert Johnson saw not only the growth of cable television but the importance of the urban African-American audience to any coming entertainment trend, and the role that political lobbying could play in this emerging market. Foresight is not a linear process; it is thinking in terms of the interdependency of many forces and how they could play out. It involves the next element of strategic intelligence: systems thinking.

Systems Thinking

My seminar with Collert taught me that systems thinking is not something that is easily taught in a five-day course or picked up in a business book. It's an entirely different way of seeing the world, an ability to synthesize and integrate, to conceptualize the whole rather than a collection of separate parts. Some people have a natural talent for systemic thinking, something I saw when I gave a series of Rorschach tests during the *Gamesman* study. The systems thinkers have a tendency to tell a story about the whole inkblot, to see it as an integrated narrative, a landscape or entire terrain where the parts are acting or things are happening to them, whereas non-systems thinkers pick apart the details, seeing a character here, an animal there, none of which relate to each other or tell a story. When Craig Venter took the Rorschach, he told me that he was trying hard to integrate all the blots into a story, whereas his wife, Claire Fraser, saw a flower, and in one case, nothing at all. This is the difference between the productive narcissist, who needs to integrate all the elements into a source of meaning, and the other types: The obsessive wants to get the "right" answer, the marketing type wants to please the examiner, and the erotic wants to be liked by the examiner.

My theory of strategic intelligence is in itself an example of systems thinking. Rather than describing a list of traits with no apparent relation to one another, it's my goal to show how these competencies fit together in ways that equip a CEO to lead a company in new directions. You can't pluck one or more competencies away from the others without affecting the whole; in other words, the whole is *different,* not just *more* than the sum of its parts. Or, in practical terms, say you are a CEO who scores high on every element of strategic intelligence but one: partnering. Your strategic intelligence doesn't automatically go down by one-fifth—it's not like missing a question on an IQ test, decreasing your score incrementally—your entire ability to think strategically about your business would be affected negatively, and in ways that are hard to predict or measure.

This is one of the many lessons about the interdependent nature of systems thinking that I learned from Russell Ackoff, professor emeritus at the Wharton School and a pioneer in the field of strategy, systems thinking, educating, and consulting. I worked with Ackoff in weeklong seminars, teaching visioning and leadership to executives of hotel, transportation, oil, and mining companies. During a seminar to senior management at Ford in the early '90s, I heard one of the most instructive ways of thinking about systems: Ackoff went around the room and asked everyone what they thought was the best car part from the best cars in the world—the brake system from a Lexus, the engine from a Ferrari, the steering system from a Mercedes, the drive train from a BMW. Now, if you took all these parts and put them together, what would you have? The answer: junk. The only way to evaluate any part is how it serves the purpose of the whole. Whenever you take apart a system and break it down into its components, the system no longer functions in the same way. This is why the to-do lists of the analyzers simply do not work; they miss out on the strategic understanding of the importance of the system as a whole.

Let me give you a simple example of a business model based on systems thinking. In an article in *Business Week*, Larry Ellison said that a lot of companies waste money buying software that helps them run each separate part of their operation—sales, accounting, marketing, and so on—and then have to hire consulting companies to get them to work together. While Oracle may not make the best software in any one area, it excels at creating software *systems* that work together, doing away with the need for outside consultants and piecemeal components, saving the business consumer time and money. Another example of a highly successful business system is Southwest Airlines; as Michael Porter describes the company, all of the parts, including the kinds of people hired, reinforce each other to serve Herb Kelleher's strategy of a low-cost, customer-focused airline.

Consider, by comparison, this case of a brilliant narcissist's career that was cut short by a lack of systems thinking: Robert Shapiro, the former CEO of Monsanto, didn't understand the broader social and economic systems of bioengineered food, a competence that can't be overestimated when operating in an entirely new industry such as the life sciences. A comparison to the early auto industry will help clarify my point. To create a new industry, Henry Ford had to think in terms of the larger systems that support and maintain car ownership: the overall economic climate and wage and employment rate; car dealerships; the network of roads, road signs, and signals, and their maintenance; the accessibility of trained mechanics and repairmen; the price and availability of gas; government standards and safety approvals. Now apply these lessons to Shapiro's career. Although he has an abundance of foresight, visioning, and motivating skills *within* the company, Shapiro neglected to look outside the company at the vast and complex global food market and the environment that supports it:

the farmers who must adapt to different technology and crop patterns; consumer needs, buying patterns, and fears; the strength and growing voice of the organic-food movement; NGOs (nongovernmental organizations); food lobbyists; the effects of global food trends; the conflicting fiscal responsibilities of the shareholders; and so on. On almost every outside front, Shapiro was met with resistance, much of which I believe could have been anticipated had he considered the broader social system of the global food industry and consumer concerns.

The first two elements of strategic intelligence—foresight and systems thinking—are pure intelligence skills. The other elements— visioning, motivating, and partnering—are what I call "real world" skills. When you get past the "pure" imaginings—the creation of a company, an idea based on your own foresight, the other forces that make up the overall system that your business ideal operates in—you enter the real world of business, where unforeseen events, the quirks and qualities of the people involved, the messy interactions with other companies, and the economic climate, enter the picture. Many businesses look great on paper: The business model adds up, the diagrams and notes and graphs are in order, and even the visionary CEO has an agenda that makes sense to the board. But how do you make this business model a reality, turning the paper idea into a competitive and profitable business? How do you *implement* your vision? Here is where so many leaders, such as Armstrong, Messier, and Middlehoff, fall short, a failure that can be attributed to a lack of the three real-world elements of strategic intelligence: visioning, motivating a social system, and partnering.

I want to stress that any leader who combines the intelligence skills and real-world skills into all five of the elements of strategic intelligence, especially motivating—the most rare and elusive of business skills—is truly exceptional.

Visioning

Visioning is combining foresight and systems thinking into a holistic vision, then creating that vision in the real world of business. It goes to the heart of business leadership, and it can't be considered separately from the other elements of motivating and partnering.

There's a lot of debate about the enduring value of Jack Welch's leadership and whether his tenure will be remembered for its business contributions: Did he really create shareholder wealth, or was it just a product of the times? Was all the downsizing worth it? Did he miss out on the Internet revolution? Will GE's share price continue to decline, a clear indication that Welch didn't set the company up for the future? I believe that these questions, while valid, miss the point, the essential achievement of Jack Welch: He implemented a vision within a huge organizational system, understanding that each separate GE division may have a different business goal, but every single person in each division must be motivated to work toward the overall GE goal as Welch defined it. Or to put it in terms of strategic intelligence, Welch has highly developed visioning skills; he had a systemic vision of GE as the greatest company in the world and built the mechanisms to realize that vision. His focus on integrating business differentiated

GE from other expanding companies. What does that mean, and how did Welch do it?

Welch had the foresight to see that the marketplace was moving from a production economy, where you are selling products, to a knowledge/service economy, where you are selling solutions or products wrapped in services. Recognizing that the profit margin on the production and sale of any commodity, even the most popular lightbulb in the world, is limited, Welch had a strategic vision of taking GE from an appliance company that dabbled in a few other industries to a conglomerate that sells solutions in almost every area of its operation. In order to accomplish this massive restructuring of business priorities, Welch needed to break down the barriers between divisions and sometimes even within divisions, busting the bureaucracy that separated the company into little fiefdoms, each carefully guarding its own bottom line. Early in his GE career, Welch saw the company schematically, comparing it to a house: The floors are hierarchies, the walls divide departments; in order to "get the best out of an organization, these floors and walls must be blown away, creating an open space where ideas flow freely, independent of rank or function." This systematic vision of the company finally came together in his clearly articulated theory of the "boundaryless" organization: "The boundaryless company that I saw would remove all the barriers among functions: engineering, manufacturing, marketing, and the rest. It would recognize no distinctions between 'domestic' and 'foreign' operations." Along with a more fluid, boundaryless organization, Welch demanded that managers educate one another. Learning became a key value essential to implementing the vision.

A focus on learning ensures that visioning constantly evolves with the times; a leader cannot have a vision that becomes frozen in a particular moment in business history, or it is doomed to fail. Welch's vision for GE was under constant revision, open to change and learning. At first, Welch required every GE division to be number one or two in its product market or get out of it, the famous Welch-ism of "fix it, sell it, or close it." But when his managers figured out how to define their markets more narrowly in order to come out on top, Welch upped the ante by defining the markets globally, forcing managers to think in terms of broader, unbeatable forces, forcing them toward growth.

Another CEO who understands the critical importance of a continually evolving vision is Bill Gates: In 1999, Microsoft changed its corporate mandate from "a PC in every home" to "empower people through great software—any time, any place, and on any device," and then, in 2002, it announced its new mission: "to enable people and businesses throughout the world to realize their full potential." The company spent $4.2 billion on research and developing new products in 2001, which *Business Week* reports is more than AOL, Sun Microsystems, and Oracle combined. This is a partial list of some of the new Microsoft products to hit the market in the last few years: Office XP, an updated version of its word processing and spreadsheet program; Stinger, an operating system for cell phones; Windows XP, the latest version, which offers new Internet messaging, mail, media, and personalized services; the related Internet Passport service, which allows identification and payment on the Net; Ultimate TV, a satellite-based set-top box that offers interactive services and TiVo-like recording capabilities (in an effort to reach the most satellite consumers, Microsoft has partnered with DirecTV, Mike Armstrong's brainchild at Hughes); the video-game console Xbox, Microsoft's first foray into making hardware itself in order to develop the most advanced, technologically sophisticated gaming system to compete with the Japanese in that $9.4 billion market. In addition to tapping the video game market, Gates anticipates that Xbox will turn your TV into media central, all connected and wired to the Internet, your PC, and your cell phone—a strikingly similar vision to Jim Clark's "interactive television" that he started and then abandoned; Gates just might be able to pull off what Clark didn't have either the patience or strategic intelligence to accomplish. Whether he can bring about these changes or not, Gates has taken a huge corporate monolith and steered it in new directions, rather than allowing it to remain fixed on an anachronistic vision.

In contrast, Henry Ford's career trajectory is a reminder that visioning must continually grow and adapt. Ford may have had a clearly articulated vision for the car—one model, one color, one size—a vision that ensured his success in the early days of the auto industry. But what worked for him at the start of his career stopped working later. When faced with a decline in sales and the competitive challenge of GM and other carmakers, Ford dug in his heels, sticking to his original vision, even hiding design changes and modifications from the public, fearing that they wouldn't accept any alterations to his "winning" formula. When Ford's son, who had been running the company, died of cancer in 1943, the eighty-one-year-old Ford resumed control, returning to the only vision he knew, the one-make business model, even though it had stopped working many years before: "We've got to go back to Model T days. We've got to build only one car. There won't be any Mercury, no Lincoln. No other car." In some respects, Henry Ford's company continues to be hampered by its highly successful blueprint and the inability of its CEOs to look beyond that formula to compete with the ever-changing vision of its rivals.

Henry Ford's vision included a production system that made workers into parts of an assembly line that delivered cars at regular intervals. Uniform jobs were measured and choreographed, coordinated and controlled in a hierarchy ruled by the CEO. In this business system, relatively uneducated workers accepted their limited roles and were motivated by what was then the industry's highest wages. The Fordist production system became the model for the auto industry until Toyota's management developed a different socio-technical system that cuts waste, improves productivity, and engages assembly line workers in continuous improvement or what Toyota calls "giving wisdom to the machine."

A constantly evolving corporate vision is not a simple or straightforward task; with all the talk of synergy these days, how many corporations with holdings in diverse businesses have anything that approaches cooperation—or better yet, idea and profit sharing among departments? The reason that this is so rare in corporate culture is quite simple: It is incredibly difficult for any leader, even with the benefit of foresight and a strategic vision, to get a differentiated and fragmented culture to embrace his ideas, goals, and values. In other words, it is exceptional when a leader excels at the next element of strategic intelligence: motivating.

Motivating

This is the ability to get people—a social system—to embrace a common purpose and implement your vision. Before I get into the specifics of motivating, let me explain how I'm using the term "social system." Russell Ackoff makes a useful distinction among three kinds of systems: A *mechanical* system like a car is designed so that its parts work together to further the purpose of the system, which is transportation. Every wheel and cog and crank works toward making the car go. An *organic* or biologic system is genetically designed to work together; your heart and brain and blood work in concert to keep you alive and functioning. The parts of an organic system can develop only within the system. The parts of a *social* system, such as a company, include people who can develop outside as well as inside the system, all of whom have purposes of their own. It's up to leadership to motivate them toward a common goal.

It is the social system that is especially important for our purpose of understanding leadership. How do you get a company to follow your lead, especially when it involves changing directions or taking new paths? If you read *Who Moved My Cheese?*, it's as simple as steering mice to new piles of cheese. But what's missing in this overly simplistic model is the basic premise that any company is a complex social system filled with people, all of whom have their own purposes and values, who have to be motivated to work toward the corporate goal and act according to shared values. Motivating is perhaps the most misunderstood and most elusive element of strategic intelligence.

Many CEOs are strong in the areas of product and financial strategy, what I call the "hard" skills of understanding the numbers and the technology needed. But it's one thing to talk tough about a new corporate initiative to improve sales and profits, to put on a macho public face about how you're going to crush the competition with market domination, and it's quite another to grasp the importance of the "soft" skills, the ones that can't be measured or put on a profit-and-loss sheet.

These soft skills, the messy and amorphous work with the people who need to make your vision happen, are, in many ways, more important and harder to change than the hard financial strategy of a company. This is where many CEOs, especially narcissistic and obsessive personality types, fall short; their business models often lack any focus whatsoever on the human, and people need to be motivated to make the CEO's vision a reality.

Many CEOs believe they can motivate people by a combination of speeches, rewards, and threats. Most employees are afraid of the boss, and an astute CEO like Goran Collert directs this fear away from him and toward the competition. But as an overall strategy for motivation, exhortations and carrots and sticks don't engage the whole person. They may work well enough for motivating simple tasks in a Fordist system, but when you need to motivate knowledge workers to think in the same way, use their brains, and act enthusiastically, they are overly simplistic. In my work I've found it useful to think of motivation in terms of the four "R"s: reasons, rewards, relationships, responsibilities. The *reasons* why workers decide to follow management's lead and feel their work makes a difference are crucial for understanding motivation. In the last chapter, I showed how each personality type is motivated by different social mechanisms: Obsessives want to be recognized for the excellence of their work, particularly by father figures; erotics want to help people; marketing types like to build a cache of job skills and increase their market worth; and narcissists want to change the world. Workers who believe that their job is more than just a paycheck are motivated to do more than just show up. A leader with strategic intelligence understands exactly what motivates different workers and communicates a sense of meaning that each type can relate to, such as defining a company or country, being part of something "insanely great," getting a "PC in every home," or "bringing good things to life."

The reasons are intimately tied to *rewards*. While every worker wants money, unless the financial reward is enormous, most employees see money as part of the deal, the compensation for giving their time and energy. The rewards that are highly motivating are different for each personality type. Erotics want appreciation and recognition that they are needed by customers as well as bosses; obsessives love certificates that they can frame and put on the wall (just look at the office of your doctor or lawyer); marketing types want signals of their worth, such as an invitation to an important event or key meeting that validates their importance; and narcissists want the independence and power to achieve their vision. Strategic intelligence means rewarding the behavior needed to further a vision. But many leaders think only about motivating those who report directly to them, often ignoring the frontline workers and lower-level employees. A CEO with strategic intelligence recognizes that he or she is responsible for creating a motivating social system. A good example of companywide motivation is Toyota, where front-line workers are rewarded when they help others and suggest improvements to the work process. Another is Southwest, where Herb Kelleher seeks out and hires erotic personalities who are motivated toward service, reinforcing helping and teamwork in a familylike spirit.

Relationships are the interactions between bosses, coworkers, and customers that create teamwork, trust, appreciation, security, and give-and-take at work. Again, different personality types respond to different relationships: The manager with strategic intelligence knows what relationships motivate their staff. This is one of Phil Jackson's greatest skills as a team coach; according to Michael Jordan, "Phil gets under your skin when he needs to. Then he pulls right off when he has to. Other coaches will go too far or not nearly far enough. Phil knows exactly how far to go." Jackson surprised fans by publicly chastising his two biggest stars—Kobe Bryant and Shaquille O'Neal—but he understands that each player needs different incentives. In Jackson's defense, Bryant said, "It's the combination of Phil being the great coach he is, and me and Shaq responding to the criticism but not being threatened by it. We know what Phil's up to, what buttons he's pushing." This emphasis on the "soft" side of motivating, of using different relationships and reasons with each player, has also been faulted in the press: Jackson is criticized for sitting quietly on the bench, not taking issue with the referees' calls, and not jumping up and yelling the way so many other coaches do. Instead he focuses on each player, strategically using his anger when he has to. Contrast this with empathy, really understanding the other person's feelings. A person with acute motivating skills doesn't "feel your pain" for the purpose of empathy; the other person's feelings are important only for your own purpose, for gauging how you can get that person to do what you need, a skill that Bill Clinton used to his great advantage.

Management needs to pick the right person for the right job, pairing skill level, interests, and abilities with the position within the company; this pairing falls under *responsibilities*. Seen in this way, it's management's responsibility to endow workers with tasks that they can, in turn, take responsibility for. These tasks should be neither too much of a stretch of their abilities nor too far below; first-year medical students should not be given the responsibility of brain surgery, but do need to acquire new medical skills that push their capabilities and learning. To use another example from the sports world, management made a brilliant strategic move when they moved Babe Ruth, then a league-leading pitcher for the Boston Red Sox, into the everyday lineup and outfield, which allowed him to become a record-breaking hitter. This was not a natural move; management knew it was a stretch of Ruth's abilities: "It was manager Ed Barrow, at the suggestion of Harry Hooper [who] switched the Babe to the outfield. That move alone should earn Barrow Hall of Fame consideration." Likewise, the business leader with strategic intelligence knows who to place where, and how to make them responsible and accountable for their work. This is the goal of Steve Ballmer's management initiative at Microsoft, which he calls Executive P&L. In the past, each one of the executives of Microsoft's seven business units reported directly to Ballmer. With the Executive P&L, which was launched in April 2002, each unit is given detailed information about every cost and expenditure, from conception to sale, making each executive responsible for the financial health of their own division.

The model in the business world of a leader who strategically employed each one of the four "R"s, who engaged the whole organization in a complex vision/system that transformed a company from a product focus to solutions, is Jack Welch. GE's old system, pre-Welch, was based on rewarding each division for its success. If your division did well, you made money at the end of the year, no matter what happened with the company's overall performance. In 1982, Welch changed all this; he broke down the segmented reward system and tied bonuses into the entire company's performance. He combined financial rewards with a complex set of psychological threats, opportunity, fear, dialogue, persuasion, meeting after meeting, and even brainwashing—anything he could to make the organization not only do what he said but think the way he did. Managers who demonstrated learning were rewarded; those who didn't share his values were fired. Ratings and the threat of failure backed up his purpose; when he instituted Six Sigma quality, he allotted 40 percent of a manager's bonus to the execution of the program. Welch may claim to be a teacher, but a teacher allows students to arrive at their own conclusions. Welch drilled managers in *his* way of seeing things, saying that "every day I tried to get into the skin of every person in the place. I wanted them to feel my pressure." (Sounds almost exactly like Michael Jordan's description of how Jackson "gets under your skin.") Welch describes his overall strategy to motivate change this way: "Stock options got us a start. An operating system connected the dots, creating a learning cycle out of what otherwise would have been a series of routine meetings."

This may be Welch's own description of incentivizing, but I call it brainwashing, a tough but effective way of motivating, of engaging the GE machinery in Welch's way of seeing things. My view of this was confirmed in an interview with Jack Welch in the *Harvard Business Review*, in which editor Diane Coutu said that there are "business observers who say GE is a cult, that the teaching you do there amounts to brainwashing" (a term that was taken directly from my article on productive narcissists in the *Harvard Business Review*). Welch immediately became defensive: "Without question, that is the craziest thought in the world." But then he went on to describe exactly what I mean by brainwashing rather than teaching: "I'll throw Six Sigma out and say, 'Here's my vision.' I'll exaggerate the case to create a sense of urgency, and I'll insist that only the best people be assigned to work on it. I'll make these pronouncements about every initiative over and over again. A relentless drumbeat." And if people dissent? Welch says, "There's no value in dissent for its own sake." Sounds exactly like brainwashing; everyone has to be on the exact same page as Welch, internalizing the GE way of doing this, without any chance of offering a conflicting view.

Very few leaders are able to get an organization to embrace their way of thinking; brainwashing is one technique that has been extremely successful for Welch. But another tactic that has been tested and proven in the economic playing field is Herb Kelleher's model of an interactive dialogue with employees who share his company's core values. Kelleher understands that every single person within the organization has to share his vision; to accomplish this, the company weeds through its applicants, picking people who, right from the start, embrace the Southwest ethos of sharing and cooperation. They encourage multiple members of families to work for the company. Southwest works closely with the union, maintaining strong relationships with union leaders and pro-union contracts. Employee stock ownership is encouraged. This is an ethos that extends from the front-line workers—the line men, baggage handlers, and ticket takers—right on through the upper levels of management—all of which fits into Kelleher's systemic view of how to engage the organization in his way of thinking.

Jan Carlzon, the widely acclaimed former CEO of SAS, provides a cautionary lesson in contrast to Kelleher. In the early '80s, Carlzon showed great foresight and systems thinking in bringing service management to SAS, creating business class and empowering front-line ticket sellers and cabin attendants to respond to customer problems. The front line was enthusiastic, but Carlzon never persuaded or motivated senior management to fully implement his vision. He once invited me to a meeting of his executive team in Oslo, where I asked him to describe his view of an ideal organization. His answer: the Brazilian football (soccer) team, where players improvise and there is a great spirit of fun. He contrasted this to German soccer teams, where players stick to their roles and positions. I turned to a vice president who had been an air force general and asked him his view of the ideal organization. He said, "I still think the military is the best." How did Carlzon respond to that? "That's right," he said, "if your goal is to shoot the customer." This reply, while witty, did not engage the obsessive and hierarchical vice president. Carlzon's lack of key elements of strategic intelligence—motivating senior managers and partnering with an obsessive COO who signed on to Carlzon's the vision, but soon resigned—led to his eventual ouster from SAS, which lost the excitement and luster he brought to it.

Bill Gates is a leader who combines the motivating techniques of Welch and Kelleher, using both brainwashing and fear, as well as profit sharing on a large, corporate scale. Gates has created a unique social system that caters to a workforce that has never felt at home in the buttoned-up, top-down hierarchies of companies like IBM and Texas Instruments. Famously known for a lack of any dress code and an individual, make-your-own-hours ethos, Microsoft employees are motivated to work longer and harder. Microsoft does not try to make smart or beautiful designs for the pure poetry of it (something that could easily be said of Apple under Steve Jobs);

throughout its early years, the company placed its highest emphasis on the "ship it" plaque, or actually moving product into the marketplace, a result of the highly competitive, individualistic workforce that Microsoft self-selects. To move the corporation into its next phase of growth, Gates turned over the CEO position to Steve Ballmer in 2000, signaling a shift in focus from product innovation to the creation of a corporate system that embraces new management processes. Learning from Welch, Ballmer has instituted a rigorous set of meetings, intensive weeklong management retreats, brainstorming sessions, an "organizational health index," in which employees are asked to give no-holds-barred ratings of their superiors, and what *BusinessWeek* calls the "final touch . . . making adoption of the new corporate values part of every employee's annual performance." Gates is that rare productive narcissist who understands exactly where his strengths lie; he currently spends 65 percent of his time working on product development, and he has turned the Microsoft social system over to Ballmer, an obsessive personality who also possesses an abundance of strategic intelligence.

I would like to contrast the superior motivating skills of Welch, Kelleher, and Gates with three narcissistic CEOs who are known for the grand pronouncements in the press about their overarching business plans but have been unable to implement them because of their lack of motivating skills and their inability to understand the "soft" side of engaging the organization. Their critics often focus on personality problems or business model failings, but I believe their Achilles' heel was the lack of an interactive model that got the entire organization working toward the same goal.

MIKE ARMSTRONG

Mike Armstrong's systemic vision for AT&T was integrating voice, data, high-speed Internet connections, and cable in order to compete with the Bell Operating companies. However, he has been unable to get past the "pure" vision and move into the real-world visioning, motivating, and partnering that could make it happen. Armstrong lacks deep knowledge of telephony or the telecommunications industry and seems to make decisions based on the advice of consultants or experts, or on his own superficial responses to the market. I believe his lack of knowledge caused him to spin off what may well have become the most profitable division of AT&T, the part best able to compete with the Bell companies if integrated with the Internet: wireless services. He is roundly criticized for overpaying for the cable companies that he thought would provide the wiring and services that AT&T lacked. Unlike Welch, he has been unable to get AT&T's separate units to work together, to move past the boundaries that make idea and profit sharing possible. Cable and telephone people have not coordinated technology. Armstrong has never taken the problem of creating a corporate culture seriously; management does not cooperate with him, nor is it motivated toward his goal. His partnership with BT for global business collapsed because his VP of business services was resistant to his overall strategy. Armstrong is known for delegating problem tasks and barking out orders, but he offers little in the way of incentive or motivation to implement his massive reorganization. He does not persuade; he blames. The only internal partner whom Armstrong relied on was his CFO, Chuck Noski, who followed him from Hughes. This lack of trust is apparent in a corporate culture that is rife with paranoia, distrust, and divisive "spying."

Armstrong is a real charmer, as befits a narcissist, and has convinced the business press that he has "saved" AT&T from total annihilation with the Comcast deal. What he has done, in fact, is lower the large debt he took on and negotiate a continued role for himself as chairman of AT&T Comcast. His greatest skills are foresight and systems thinking; at Hughes, he had the foresight to switch the corporate strategy from defense contracts to satellite television, and at AT&T, to envision one-stop telephony shopping for consumers. But he lacks the real-world visioning, partnering, and especially motivating skills to turn his vision into a reality.

JIM WOLFENSOHN

I have been a consultant to different parts of the World Bank, and although I never worked directly with James Wolfensohn, I have heard from a number of executives who worked closely with him. Some have come up to me at meetings to say that the *Harvard Business Review* article described him precisely. Wolfensohn took over as CEO of the Bank in 1995, and despite what many experts considered a disastrous tenure, his contract was renewed in 2000 for another five years. A former corporate finance wizard who distinguished himself by his support of the arts, such as Carnegie Hall and the Kennedy Center, Wolfensohn came into the job with a bold and overarching strategy for reducing poverty in Third World countries. In the past the World Bank's mandate has been to go into different countries, putting money into the infrastructure—dams, roads, factories, and so on—thereby saddling them with debt and loan repayments. Wolfensohn's vision is to get the Bank to collaborate with less-developed countries to invest in programs that alleviate poverty—for example, spending money on nutrition, improved agricultural and water standards, education, and health care, preventing illness instead of simply building a hospital. This is a complete turnaround in the World Bank's mission, requiring a massive reorganization and change in corporate priorities.

The problem is that Wolfensohn is not a leader who can make it happen. His colleagues tell me that he is a prototypical productive narcissist, embodying many of the strengths—especially vision, passion, and energy—but also all of the weaknesses of the type: He's capable of flying into uncontrolled rages, ranting and raving at his managers and blaming them for mistakes, taking everything personally, overreacting to criticism while heaping it on his staff. An internal memo from the bank's Middle East and North Africa department revealed that Wolfensohn is "quick to rebuke and humiliate managers, often in open meetings" and "He does not welcome criticism or tolerate dissent, be it from the board, or the managers, or the staff association. Managers at all levels live under fear." Wolfensohn is not only incapable of partnering with an obsessive COO, he has never even hired one to work under him and implement the changes that his vision requires. There are no systems in place that reward managers or incentivize them. Unlike Welch, who broke down internal barriers, Wolfensohn's intimidation and rage serve only to polarize the company. To be fair to Wolfensohn, he faces more challenges to "boundarylessness" than Welch did; the bank is highly politicized, the donor countries carefully guard their own interests, and many of the recipient countries lack the institutions and personnel required to make a partnership work. Even so, Wolfensohn offers little motivation for managers and other countries to work together.

This is a classic case of the pitfalls of narcissistic leadership, or, as Stephen Fidler of *Foreign Policy* puts it, a "tragic deterioration of the world's premier development institution." I believe the real tragedy is that Wolfensohn's vision is far superior to those of his predecessors; he is a man who could literally make a difference in millions of lives around the world, but he is crippled by a lack of strategic intelligence in general and the total absence of any motivating skills. He quite simply can't get his vision across, either within the bank's organization or in the separate countries, where local politicians like to take credit for big projects rather than the incremental advances that are part of Wolfensohn's vision. He is known for glomming on to fads and pet projects, such as the slightly loony World Faiths Initiative, a plan to gather together the Archbishop of Canterbury, John Paul II, and the Aga Kahn to promote religious tolerance, which the Bank's board quite rightly squashed. But the board needs to take more action, appointing strong generals who can stand up to Wolfensohn and implement his vision. Even if they do step in during the next few years, I doubt that the World Bank can save itself from a visionary leader so lacking in strategic intelligence.

PERCY BARNEVIK

I was a consultant to ABB, the global engineering company, over the course of ten years, and while I did not work directly with Percy Barnevik, I did coach his successor as CEO. One of my roles was to interview managers in twenty different markets in Europe, Asia, and North America in order to understand their values, how they approach their customers, and to improve the relationships between local managers and expatriates. In Canada, I had a more focused goal: I was a consultant to a five-year strategic change process, and worked with managers to help them adapt to an evolving marketplace. ABB products were losing money and market share to their competitors, and management wanted to know why and what they could do about it. I instituted a systematic set of interviews with the largest customers to find out what they thought about ABB products and what they wanted from ABB; instead of hiring outside consultants to talk to the customers—their reports almost always end up on a shelf, unread—we had managers interview the customers themselves, hear what they had to say and how they thought about their own businesses. What came out of the interviews is that the customers didn't need to go out and buy more product, simple commodities; they wanted partners for strategic solutions. For example, rather than buying a new power transformer, a business consumer wanted to partner with ABB to cut energy costs and decrease air pollution. On the surface, it makes business sense. But putting it into practice is another thing entirely. It would require a complete restructuring of ABB's 2,000 business units, each of which had its own profit-and-loss responsibility that was presided over by Percy Barnevik.

The career trajectory of Barnevik is a case study of a lack of adapting a vision to the changing business environment, a failure of strategic intelligence. Throughout the 1990s, Barnevik was considered the most respected and talented businessman in Europe. He was recently pushed out of his position as chairman of Investor, the

Wallenberg holding bank, and the year before resigned as chairman of ABB. He has been vilified in the Swedish press for his huge pension from ABB at a time when the company is floundering. Although he gave part of it back, his aura has faded. What went wrong?

I believe that the problems at ABB, with its inability to integrate divisions and provide solutions, stem directly from Barnevik's belief system. When I first met him in 1982, he had just become CEO of Asea, a Swedish electrical engineering firm. He told me about his transformation of the company from a bureaucracy where the CEO had the only bottom-line responsibility to a structure where each business unit had its own profit-and-loss accounting, fostering a competitive, entrepreneurial spirit. Barnevik orchestrated a successful merger with the Swiss-based Brown Boveri in 1988, then moved on to head up the newly formed Asea Brown Boveri (ABB), where he instituted the strict P&L responsibility among the 2,000 entrepreneurial units he designed.

While this structure worked for products, it was not suited to a changing market calling for solutions. Unlike GE, where Welch broke the boundaries between business units and forced them to learn together, ABB's business units resisted the kind of cooperation that would have made partnering with customers possible. There were larger, strategic visioning errors: Barnevik and Goran Lindahl, the managing director who followed him, bet too heavily on technology, selling off the profitable power products division that is essential for building a service business base that cooperates with customers. Later, Barnevik made the same kind of costly mistake as CEO of Investor, valuing technology over the core businesses, with his unsuccessful investments in the dot-com and e-commerce world. By not responding to large business customers who asked ABB for solutions, Barnevik showed a lack of the final element of strategic intelligence: partnering.

Partnering

P artnering is making strategic alliances. Someone with emotional intelligence is able to make friends; a person with strategic intelligence makes allies. This can be on both a personal and a corporate level. Andy Grove was able to dominate the microprocessor market by partnering with Microsoft, Compaq, and Dell. Inside Intel, Grove has partnered with Craig Barrett as CEO, knowing that Barrett has the emotional intelligence that he lacks. Jorma Olilla built Nokia by partnering with suppliers, competitors, and universities to further research on mobile telephones. Larry Ellison partnered with COO Ray Lane to operationalize his vision. Right after his departure, Lane said: "The difference between us was good for shareholders." Since Lane, critics say Oracle is faltering and Ellison needs help. Observers think that Michael Eisner was most creative at Disney when he had Frank Wells as a partner and buffer. Daphne Kis is CEO of Esther Dyson's EDventure; Bill Gates has partnered with Steve Ballmer at Microsoft; Colleen Barrett was COO under Herb Kelleher and took over the CEO position when Kelleher left; Bob Pittman, an operational expert, was allied with visionary Steve Case during the rise of AOL. When I described these partnerships at a seminar of business leaders, Per Mosby, a Swedish entrepreneur in his twenties from Melody, a company producing mobile Internet software, recognized that he is a narcissistic personality who needs to partner with an obsessive

("I'm not an operations leader") and wants the freedom to be the "chief visionary." Even early in his career, he saw himself as helping employees with great ideas start new companies where he could be chairman, influencing the direction and overall strategy. Another young narcissistic CEO, Max More of manyworlds.com, partners with operational obsessives as well as business experts who are showcased on his Web page, www.manyworlds.com.

Partnering means understanding how each alliance, whether personal or corporate, fits into your vision for the company. Corporate acquisitions must add value to the overall vision; likewise, managers must add value to their particular CEO. A CEO can't underestimate the importance of partnering when determining the strategic value of corporate acquisitions. Jeffrey Sonnenfeld, a dean at the Yale School of Management, singled out partnering failures in *The New York Times* in which he calls Dennis Kozlowski of Tyco, Ken Lay of Enron, Bernie Ebbers of WorldCom, and Gary Winnick of Global Crossing "serial acquirers," tacking different companies on to their core business in order to bolster overall financial holdings, rather than create and manage companies that reinforce and complement one another: "These serial acquirers did not build businesses around core competencies but were scavengers for good deals, a strategy that rarely pays off in the long run."

These men are the modern equivalent of William Durant, the founder of General Motors and Henry Ford's main competitor. Of the two carmakers, Durant was the one who seemed destined for lasting success before he started making cars. A millionaire by the age of forty, Durant made his fortune from the car's forerunner, the cart and carriage. But once he moved from carriages to cars, Durant seemed to change business strategies entirely. What had worked so well for him in the past—streamlining his company's operations, cutting costs, spending money on marketing and advertising, and making only select high-profile models—was exactly the opposite of what Durant did in the car industry. He went on a corporate spending spree, acquiring new car and parts companies at an astonishing rate. After his efforts to build a "dream team" car conglomerate of four of the largest manufacturers fell through, he formed General Motors in 1908, drawing together Buick, Oldsmobile, Cadillac, and a number of other carmakers and parts manufacturers. Throughout it all, Durant didn't know what car model would take off, so he decided that he would try to sell every model, at least all that he could get his hands on, betting that one of them had to hit. This strategy, if it could be called that, is akin to playing every single number on the roulette wheel, ensuring that there will never be a big payoff. Like today's serial acquirers, he ended up amassing huge debt. Durant may have had the foresight to know that the buggy was about to give way to the car, but he had no real-world visioning skills, no way of turning a good idea—the car—into a profitable business. On the corporate level, Durant's holdings, whether they were car lines or parts and accessory manufacturers, went up against one another in the marketplace instead of working together as part of a systemic whole. This is exactly the same lack of partnering skill that Sonnenfeld attributes to Bernie Ebbers, who "cares more about snaring new companies and less about making all his acquisitions work together." The serial acquirers lack several essential elements of strategic intelligence: knowing how to partner well internally, with advisers who complement their own personality, and externally, with companies that add value rather than size. Although they may have a seductive vision of product synergy, they show no understanding of how the companies work together and how to motivate a company, a social system of people, toward their vision. This is the case with Mike Armstrong's overarching vision for one-stop telephony, which seduced shareholders and creditors but was nothing more than a beautiful idea, conceived and executed without any concern for the integration of the separate divisions and how they could offer more than the sum of their parts, or the interests of the customers, who never saw the benefit of bundled telecom services.

The inability to partner effectively within a company, as well as with outside acquisitions, can cut short a visionary leader's career. Craig Venter's career is an interesting case study of a person who has demonstrated most of the elements of strategic intelligence but hasn't been able to turn his innovative and brilliant vision of mapping the human genome into an income-generating business. Venter likes to call himself the Henry Ford of biotechnology, but it remains to be seen if he can go beyond his scientific discoveries and apply them to the broader social and economic forces to create a profitable business model. When I spoke with him in the fall of 2001, Venter planned to use genetic information to develop drugs that target tuberculosis and pancreatic cancer. He had a staff of distinguished scientists who he said were motivated by the opportunity to be part of greatness, getting in on the ground floor of a highly innovative and potentially lucrative business. Then, in January 2002, we learned that Venter had been forced to resign as CEO of Celera, the company that he cofounded and brought to international attention.

What happened at Celera? The official explanation from Applera, the owners of Celera, was that Venter was scientific rather than industrial, and lacked the necessary pharmaceutical experience. That may be true, but I believe Venter's greatest weakness is his inability to partner well. That can't be said of his personal life; he is married to Claire Fraser, a productive obsessive who is strong on details, organizing, and implementation. They met when she was a research assistant, and over the years made a great research and money-raising team, founding, among others, TIGR, the non-profit company that Fraser now heads up. Venter told me that "she's running it better than I ever did." Venter left TIGR because he saw the possibilities of mapping the human genome and knew that he could get it done faster than anyone else thought was even possible. He partnered with the industrialists Tony White and Michael Hunkapiller at Perkin-Elmer, now called Applera, a company that had the technology and Wall Street backing to get it done. But without Fraser by his side, Venter lacked an internal partner, a trusted sidekick who could complement his narcissistic personality. His staff told me that he had great difficulty with his COO, an Englishman with a background in manufacturing nasal sprays whose role was to provide the drug experience that Venter needed. But their personalities clashed: The COO spoke slowly and was excessively polite; Venter talks fast and is outspoken to the point of being rude. The COO liked to show Venter his methodical, carefully laid out plans, a habit that Venter found maddening. The COO lasted only a year, and Celera executives complained that Venter made it impossible to find another COO who could bring the research into the marketplace, an experienced player in the drug world who wouldn't mind playing second fiddle to Venter's large and very public persona.

What will be Venter's future? Scientific adviser? Or a new business approach? Venter has announced that he plans on starting three institutes—a large-scale nonprofit genome-sequencing center that will compete with Celera; The Center for the Advancement of

Genomics, which will study the issues surrounding genetic research; and the Institute for Biological Energy Alternatives to develop nonfossil fuel sources. Venter told Andrew Pollack of *The New York Times* that his plan for the sequencing center is to bring the cost of sequencing a person's genome down to $2,000 from $3,000, making it possible to use the genetic information for patient-specific medical treatments. A bold undertaking, and one that could have enormous medical benefits if Venter can make it happen; but unless he is able to partner strategically on a corporate level, with a company that has a track record in the drug or energy industry, and on a personal level, with a COO or other, possibly obsessive, sidekick, I think that his brilliance will be limited to the lab rather than the marketplace.

I saw a similar lack of partnering ability in the career of Pehr Gyllenhammar, the former CEO of Volvo, who was forced out by shareholders who rejected his attempts to merge Volvo with Renault. Gyllenhammar had the foresight to see that the Volvo car corporation was too small to compete in the global market. His failure of strategic intelligence was in the area of motivation and internal partnering. Gyllenhammar never got into the heads of his managers. He didn't understand the importance of having them share his values. Gyllenhammar was most effective at Volvo when he had an obsessive COO, Hakan Frisinger, to focus on improving quality and cost, as well as an obsessive HR director, Berth Jonsson, to implement his vision of changing the workplace. His new factories at Kalmar and Uddevalla transformed the assembly line, providing workers with more challenging jobs. (Volvo's innovative approach was superseded by the Toyota lean manufacturing system). When Frisinger, Jonsson, and Bo Ekman, Volvo's creative vice president of strategy, left, Gyllenhammar became even more isolated from the organization. Volvo managers who worked with Renault on engine design and production thought the French were arrogant and uncooperative. They spoke out against the deal and appealed to Swedish nationalism. Gyllenhammar's early foresight was shown to be right—Volvo sold its car corporation to Ford—but by then it was too late for Gyllenhammar, who was forced out years ago, the victim of his own poor motivating and partnering skills.

Summarizing Strategic Intelligence

It's impossible to gauge strategic intelligence from a simple test (unlike IQ, which is quantifiable), but the following statements summarize the elements of strategic intelligence. Ask yourself how well these statements describe you. Be sure you come up with specific examples and scenarios that support your answers. It doesn't matter if you're not in a position at your workplace to make policy changes or shape corporate strategy; you should work on your strategic intelligence and develop it, no matter what role you play at your company. Strategic intelligence can strengthen you in any position, in any career. For example, an element of Nokia's success is that people at all levels are encouraged to think about the future and partner within and outside the company.

These statements are especially useful for investors and board members who need to evaluate a visionary entrepreneur; before interviewing or deciding upon a potential manager or executive, try to frame these statements in terms of your company and particular field. Can your candidate affirm them? Can he give examples from his previous experience or come up with scenarios for your business?

FORESIGHT

- I scan the business environment for trends that present threats and opportunities for me and my organization.
- I listen to my gut or intuition about the future.
- I seek out and listen to people whose knowledge helps me foresee future trends.
- I have a deep knowledge of my business.
- I construct scenarios of possible futures and think about how I would deal with each scenario.

SYSTEMS THINKING

- I evaluate parts of the organization and its systems in terms of how well they further the overall purpose.
- I manage the interactions among different parts of the organization.
- When I have a problem, I look for all the factors influencing it before I try to solve it.
- When I have a list of things to do, I try to understand how each action will impact the others before I act.
- When my theories don't work, I question my assumptions.
- I think of my own well-being as an interaction of my physical, mental, and spiritual selves and I work on all three.

VISIONING

- I can describe how my vision uniquely positions my company in the market.
- I can describe how my vision will change our reputation and brand.
- I can describe my vision as a socioeconomic system.

- My vision for the organization includes how people will interact with one another.
- My vision for the organization includes the shared values essential for its implementation.
- I can describe the competencies we need to implement the vision.
- My vision takes account of how the organization will interact with political and social forces.

MOTIVATING

- I have thought out what people will have to do and what has to change to realize my vision.
- I understand the values of the customers who are essential to my business.
- I understand the values of the employees who are essential to my business.
- I understand the values of the investors who are essential to my business.
- I use this knowledge to shape a message that inspires people.
- I engage my key managers in a dialogue about how we need to think and act and why this is important.
- I can tell when people are only paying lip service to the vision.
- I make sure the rewards given to employees reinforce the values and behavior needed to realize the vision.
- I do not punish honest mistakes but use them as an opportunity for learning.
- I make sure that we are hiring people with the competence and values needed to realize the vision.
- I put people into jobs that are challenging.
- Once I know that people are not adding value, I am quick to get rid of them.

PARTNERING

- I partner with key customers.
- I partner with key suppliers.
- I build trust with partners by making sure we share the same goals.
- I make sure that my partners will also benefit from the partnership.
- I seek internal partners who aren't just yes-men, who will tell me hard truths.
- I form partnerships with people who share my values.
- I know what my strengths and weaknesses are and look for partners who can complement them.
- I am quick to break off ineffective partnering relationships.

FIVE

WORKING WITH A PRODUCTIVE NARCISSIST

With everything we've learned about the narcissistic personality, why would anyone want to subject him- or herself to
working with this type? And if you make the decision to align yourself with a productive narcissist, how do you work for, with, or
around him without losing your mind or letting your own ego take
a battering?

Before I give some answers to "how," let's get at the "why."
When I look back at my thirty-year immersion in the business
world, it turns out that the majority of CEOs I've coached are productive narcissists. How is it that I ended up working with so many
narcissistic CEOs, and why did I think it was worth it? I didn't
plan on it. My academic training was entirely focused on human
development, preparing me for a natural career path of teaching,

writing academic papers for journals, participating in conferences, and working with individuals in psychoanalysis, all of which I've done. But my career took an interesting twist after I lectured to a church group in Palo Alto on the relation between the sexes: love, war, or indifference. After the lecture, I was approached by a manager at a large technology firm who was intrigued by the idea of applying my concepts of social character to his own workplace. How did work and relationships both reflect and shape their values? One introduction led to another, and soon I found myself meeting with top managers and CEOs of innovative firms while working on the *Gamesman* study. I found it exciting and even inspiring to be among people who weren't sealed off in a classroom, limiting themselves to writing about their theories, discussing them as if they were divorced from any kind of work, practice, or the everyday realities of people's lives. They were struggling to take their ideas and give them a shape and form in the messy and unpredictable world of the marketplace. I came to see that the real test of people's productivity is in the workplace, challenging their abilities, how they handle relationships, how they see themselves participating in the world. I believe in the possibility of human development within a capitalistic, democratic society, and as it turns out, so do many productive narcissists. They are the ones who are pushing themselves and the people around them to the limit, stretching their capabilities.

Productive people have a project or a series of projects. Their work is an effort to grapple with their projects, to try to make their projects come to life. The narcissistic CEOs I met and worked with all had inspiring projects, whether they accomplished them or not. They didn't just want to go through the motions at work, make some money, have their "real" lives outside of the office. You may want to take a look at your own project. Do you have one, and what are you doing about it? Your project may not have to do with changing the world, but if it engages your passion, it will be true to your personality type. If you are an erotic personality, it may be about helping people and feeling needed. If you are an obsessive, it may be about breaking records, scientific discovery, or engineering an elegant solution to a problem. If you are a self-developing marketing type, it may be organizing a team for a campaign or achieving a healthy lifestyle. You need to ask yourself whether working for a productive narcissist will help or impede your own project, and whether you can support and believe in his project.

You need to decide for yourself if it's worth it—do you want to be close to someone who is pushing himself to the limit, who has the possibility of tremendous growth and, quite possibly, tremendous wealth? If so, you have to be willing to go along with all of the negatives, the personality problems, the volatility, the threat of total failure. No matter what their strengths, productive narcissists are incredibly difficult to work for. They don't learn easily from others. They are oversensitive to any kind of criticism, which they take personally. They bully subordinates and dominate meetings. They don't want to hear about anyone else's feelings. They are distrustful and paranoid. They can become grandiose, especially when they start to succeed. Perhaps their most frustrating quality is that they almost never listen to anyone. But look at it this way: After Sancho Panza traveled with Don Quixote, saving him from his wild fantasies, he achieved his lifelong goal, becoming the governor of an island. In like manner, Ray Lane left Oracle with a net worth of $850 million, and now is a general partner at the venture capital firm of Kleiner, Perkins, Caulfield & Byers (as well as a board member of several other companies), working relatively "normal" hours while gaining the financial benefits of a partnership, a position that would have been tough to land without trading on the Oracle name and brand image. Lane aligned himself with a productive narcissist, partnered effectively, took it as long as he could, and then left with the cash and bankable experience. Daphne Kis, who is Esther Dyson's CEO, told me that she has stayed for thirteen years because of her involvement with cutting-edge thinking and technology, the constant innovation and new ideas, the access to important and influential thinkers. Why stay? Because, she says, "it excites me."

If you decide it excites you, then you need to understand the challenges of the narcissistic personality and how to handle them in a work setting. This chapter provides specific strategies for anyone who works with, for, or around a productive narcissist, as well as board members and shareholders who need to know how to handle their narcissistic CEOs. The chapter follows this structure: First, it describes five general guidelines, the emotional tools that are essential for anyone who works with a productive narcissist,

FIVE PRINCIPLES FOR WORKING WITH A NARCISSIST

- Know yourself and your type
- Acquire deep knowledge in your field
- Learn how to partner effectively
- Don't invest your own ego
- Protect the narcissist's image

after which it gets more specific, taking on the weaknesses of the narcissistic personality that were outlined in the third chapter—the negative ways that a productive narcissist typically behaves in the workplace—and provides ways to deal with each of these negative traits, including when you need to shut up and just take it, and when you know it's time to walk.

Know Yourself and Your Type

B efore you can understand how to work with others—especially narcissists, who are notoriously lacking in self-reflection—you have to know yourself. I learned this the hard way. Before becoming a business coach, I underwent psychoanalysis for eight years with Erich Fromm in an effort to understand myself, my motivations, and what prevented me from realizing my own potential. While a productive narcissist may not need much emotional intelligence, or what I prefer to call self-awareness, a coach to a productive narcissist certainly does. The same can be said of a business associate of a productive narcissist. The point is that your own personality type influences all your relationships and interactions. Before you can listen to any advice about work relationships, you need to know yourself. If you understand your own type, you will be better equipped to know why you do what you do, your motivation, your typical reactions and behaviors. There's no way that you can evaluate your own goals, and decide if they're in line with your narcissistic CEO's, without some degree of self-knowledge. Otherwise, as we'll see, you may become extremely frustrated. The narcissist can be very intuitive in seducing people he thinks he needs.

As long as you are useful, he can be enthusiastically supportive and make you feel you can do practically anything. But in the long run, a narcissist won't satisfy the erotic's need for love, the obsessive's need for recognition, or the marketing type's need for affirmation. Knowing your own type will ensure that you get these needs met elsewhere.

Acquire Deep Knowledge in Your Field

Be strategic about acquiring deep knowledge in your field. Learn where your boss or CEO is weak, and build your own strengths in that area. This seems like good advice for working with any personality type, but that's not the case. Some obsessives are threatened when you know more than they do; erotics like to "share" information, particularly when it is served up with juicy gossip, and marketing types want only information they can use right away. Productive narcissists, on the other hand, don't have time for you unless you fill in the gaps in their knowledge and skill set. A former Apple executive said about Steve Jobs: "Quite honestly, no one is Steve's friend. Either you are useful to him or not." Regis McKenna, who was a marketing consultant to Jobs in Apple's early years, put it another way: "If you know something he doesn't, you're in great shape."

If you think about the relationship that productive narcissists have to information, it explains a lot about their relationships with people. They *use* people the same way they use books, information, and knowledge. They pump them for information. This is very different from having a real conversation with someone, actually asking about another person and listening to what they have to say. The productive narcissists I've worked with want one of two things out of me: They want me to listen to them monologue, let me in on their internal dialogue, play Horatio to their Hamlet, or they want me to give them some understanding that they can use for their purposes, information that runs deeper than the readily usable information that would satisfy a marketing type. This kind of relationship to others, where they're kept close by as long as they serve a purpose, can be found in the work of the prototypical productive narcissist St. Augustine. Consider this passage from *Dialogue with Myself*, an internal dialogue committed to the page, between Augustine, on the one hand, and his counterpart, "Reason," on the other, where he considers friendship as a vehicle for his own spiritual journey:

> REASON: But what if [your friends'] presence distracts you from your own search? Won't you take steps, or hope to, to be rid of them?
>
> AUGUSTINE: You are right, I confess it.
>
> REASON: So you do not want them to live or be with your friends for their own sake, but to help you find wisdom.
>
> AUGUSTINE: I agree entirely.

Let's take this insight and put it into practice in a business setting: Pretend you are a book that has data and facts scattered throughout it that are useful to your boss. When your boss needs this information, he skims you, the same way he would skim a book to find just the right piece of data that will help him develop his strategies. But he'll skim you only if he believes the book is based on solid research. This is how productive narcissists "read" people who are worthwhile to them. It's not what you would call "pleasure reading," and it's the reason productive narcissists usually have no time for the usual social greasing, or what we call "niceties." Rockefeller, for example, was extremely focused on whom he was talking to and what they could do for him. Even in his late twenties, when he was the director of an Ohio bank, he had no use for the bank directors and their thumb-twiddling meetings: "I used to go at first, and there were some nice old gentlemen sitting stolidly about a table discussing earnestly the problem offered by new departures in vault locks. It was all right in its way, but I was a busy man even then and I really didn't have the time for it. So they got rid of me speedily." Henry Ford had his right-hand man, Bennett, take meetings with people in his office rather than Ford's, "because he could always get up and walk out whenever he wanted to," which turned out to be pretty often. Patty Stonesifer, the cohead of the Gates Foundation, says that "Bill by his own admission doesn't spend a lot of time on niceties. You don't go into a meeting with him asking 'How are your kids?' He's very targeted." The bottom line: Make yourself "skimmable," offering up the essential tidbits of information to your narcissistic boss. Realize that your usefulness to him depends on discerning what he needs, then offering it to him in the most expedient way possible.

This may sound cold or exploitative, and it would be if it went only one way. But you need to realize that any relationship involves an exchange; it is not just the narcissist who is "using" you. For example, I am "using" the people whom I coach just as much as they use me. I am inspired by them, surrounded by creativity and excellence, learn from them, and am well-compensated. They use me because they want someone who understands them, shares their vision, listens to them, gives them information or knowledge that they may need, and tells them the hard truths that an employee often cannot voice. I don't feel resentful or angry even when they decide they don't need me anymore. The question I ask myself, and so should you, is: Can we use each other in ways that are decent, honest, and productive?

Learn How to Partner Effectively

The previous two strategies lead directly to the third: After you gain self-knowledge, you are better equipped to partner strategically with your narcissistic boss. If he is convinced you have knowledge or skills he needs, he'll see you as a potential partner. Look at how these partners talk about their role in relation to a narcissist: Daphne Kis says that "I had skills that Esther didn't: managing, organizing, taking care of the details, the steps involved in making them come together." And: "I know the details of the employees' lives that she doesn't know." Claire Fraser says about her partnership with Craig Venter that he could never stand the details, whereas she loved "being challenged by the technical aspects, the painstaking work." Remember the quote from Colleen Barrett, who said that Herb Kelleher had no idea how to get from A to Z, but *she* did, turning Kelleher's ideas into practical business solutions. Deborah Lee handles all of the staff management at Black Entertainment Television, including motivating the workforce and making the hard decisions about who needs to go and who should be nurtured, all things that Johnson has never been good at. These successful sidekicks, people who have outstanding careers in their own right, know exactly where their CEO is lacking, and have the skills to step in and take over, relieving the narcissist from the day-to-day minutiae, the implementation, the personnel management. As one narcissistic CEO put it, "I need sidekicks, not hangers-on."

If you want the job as a top manager, CFO, COO, or adviser to a narcissist, you need to ask yourself this series of questions: What does my boss need within the organization? Can I fill that need? What specific knowledge can I provide? Can I give him well-researched, documented facts that are crucial to the strategy? What areas of his strategic intelligence are lacking? What about my skill sets—where are my strengths and weaknesses? Can I provide information, the meaning of information, a service, a skill set that he doesn't have? Does he lack emotional intelligence in his deal-ings with the organization, customers, and other companies that I can provide? Can he use me as a speaking partner? Can I help him better realize his vision?

Reflect on your own personality type and what skills you need to be an effective partner to a narcissistic leader. This doesn't mean that you have to contort yourself, mold your own image to conform to a narcissist's whims. Far from it: You need to build on your strengths and develop skills that are useful in other partnering rela-tionships.

If you're an obsessive, you may have to learn that you won't get any approval from the CEO, the authority figure in your life. While your knack for details and processes is what makes you valuable to a productive narcissist, you need to curb the impulse to take your paperwork to him, to try to involve him in the details. That's your job, so take care of it with some independence. One characteristic of obsessives is what I call "downloading" information—instead of telling a quick story that's punctuated with a point, obsessives often dump the entire story, filled with digressions and irrelevant details, before arriving at the point. Productive narcissists can't stand this. So, before talking to your narcissistic boss about an idea or proposal, ask yourself, "What is essential for me to communicate, and what is the best and most efficient way to get to the point?" Avoid kissing up to the boss; insincere flattery will get you nowhere. A productive narcissist sees right through it, and finds it annoying and lacking in independent thinking, a trait he values in himself. However, productive narcissists like to be congratulated for things you truly believe are great. They may remark that it's flattery, but they bask in the sincere admiration.

If you're an erotic, you have to understand that you're not going to be "liked" by a narcissist—they may fall in love with you for a while, but they can't stand dependent people. Freud pointed out that it's more important for the narcissistic personality to love and seduce than to be loved. If you want to work for a productive narcissist, you should create a warm, cuddly family elsewhere—at home, with friends, doing volunteer work. Erotics should try to focus on the results, the numbers, their contribution to the company rather than their relationships.

If you're a marketing person, you need to learn how to make commitments, to acquire deep rather than superficial knowledge, if you're going to be of use to your narcissistic boss. You have to be the real goods. If you try to sell yourself and your personality over and over again, a productive narcissist will end up disgusted, tired of your people-pleasing. Remember how the ombudsman became a thorn in the side of his narcissistic boss, who saw him as wishy-washy and, in the end, useless? This may sound harsh, but marketing personalities must recognize that a work relationship with a productive narcissist is an opportunity for self-development and growth, a chance to see if they have what it takes to reach inside and add something of *true* value, not just a shiny and attractive image.

And if you yourself are a narcissist who works for a narcissist, you need to let him run the show. Step back and learn from him. However, you may want to consider getting your own coach; your boss doesn't want to hear about your problems, and you really don't want him to know them anyway. He wants you to help solve his.

Don't Invest Your Own Ego

This is the most important strategy for working with a productive narcissist: Don't invest your own ego in the relationship. What does that mean in practical terms? Don't look to your narcissistic boss for empathy, understanding, interest in your life, congratulations, praise for your work, or recognition of your loyalty and good qualities. You're not going to get it. Check your ego as soon as you walk into the office. Does this mean that you have to completely submerge your own ego and take whatever comes along from a narcissist? No, but you have to accept that while working with a productive narcissist offers some benefits, feeding your ego isn't one of them. Expecting it will just feed your frustration.

Once you accept that, you can look for ego gratification elsewhere—your home life, hobbies, outside interests, sports, classes, artistic pursuits, mentoring relationships, and so on. One of the reasons that Daphne Kis has had such a long and productive relationship with a narcissist is that she has this figured out: "Esther is happy that I have this whole other big life. It would make her unhappy to know that I was dependent on her, it would make us unequal." Her "other big life" is her family, which gives her great satisfaction and joy. If she expected that kind of approval and satisfaction from Esther, she would be sorely disappointed, and their working relationship would suffer. Same is true in my work. I don't invest my ego in my relationships with narcissistic CEOs. I have my other work—research, writing, lecturing, working with nonprofit boards, as well as my family.

An important caveat to this: While you need to develop your own interests outside of the office, remember that a productive narcissist works around the clock and expects everyone who works for him to do the same. He will call you at all hours, arrange meetings at the drop of a hat, bounce ideas around at midnight. Be ready for it, and accept it. It's that simple: Just take it and try to roll with it. Don't try to lay down some kind of law and explain that you have "boundaries." This will not go over big with a productive narcissist, who has no understanding of you and your life—it is, in the end, all about him. A brief story illustrates this: A VP put together an important meeting with key people. When the VP was interrupted by a phone call from his narcissistic boss, saying "I want to talk to you. It'll take about an hour," the VP told his boss that he was in the middle of a key meeting, that they could talk when he was done. The narcissistic boss came back with "My time is more important than yours." The VP excused himself from the meeting and took the call. And so should you, unless you can persuade him that missing the meeting will hurt *him*.

Protect the Narcissist's Image

The image of the CEO or the boss is extremely important to the company as well as himself. It's your job to protect the productive narcissist's image. Consider this anecdote: I once accompanied a CEO and his staff to a televised interview, where I sat back, said very little, only prodding the staff with suggestions. After we taped the show, the CEO told me that he was surprised by my behavior—why didn't I speak up more, why did I let the others take over? This was strategic on my part—I was trying to let the staff and CEO shine, so I needed to recede, let them take center stage, be seen and appreciated. My job wasn't to grandstand; my job, at that point, was to enhance the image of the company that was projected in the interview. Remember that a productive narcissist cares only about his own *personal* image and reputation; don't confuse it with concern for the company, or product, or how the rest of the company looks to the outside word. The image to protect is the narcissist's, and his alone.

You need to look for ways to let your CEO shine, to be his best self. How do you do this? First, let him take credit for all of your good ideas. Second, let him blame you for his bad ideas. Sounds brutal, but you need to swallow some humble pie, realize that this is part of the bargain you make in working for a productive narcissist. Narcissists *always* blame other people for their failures. And all the good ideas become theirs. One of Larry Ellison's lieutenants told me that whenever Ellison gets an idea from his staff, he tries it out, tests it in some meetings and talks; if it's working, he takes credit, assumes the idea as his own. If it's not working, he shunts it off on one of his underlings. Similarly, a manager at World Bank told me that Jim Wolfensohn is constantly blaming others for his mistakes; same for Jürgen Schrempp. Harry Bennett sums up his most important job at Ford: "It was my role to protect Mr. Ford against himself. I knew that all this stuff was hurting Mr. Ford personally, and was hurting the company. When I could prevent some rash act on his part, I did so. When I could not prevent it, I tried to make Mr. Ford's plunge off the deep end as restrained as possible. And when I could not do even that much, then I tried to patch up the pieces."

There is a lot of business literature today that's focused on building your own brand. I consider most of this a waste of time—how many people can really build a brand? Very, very few (try to name twenty name brands based on one person, quickly, right now—you'll probably start slowing down before you reach ten). But if you *attach* yourself to a brand, you have your own kind of calling card, instant cachet. This is what happened with Ray Lane. Same with every single person who worked at GE under Jack Welch and went on to a CEO job elsewhere based on Welch's stamp of excellence: Larry Bossidy at Honeywell, Jim McNerney at 3M, John Blystone at SPX, Bob Nardelli at Home Depot, Dave Cote at TRW and then Honeywell, and Larry Johnston at Alberston's. If you protect and enhance your CEO's image, you can benefit.

Dealing with the Narcissistic Weaknesses

THEY DON'T LISTEN

There is one anecdote that I always use whenever I write or lecture about narcissism; it's the story of the CEO I was counseling who told me: "I didn't get here by listening to people!" and it always strikes a chord with the audience. I think this simple story appeals to so many readers because it's true, but it hasn't really been explained in a way that makes sense of the personality type. That CEO is right—he didn't get to be the CEO by listening; he got there by shutting people and their conflicting voices out. In telling everyone that he doesn't listen—and, in fact, has *never* listened—he's doing only what has always worked for him. Of course, he listens when he wants information or senses something is wrong that may hurt him personally. But he won't empathize with your concerns, especially if you question what he wants to do. He'll ignore your memos if he's not getting the information he wants. So what are you to do?

First, recognize that productive narcissists are strategists. As we've seen, they form strategic alliances and are interested only in people they can use. If you want to be heard, you need to put your personal feelings aside and be useful—or, better yet, "usable." Become an expert, learning more than your boss about one area of an operation—the competition, technology, and so on. Decide which element of his strategic intelligence is lacking, and fill that void. Second, understand that narcissists do listen, but only to themselves. They are always engaged in an inner dialogue. Your job is to figure out how to participate in the narcissist's inner dialogue. This isn't as hard as you may think; you can take the tack of the character Kramer in Michael Crichton's *Timeline*. A lawyer and confidant of a narcissistic technology billionaire, Kramer recognized that there were times when her client was completely caught up in his own internal dialogue. Instead of trying to get him to listen to her, she entered his dialogue. How? She repeated back to him whatever he said, giving him the chance to consider, debate, and disagree with his own ideas. Kramer was there to facilitate his own conversation with himself, and she knew exactly *when* he needed her help and *how* to give it to him. This is key: You need to pick your moments. Be strategic about when to present him with an idea, when it seems he can take it on as his own. Try to gauge when your boss is in what Crichton termed a "pacing mood," times when he seems to be in his own world or tossing out ideas. Repeat back his best thinking; add to it with your own deep knowledge. And remember that there is a difference between a sounding board and a suck-up; a productive narcissist can always spot a syco-phant, so steer clear of insincere flattery when you use the "repeat back" tactic. Only if you truly are inspired by his ideas will he accept your affirmation and elaboration of his thinking.

If you have a great idea and can't get his ear, you have to frame it in a way that shows him how he will benefit personally. Also, if you are trying to stop him from an action that could damage the company, you have to show how it will damage him personally.

As a coach, I was able to get one CEO to listen (at least for a little while) by engaging him and his top team in an exercise called Desert Survival. He was CEO of a high-tech company that, all of a sudden, faced growing competition. The CEO knew he had to make some changes, fast, but thought he had all the answers. An equally narcissistic VP introduced me to him. Needless to say, the two clashed and the VP complained that the CEO never listened to him and his innovative ideas, breeding fear and competition among divisions. And not without reason: The CEO was a know-it-all who made everyone feel stupid by asking questions they couldn't possibly answer. When I met the CEO, he asked me why he should hire me; he had never needed an outside consultant before, so why now? It was only after I showed him that he wasn't able to get people to implement his vision—that I could help *him*—that he hired me.

I began the way I usually do, interviewing the top ten officers and holding an off-site meeting where we talked about how to get better results with customers. A VP came up with a new approach to customers, and the CEO jumped on him, making it clear that he set the agenda, not his VPs: "I don't have to listen to other people's solutions. I'm hired to make the decisions." Narcissistic leadership in a nutshell.

That night, I decided to play the game Desert Survival. I divide the group into teams that have to survive a plane crash in the desert, deciding whether to stay with the plane or try to hike to safety. The group is given fifteen objects—a blanket, a knife, water, a compass, and so on—that they have to rank in order of importance for survival. Each person ranks them, and then the team comes up with a group ranking. Observers take notes on how well everyone works together and how decisions are made. In the best cases, the team score is better than, or at least as good as, the best individual score. The result was exactly what I expected: The CEO's team lost. One of his team members had the best individual score of anyone playing, but the CEO wouldn't listen to him. The CEO made the decisions, even if it meant killing all of his team in the desert.

The game got the CEO's attention, but I was never fully able to get him to listen, even when it was in his interest, when his own survival was threatened. This was obvious to me after one meeting in which a terrified VP stood up and presented the results of the latest employee survey, showing a lack of trust in top management and little understanding of the company's strategy. The CEO didn't want to hear it, and became furious, railing against his employees. "I've done everything I could, and I've explained things to them. They just don't appreciate how much I've done." This CEO went on to break up the company, splitting off and heading up the division that he was sure would go on to great success. The result? The division he left behind, while not a visionary company, is a successful and sustained business, whereas his own company failed and he left to become a university professor.

THEY ARE OVERSENSITIVE

Like the princess who felt the pea beneath a stack of mattresses, narcissists are supersensitive to every slight and have a tendency to take everything personally, despite the fact that they can be brutally insensitive to their employees. A World Bank executive told me that in a private meeting, he asked Wolfensohn whether he had considered the possibility of a negative outcome. "So," Wolfensohn shot back, "you don't support me." When I gave one narcissistic CEO I was counseling some unwelcome feedback, he said to me, "I can fire you at any time!" My answer: "Of course you can." I acknowledged that he was right; he could get rid of me in a second. He found my response calming. It would have been a big mistake to argue with him or try to gain some ground against him. In most situations like this, it's best to take what a productive narcissist dishes out. Generally they are unaware that they've hurt your feelings (and if your ego isn't so invested in the relationship, it won't hurt too much). After they have blown off steam, they feel better, so why don't you?

THEY ARE PARANOID

The most important rule about the paranoia of a narcissistic boss is that you should always take it seriously. It's often an awareness of a very real threat to the business. Productive narcissists have a good sense of who or what is about to attack them and undermine their position. Other businesses and competitors *are* out to get them, to find out about new product development, to take over their market share—or, in Bill Gates's case, haul them into court. Listen to their fears, and try to understand and learn from their gut reaction to threats.

I've found that the most effective way of dealing with mildly irrational narcissistic paranoia is with humor. Humor is the emotional reality principle, and it takes the air out of a puffed-up paranoiac. One CEO I worked with said about an underling: "I don't trust him—he wants my job." I told the CEO that he should be grateful for anyone who would actually want to take on his burdens; he understood that I was poking fun at him and smiled back at me, a sign that he was not too far removed from reality. The humor tactic works, though, only if you have a close working relationship to the productive narcissist. It's trickier, for example, if you're an underling, far removed in the company hierarchy from the narcissist. He will take your attempts at humor as insubordination. But if you are a coach, a board member, a COO to a CEO, try well-timed and gentle humor to puncture his irrational paranoia.

Problems arise when the narcissist's alertness to threats tips over into irrational, unfounded, or out-of-control paranoia. I remember one case in which a VP was told to sue a reporter who made a disparaging remark about the CEO. He ignored the request and the CEO didn't mention it again. I've never worked for someone whose paranoia became out of control. However, if I worked with someone who demanded that I do destructive things and responded to my concern without reason or humor, I'd quit in a hurry.

THEY ARE OVERCONTROLLING AND OVERCOMPETITIVE

A certain amount of control and attention to detail can be beneficial to a productive narcissist. In fact, Freud considered the narcissist/obsessive to be the "ideal" personality type, combining the narcissist's disregard for the status quo with the obsessive's exacting standards and need for order. In business, a productive narcissist/obsessive personality is focused on both vision and implementation, creating new worlds *and* making them a reality. Well-known examples of this combination include Jack Welch, Henry Ford, Bill Gates, and Andy Grove.

In my experience, Sidney Harman was a productive narcissist/obsessive, combining business vision, idealism, and concern for the details. He could definitely be overcontrolling, but more often than not his high standards and demand for control helped the business rather than hurt it. Once, during one of his routine tours of a factory, he ripped all the address labels off an entire shipment of boxes, complaining that they were crooked, ordering his staff to reapply every single one, making sure they were neat and straight. You could say that Harman was too controlling, too focused on the details, letting his obsession with the little picture get in the way of his goals. But Harman's belief was that shoddy work habits were infecting every level of the organization and it was his job to impose strict quality control, starting with the application of shipping labels. From where I sat, Harman was right. After the labeling outburst, there was a change in the workers: They put more care into their work, knew that every aspect of their work was important to the overall success of the business. The result? Harman's staff internalized his values. When you think a productive narcissist is being too controlling, ask yourself if you're resisting him out of your own ego or because you think his actions are impeding his vision.

There are times when a narcissistic CEO takes direct control too far, threatening the survival of the business. For example, I counseled one narcissistic CEO whose meddling in every detail was getting in the way of his corporate goals. His lieutenants were afraid to act unless he first approved of their plans, which demotivated them. In this instance, you need to show the productive narcissist that his control is hurting *him*, as opposed to the people who work for him, and that it's in his interest to delegate or to engage the organization in focusing on the details.

This need for control sometimes plays out as overburdening employees with direct orders. Productive narcissists often pile on more work than anyone could possibly accomplish. In these cases, don't do everything the boss tells you; it's likely that he'll forget about any number of assignments. One executive told me that his narcissistic boss asked him, among other things, to hire people for nonexistent jobs. The executive ignored the order and it was never mentioned again. Heed the advice of Harry Bennett, who responded to a silly command from Henry Ford with this: "I just ignored this order, as I did others of a similar nature." But be strategic about what you decide to ignore. Carry out the tasks that you think are important to *him*, not necessarily to you or even the business.

THEY EXPLODE IN ANGER

I've found that almost every productive narcissist I've worked with explodes in anger when key buttons are pushed. When this happens, I try to understand the reason for the anger, breaking it down into three main categories. The first is when a productive narcissist doesn't feel supported by his team for his daring and risky maneuvers; he believes that he's out on the edge all alone. When he hears "You can't do that," "That'll never work," or "I'm not sure that's the best idea," he becomes furious at what he thinks is temerity, nay-saying, or a "bunker mentality." At times like this, the worst thing you can do is say that his strategy "doesn't feel right." If you are going to shoot down a productive narcissist's big plans, don't go on your gut (although he can, because it's worked for him). He needs facts, clear logic, specific reasons why his idea will hurt him and the company. If you can't get him to listen to a reasoned argument, then just swallow it and move on.

The second main reason a productive narcissist gets angry is that he's confronted with something that may be true but he doesn't like or want to listen to. In instances like this, either take it and wait until the storm passes, or present him with your argument. In the latter case, you may be respected or you may be fired. There are only two times in my career that I have been fired by a productive narcissist, and in each instance it was for telling the CEO the hard truths that he couldn't bear to hear.

What about when he explodes in irrational anger and neither you nor your coworkers seem to have anything to do with it? For example, Jim Wolfensohn screams at his vice presidents that it's their fault he hasn't won the Nobel Peace Prize. Sounds silly, but it's true. In a case like this, you should ignore it and try to forget about it—he usually does. It's the same as getting orders to do stupid tasks; most VPs just let them pass. Whatever you say will just feed his anger. Also, never apologize to him after one of his irrational outbursts, or he'll think he's justified, you're a weakling, and he can keep using you as a punching bag.

THEY EXAGGERATE

When a narcissistic boss exaggerates about what the company offers, he will look to his employees to make him honest, to make his claims true. If you're in a managerial position, the best thing to do is humor him and his claims, then tell the rest of the staff that you know the boss is padding or inflating but that he has sometimes been proven to be prescient. Try to prevent your boss's claims from infecting the whole staff or turning into a resigned, "We can *never* do that" attitude. Ride on his enthusiasm, even if you know it's not realistic or might be out of the company's reach.

Seen in the best light, narcissistic exaggeration is a way of stretching the company's capabilities. But when exaggeration tips over into lying to board members, consumers, and customers about accounting, profits, and financial projections, it's time to take a good, hard look at the company and consider whether you should get out. A colleague of Mike Armstrong's told me that Armstrong completely revises what he says depending on the audience and context; what he tells customers is totally different from what he says to employees. This executive said that the "revisionism" and exaggeration became untenable, that "I wouldn't front for the guy anymore. There was a limit." In some cases a CEO goes beyond revisionism to breaking the law. The last thing that you want to do, as an employee, is get caught in another Enron. If you see something that is patently illegal and have the guts, it's time to call the SEC or the U.S. Attorney's office on your way out the door.

THEY HAVE A LACK OF SELF-KNOWLEDGE

Jack Welch's autobiography has been met with a lot of criticism, much of it for Welch's lack of self-reflection; the superficial recitation of this deal and that acquisition; little in the way of insight into how he did what he did; a deeper understanding or explanation of his overall business strategy; and how he was able to systemically overhaul not only the corporate GE structure but also the culture of GE. What the critics don't understand is that it is entirely unreasonable to expect a productive narcissist to take a look at himself and analyze his business strategy, thought process, and, most of all, his feelings. When asked by Diane Coutu of the *Harvard Business Review* if he has a tragic flaw, Jack Welch said: "That's something I've never thought about. I don't think much about myself." Welch is right about that, and he is perfectly in line with the personality profile of a productive narcissist.

In the last chapter, I described how Diane Coutu challenged Welch, saying that there are some business theorists who describe GE as a cult, to which Welch immediately became defensive—his response: "Without question, that is the craziest thought in the world." The upshot of this story? Don't try to point out personality traits or make psychological observations about your narcissistic boss. He doesn't know why he does what he does, and he certainly doesn't want to hear your explanation of his psyche or insights into his personality. He's sensitive about any kind of personal commentary, and will shut down, or react angrily to your efforts at analysis. He takes it as needling or unnecessary power games. In addition, don't ever go to him with gossipy information about him or his personal life, or say, "I heard from so-and-so that you are thinking about this." He hates it when he's confronted in this way, and feels betrayed and even more isolated. If it's your goal to be part of his inner circle, this kind of gossip-mill information will only alienate you from him.

Because productive narcissists are lacking in self-reflection, you need to adopt the now-familiar tactic of showing how his behavior is hurting him, rather than telling him to evaluate his actions or think about why he's doing something. He doesn't care. But he does care if, in the end, it's going to get in the way of his goals or affect his stature. For example, the Harvard Business School approached Mike Armstrong because they wanted to do a case study of AT&T under his management. Armstrong was flattered by the attention and thought that Harvard was planning on using his tenure at AT&T as an example of successful leadership. Little did he know that it was quite the opposite; Harvard had chosen him as an example of flawed and problematic leadership. A colleague knew that the case study would be a disaster and kept Armstrong from being interviewed personally for the article, a potentially embarrassing move. He showed Armstrong how the article would embarrass *him,* how it would make a fool of *him,* how it would hurt *him.* Armstrong turned Harvard down, and they went on to do an unflattering case history without his input.

THEY ARE ISOLATED

Here's where your partnering skills come into play. If you think that partnering with an isolated narcissist will both benefit the organization and further your career, you need to advertise your value. If your boss decides to take you on in a partnering capacity, be prepared to play the Sancho or Horatio role, recognizing that you won't have job security and can be dropped at a moment's notice. If you are a board member or trusted adviser, you can suggest that he partner with someone who will complement him. This was the case when I suggested that Goran Collert, who needed to partner with someone who understood the industrial and political world of Sweden, form a relationship with Bo Ekman, the former EVP of strategy at Volvo.

THEY ARE GRANDIOSE

Even the most productive narcissists can become hopelessly puffed up and grandiose, especially when they start to succeed and begin to surround themselves with toadying employees. When this happens, there is usually nothing and no one who can stop a narcissist from self-destructing. Be on the lookout for the signs of grandiosity, and be prepared to leave if you see that your narcissistic boss exhibits all the signs of self-intoxication and unchecked pride.

What should you look for? Over-the-top narcissists disparage other people, who are all seen as fearful, stupid, and small-minded. They stop listening to everyone, including their small inner circle or trusted sidekick. They get rid of anyone who is critical of their outrageous claims, and they surround themselves with yes-men and flatterers. They become more withdrawn and isolated. They decide the business world is too small for their big ambitions and plans, that they need to be a player in the world at large, becoming an ambassador of peace (Andrew Carnegie's guarantees that Kaiser Wilhelm would support peace before World War I, Henry Ford's Peace Ship), a political force (Ross Perot's run for the presidency), or the savior of the world (Bono).

In an excellent four-part series in the *Washington Post* in January 2002, Mark Leibovich describes all of the signs, the entire syndrome of narcissistic grandiosity, that brought Michael Saylor of MicroStrategy down. Instead of a trusted sidekick who could keep him grounded, Saylor relied on Mark Bisnow as chief of staff, a role that turned into PR toady and "unchecked agent of Saylor's ego." The business world was too small for Saylor; he wanted to build his own American version of Versailles on forty-eight acres in Great Falls and endow a free online university employing the greatest professors in the world. He declared, "I'm a political leader. I have a nation. I have constituents. I have investors." When the news broke that MicroStrategy had inflated its financial statements, declaring 1999 profits of $12.6 million that were later revised to show a loss of $34 to $40.3 million, Saylor dug in his heels, saying that "Mother Teresa never quit during a down quarter, and what we're doing is just as important." He called the press "jackals," and he blamed everything on the "bean-counter sophistry" of the accounting firm of PricewaterhouseCoopers. The result? Saylor has stayed on, against protests, as CEO of a company that is struggling to regain credibility and a sense of mission. No longer the recipient of regular invitations to the White House, Saylor keeps a low profile, performing a somewhat perfunctory position in the company he built up to dizzying heights, then single-handedly destroyed, completing the cycle of narcissistic self-destruction.

After reading this chapter, you may be asking yourself whether there will be many narcissistic CEOs around in the future. When I wrote my article in the *Harvard Business Review* about narcissistic CEOs, they dominated the business scene. Their faces covered the major magazines. Then came the corporate blowups of 2001–2002 and some of the most publicized narcissists were shoved off their thrones. What about the future? Will there even be narcissistic leaders to work for? The next chapter addresses this question.

SIX

THE PROMISE AND PERIL
OF VISIONARY LEADERSHIP

Over the past several years, the American public has been
seduced by the promise of visionary leaders, narcissistic
CEOs who trumpeted unparalleled profits, unlimited growth, and
a new economy of technology-based businesses. More often than
not, this promise gave way to dot-com disasters, failed corporate
conglomerates, and technology that never found a place in the
market. Narcissistic CEOs offered a compelling overall vision but
were unable to turn their overblown promises into an economic
reality. In the wake of these corporate disasters, we are left to
wonder if corporate boards are so traumatized by narcissistic failures that they're going to turn the reins over to the obsessive and
marketing types, forgoing risky innovation for the hope of slow
and steady growth. Or, more pointedly, is there a future in today's
world for productive narcissists, or has their time of prominence

and glory gone the way of the Internet bubble and "irrational exuberance"?

The business press, including *Forbes*, *Business Week*, and *The Economist*, has answered this question in the negative, writing off the celebrity CEO. Too quickly, in my opinion. To give a balanced and reasoned answer to this question, we need to look at narcissistic leaders throughout history and understand the social, political, and economic context that gives rise to visionary leadership. As I've argued throughout this book, effective leadership depends on context; running an innovative company is not the same as presiding over a bureaucracy. A different kind of leader is needed in wartime—think of how Winston Churchill was rejected by the British people before and after World War II—than in peacetime.

The first time I observed this correlation was not in a business setting. In 1965, Erich Fromm and I were studying how different personality types in a Mexican village reacted to the upheaval of the Revolution (1910–1920) and its aftermath. We found that the successful farmer was a traditional type: conservative, hardworking, religious. The personality of this productive and patriarchal man was like his father, and his father's father before him; what's more, it was a type that anthropologists around the world, wherever they studied traditional farmers, described in essentially the same way. For centuries, the Mexican village was run by this type of leader, the kind of productive obsessive personality who maintains tradition and resists change. But with the upheaval of the Revolution and the introduction of new agricultural technology, capital sources, and marketing opportunities, a different type of leader emerged, one who was unlike his predecessor in significant ways. Entrepreneurial, dismissive of tradition, and filled with the promise of a new kind of prosperity, these new leaders challenged the way things had always been done; they inspired young villagers to break from the past, to leave fiestas and bullfights in favor of basketball and soccer. They supported schooling to gain work outside the village, in nearby cities, and built roads and houses to bring in new business by attracting tourists from Mexico City. The villagers who wanted to prosper joined the visionaries. The ones who resisted were left behind. Fromm and I concluded that the leadership model that worked for centuries didn't work during times of disruption and upheaval, periods of crisis that cleared the way for productive narcissists to assume positions of power, leading the villagers to a new way of life.

What I experienced in the Mexican village over the course of our seven-year study is, in many important ways, consistent with visionary leadership throughout history. Productive narcissists emerge during times of economic upheaval, cataclysmic change, and crisis; they are ideally suited, as Freud writes, to "damage the established state of affairs," giving direction and meaning to societies in a state of flux. During these times narcissistic leaders, for better or worse, create a new visionary order, as in each one of these revolutionary periods: the civil rights movement (Martin Luther King Jr.), the Reformation (Martin Luther), the Cuban Revolution (Fidel Castro and Che Guevera), the Russian Revolution (Lenin, Trotsky, and Stalin), Indian independence (Gandhi), the Chinese Communist Revolution (Mao Tse-tung), and the Great Depression (Franklin Delano Roosevelt).

The prototypical narcissistic leader, Napoleon Bonaparte, rose to power in the aftermath of the French Revolution, a time when the social and political slate had been wiped clean, calling for a visionary leader to create revolutionary changes. Napoleon took the inchoate stirrings of equality that found expression in the French Revolution and turned them into a lived reality for the people of France, upending the old social, political, and legal systems with concrete reforms that endure to this day: He created the first national university system that was free; he built and maintained schools, hospitals, workhouses, and orphanages that were accessible to all citizens; he did away with centuries of legal injustice with his Code Napoleon; and he freed the Jews from laws that limited their activities.

In America's history, Abraham Lincoln is a productive narcissist who brought about social reform during a time of great turmoil. In the midst of a civil war that tore the country apart, Lincoln walked onto a battlefield to memorialize the dead; rather than simply delivering a eulogy at Gettysburg, Lincoln recast the suffering of the war, shifting it from a military struggle to maintain the union to a social struggle to establish equality. This was an act of social revolution that forever changed the way Americans understood and read the Declaration of Independence. What historian Garry Wills calls the "refounding" of the American ideal of equality was not an inevitable result of the war, an idea that was bound to emerge from the country's struggle; it was a new way of seeing the nation that was authored by Lincoln, a productive narcissist who was able to walk into the chaos of war and create a clear vision of a country committed to equality. Wills writes: "For most people now, the Declaration means what Lincoln told us it means. . . . By accepting the Gettysburg Address, its concept of a single people dedicated to a proposition, we have been changed. Because of it, we live in a different America."

The correlation between disruptive political and social forces and the emergence of visionary leaders also applies to the economic landscape. The theories of leadership taught in business schools and corporate seminars are too often based on snapshots of leaders, a freeze-frame of a particular moment in time. Different personality types assume leadership positions based on the changing economic climate. I saw this when I interviewed managers at the new technology companies like HP, IBM, Xerox, and Texas Instruments in the 1970s. Even though these places were creating some of the most cutting-edge technology, they still operated like traditional top-down companies. Most of the people working in the field fell neatly into the hierarchical structure of a large corporation. But one group stood out: the narcissistic innovators, the hackers and programmers, who wore whatever they wanted, worked at odd hours of the day and night, and ignored authority. Because of their independence, they were not seen as important players in the corporate culture of the '70s. The revolution in the technology fields has completely upended this old pecking order. The outsiders—the hackers and dressed-down visionaries—have been reborn as the productive narcissists of today, and they've made it from the periphery to a central role in corporations in just twenty years, transforming organizations and the way we work today.

I was able to observe, firsthand, the dynamic playing out of economic forces and the corresponding change in leadership taking shape at one major company; for twenty-three years, I was a consultant to top management at AT&T. Just as shifting periods of stability and disruption brought about different types of leadership in the Mexican village, so too did the economic developments over the course of several decades bring about dramatic changes in AT&T's

leadership and strategy. When I started working with management in 1977, AT&T was the epitome of a bureaucratic system in which everyone, from the CEO on down, functioned as the working parts of a machine. During the '70s, the corporation operated in roughly the same way it had since 1913, when Theodore Vail persuaded Woodrow Wilson to declare AT&T a regulated monopoly that would provide telephone service to all Americans. Its CEOs and managers embraced Taylorism, where jobs were standardized and measured to the second. The system was designed to eliminate decision making by managers as well as workers, essentially doing away with personality in the workplace. Despite the high human costs of monotony and mindlessness, this system worked reasonably well until 1984, when the justice department put an end to AT&T's status as a "natural monopoly," an agreement that was later modi-fied by Judge Harold Greene. As a result, AT&T's market position was challenged by MCI, an upstart that offered long-distance serv-ice to business customers at a much cheaper rate. AT&T's basic strategy—expand the consumer base, cut costs, increase labor pro-ductivity, and keep business rates high to offset consumer losses—wasn't enough to beat back the new telecommunication companies, hungry start-ups that used guerrilla marketing tactics and greatly reduced rates to lure customers. The company that had been *the* phone company for almost a century was in danger of being put out of business by a bunch of newcomers.

When all of this was shaking out, the CEO at the time was Char-lie Brown, an obsessive personality and an AT&T old-timer who had no feel for either the new information technology or the intense competition in the telecommunications world. Despite Brown's dis-astrous tenure, AT&T stuck with the same leadership formula, promoting the next two CEOs, Jim Olson and Bob Allen, from within the organization; both were AT&T-bred bureaucrats, the kind of consensus-seeking obsessives who were incapable of creating a strategic vision or bringing about any lasting change. AT&T was unable to establish any footing in the high-tech market, while its core business of home and business customers was dwindling. In addition, it was losing its most innovative narcissists, such as Larry LeMasters, who created American Transtech, a successful subsidiary, and Joe Nacchio, who was seen as too pushy and abrasive.

It wasn't until 1997 that the AT&T board saw that nothing short of a wholesale upheaval would help the company survive the telecommunications free-for-all. For the first time in its history, AT&T hired a visionary leader, the productive narcissist C. Michael Armstrong, as CEO. Armstrong was chosen because of the dramatic results that he achieved as chairman and CEO of Hughes Electronics, a division of General Motors. Before Hughes, Armstrong had spent his entire thirty-one-year career at IBM, where he was seen as a supersalesman, taking over global operations and increasing the company's overseas presence. Despite his superior performance and sales record, Armstrong, a Harley-riding risk-taker, never quite fit into IBM's corporate culture, and in 1991, IBM chairman John Akers made it clear to Armstrong that he would be passed over for CEO.

In a move that surprised both the high-tech world and the defense industry, Armstrong left IBM to become CEO of Hughes Aircraft Corporation, a small and slightly eccentric company (in keeping with its founder, Howard Hughes) that was known almost exclusively for its defense technology, missiles, and military contracts. Armstrong immediately shifted the company's focus from the shrinking defense industry to satellite systems for "civilians," investing millions in the satellite television service DirecTV, a direction that turned out to be right only in retrospect. Armstrong boasted: "We, against all public and industry knowledge, believed that space would commercialize." Within a few years, the company controlled over half the direct-broadcasting market, and by 2000, it was the largest satellite television company, with 10 million customers in the United States and Latin America.

It was exactly this kind of dramatic turnaround strategy that AT&T was looking for when they brought in Armstrong as CEO. He had demonstrated both foresight and vision, and the board wanted him to do the same for AT&T. Armstrong immediately set about smashing the AT&T way of doing things, breaking all ties to past leadership and the old business model, announcing an expansive vision to convert the phone company into a telecommunications and information monolith, offering one-stop shopping for customers looking for cable, Internet, wireless, and long-distance access all rolled into one. In addition to a complete companywide reorganization, Armstrong spent between $90 and $110 billion buying up cable companies in order to acquire the equipment— wiring, trucking, and technical labor—needed to upgrade and convert the old AT&T systems to cable and broadband. Almost as quickly as Armstrong's strategy was set in motion, it started to unravel; in October 2000, Armstrong announced that AT&T would be broken up into four separate divisions—business, broadband, wireless, and consumer—in order to offset the debt that he had amassed from his acquisitions. Armstrong never demonstrated the strategic intelligence needed to motivate change in a corporation as large and complex as AT&T.

Leaving aside Armstrong's inability to realize his vision, there is no escaping the fact that his career trajectory experienced a distinct and rapid rise; in only a decade, Armstrong made the leap from salesman, the kind of guy who moved product, to innovative "change artist" and "turnaround strategist" in the business press. How is it that a person can work for *thirty-one years for one company* where he is a salesman, albeit a very successful and high-powered one, and then, practically overnight, become known as the architect of bold corporate strategy, first at Hughes and then at AT&T? Some may argue that Armstrong was building experience and momentum, and had just hit his peak CEO years, when he left IBM. Others may argue that AT&T had reached a crisis point only in the past few years, and Armstrong seized the opportunity to make his mark at a critical moment. I believe that the answer lies in the pairing of the narcissistic personality with a period of revolutionary change. Armstrong is a productive narcissist who was able to execute his bold and innovative strategy, albeit with disastrous results, only during a period of economic upheaval, a time when the telecommunications industry in particular, and the economic climate in general, underwent cataclysmic change. We can see a similar trend toward narcissistic leadership in the airline industry after federal deregulation in 1978, when Don Burr of People Express, Richard Branson of Virgin, and Herb Kelleher of Southwest all capitalized on the newly created economic free-for-all.

It is the combination of productive narcissists and the corresponding revolution that creates change; but what happens when extraordinary personalities with a vision find themselves living in the wrong time? What, for example, would have happened to Napoleon had he been born too early or too late? This is exactly the fictional scenario imagined by Stephen Vincent Benét in his short story "The Curfew Tolls." Benét places Napoleon thirty years earlier, before the French Revolution; rather than an empire builder, Napoleon is a retired artillery major who never really saw military action, and he can't help but talk about his lost opportunities to the other *dramatis persona*, a British general who has come to France for a vacation. While trying to get some sun, the general is subjected to Napoleon's pathetic tirade that *he* could have saved France from the British in India if only he had been given the chance. But in the rigid prerevolutionary class system, Napoleon, despite his brilliance and vision, had no chance of rising to the top (which sounds a lot like Mike Armstrong's position for all those years at IBM when the company wanted stability). The Revolution opened the field. Napoleon himself understood how well suited his reforms were to the time, saying that: "Revolutions are ideal times for soldiers with a lot of wit—and the courage to act."

In the business world, visionaries, even ones with the wit and courage to act, have historically had a hard time trying to bring about a revolution during periods of relative economic stability and calm. Take William C. Norris, the CEO of Control Data Corporation, a productive narcissist who had the misfortune of being ahead of his time. Norris had the then crazy and slightly sci-fi idea that computers could change classrooms, offering a high level of education to a lot of people while cutting down on staffing. He was able to convince people to buy in to this idea, raising millions in 1957 for what was the first publicly financed digital computing company. He built a network of huge mainframe computers that were connected to the schools through long-distance telephone lines. He essentially invented online learning, just thirty years too early. The market wasn't ready; schools didn't have the high-tech resources and money; the equipment was far too expensive. It's a shame that Norris is not active in today's education field, an area that could benefit from the vision of a productive narcissist.

We need to recognize that we are in the midst of great social, economic, and political crisis, a period of upheaval that calls for visionary leadership, a new Napoleon, Lincoln, or King to burst onto the international scene, a charismatic personality who can mobilize society, give a sense of unity and meaning, and find solutions to the problems that threaten world peace and stability. We have entered a new era in which there is no such thing as economic or political insularity; the ailments of each society infect the global community. To date, there are no political leaders who have emerged to mobilize people to confront the systemic challenges of globalization and the new world order: growing political unrest, terrorism, the international AIDS catastrophe, environmental shifts and global warming, the development of new energy sources, the economic disparity between nations, and health care for an aging population. If we are to move forward as a society, we must rely on productive narcissists to take the risks, gather the social and economic resources and support, and push through the reforms that the other personality types could never dream of, much less undertake. We need visionary leadership for what Michael Lewis brilliantly writes is the "idea that is a tiny push away from general acceptance, and when it gets that push, will change the world." It is narcissistic leaders who take us to places we've never been before, who innovate, who build empires out of nothing.

In the economic playing field, the bubble may have burst, draining surplus capital away from risky investments, but that doesn't change the fact that we are still in the midst of continuous invention and experimentation. No matter the state of technology stocks, there exists today a surplus of technology, much more than we have either the practical or business applications to use; it is lying dormant, underutilized. This has been the case throughout history, but it is even more true during periods of technological innovation. The lightbulb, as an object, an invention, existed for years before Thomas Alva Edison saw the possibilities of a power-generation and -distribution system and transformed the lightbulb, which had been a singular engineering feat, into a household convenience. The automobile was manufactured by some very talented and smart men, in both Europe and America, for years before Henry Ford tossed aside the conventional thinking of the time—that the car was only a mechanical novelty for the rich, a grown-up toy for the moneyed few—and replaced it with his vision of affordable mass transportation that would become the dominant means of travel around the world. The engineers at Intel had the circuitry, the chips, the power source, everything they needed to make a relatively cheap home computer in the late '70s, but they had no idea why anyone would need a computer in their home, except for organizing and storing cooking recipes. It took Steve Jobs and the engineers at Xerox PARC to come up with an entire usable universe—otherwise known as the computer interface, folders, trash cans, and all—to turn the PC into the indispensable tool that it is today. The Internet was used for years by a bunch of academics and government scientists as an easy and quick way to share up-to-date data. But once Jim Clark imagined it as a way for everyone to communicate, he, along with Marc Andreeson, produced the Netscape browser, turning what was once an academic application into a revolutionary way of "talking" to others through the computer, the social and economic implications of which are immeasurable and ongoing. In every one of these cases, it took a productive narcissist to unleash the power of emerging technology, turning it into tools that changed the world. I predict that we will see the same kind of technological and social revolution over the next twenty years in the fields of nanotechnology; genomics and gene therapy; robotics; artificial intelligence; bioscience, biomedicine, and bioengineered agricultural products; environmental and energy research; and health care and medical advances—brought about by the explosive combination of narcissistic leadership and tremendous scientific experimentation and ferment.

Given the enormous financial and social stakes, there is an urgent need to understand the personality type of our leaders, to have a clear and open-eyed view of the promise as well as the peril of narcissistic leadership. Looking back to the beginning of the twentieth century can teach us a lot about what will determine the success or failure of our own narcissistic business leaders. A hundred years ago, an agrarian society was transformed into an industrial society. The revolution was fueled by new resources—coal, oil, steel, electricity, and a new labor pool. Extraordinary productive narcissists such as Henry Ford, Thomas Edison, Andrew Carnegie, and John D. Rockefeller combined industrial innovation and the vast natural resources of the era into the modern-day auto industry, railways, the global oil industry, universal availability of electrical power, and the industrial trust, building lasting empires and restructuring American society. Now we are well along the way to a full-scale change from an industrial to a knowledge-service society (my term for the information age). I believe that the Internet mania, as well as the current wave of CEO scandal and failure, has its historical precedent in the turn of the century, when the Industrial Revolution brought about a casino culture of risk, especially in the car and oil industries. At the genesis of every major industry—railroads, steel, auto—all sorts of entrepreneurs rushed in and tried to make it big, but only a handful of productive narcissists built large and sustained industries. While Henry Ford was making a name for himself, three hundred other automobile start-ups were also trying to capture a piece of the new auto market without Ford's success. Between 1900 and 1908, more than 60 percent of the auto manufacturers went out of business. Even with such a high attrition rate, money continued to pour into the car industry, prompting a speaker at a bankers' convention to caution investors away from the high-risk auto industry. Out of that playing field of more than three hundred carmakers, only two—Henry Ford and William Durant—created companies that have survived to this day.

The narcissistic leaders who have fared the worst throughout history, from Napoleon to Messier, fell prey to unbridled greed and grandiosity, were puffed up by their own vision and initial success, and isolated themselves from advisers who could help them from self-destructing. To work with productive narcissists, we must be able to distinguish between the modern equivalent of snake-oil charmers, the false visionaries who create the illusion of value, and the ideal CEO with strategic intelligence who acquires companies that support his overall vision only in order to build an organization that works or to create new products and true innovation.

A lack of understanding of the importance of personality and strategic intelligence can lead to the wrong lessons from the collapse of companies like Enron. Writing in *The New Yorker* in July 2002, Malcolm Gladwell attacks what he calls "the talent myth" as the main cause of Enron's troubles. According to Gladwell, Enron bought the view sold by McKinsey and Company, the management consultant firm, that success could be attained by finding and hiring the best business talent and supporting their ideas for improving the company. Some of these ventures were costly failures, whereas others proved profitable. With approval from the McKinsey consultants, Enron leaders held an "open market" for talent to move within the company. "When an Enron executive started the company's global broadband unit, he launched what he called Project Quick Hire. A hundred top performers from around the company were invited to the Houston Hyatt." Recruiting booths were set up outside the meeting room, and fifty top performers were hired from other parts of the company. Gladwell tells us this left fifty holes in the company that presumably hurt the units that lost the talent. But did it? We are given no evidence that this was a major problem. What we do know about Enron and other failing companies is that top management hid bad numbers, and some cooked the books. These companies made many acquisitions, paid too much for them, and were burdened by heavy debt.

Gladwell contrasts the Enron chaotic star system, where talented people are hired and then let loose, with companies that control what their people do. "The talent myth," he writes, "assumes that people make organizations smart. More often than not, it's the other way around." There is some truth in this statement, but for managers in companies that survive on innovation, it can be seriously misleading. Gladwell's exemplary organizations include Southwest Airlines and Wal-Mart. To be sure, both companies benefit from great organization and supportive systems. Both hire not on the basis of sheer brilliance but of fit with company culture. But neither is in the business of innovation; the key to the success of Wal-Mart and Southwest is doing the same thing over and over again, more effectively and more efficiently.

Gladwell also claims that Enron was a "narcissistic corporation," which he defines as taking more credit for success than it deserved, not acknowledging responsibility for failure, and lacking disciplined management. What's wrong with this view is that a company can't be narcissistic; only a leader can model this kind of behavior. Gladwell is buying in to the common misconception of the narcissistic personality; not all of them doom their companies to failure, nor are they all self-involved crooks. While Jeff Skilling appears to be a narcissistic personality, Ken Lay has all the qualities of a marketing personality, the glad-handing public face of the company who sold Enron to the press and investors. He just happens to be a marketing personality who is dishonest and lied to shareholders and employees. Narcissists can be honest or crooked, brilliant or ordinary, wise or foolish. What they share is vision and boldness, persuading others with their unshakable conviction about the value of their visions. What differentiates the most successful from the failures is strategic intelligence. Gladwell's description does not work for productive narcissists like Jack Welch, Bill Gates, and, yes, Herb Kelleher, the flamboyant self-promoter who built Southwest Airlines. These leaders have developed disciplined management by partnering with operational managers who implement their strategy.

Earlier I cited the work of Jeffrey Sonnenfeld of the Yale School of Management, who correctly calls some of these failed

CEOs "serial acquirers," tacking companies on to their core business in order to bolster overall financial holdings, rather than managing and creating companies that reinforce and complement one another. However, Sonnenfeld goes on to recommend that in making acquisitions, companies stick to their "core competencies." But what is the core competence of GE or IBM? If anything—and I don't find the concept very useful—it is integrating and managing different competencies. Both companies benefitted from leaders who used services and solutions as a way of selling products. Because of these leaders, managers in both companies work at breaking down the barriers between departments and business units. Some of the failed CEOs acquired companies in order to achieve an illusory synergy that never materialized: Enron's energy and telecommunications, AT&T's cable-voice-Internet-data, Vivendi's various media companies. In contrast, narcissistic visionaries with strategic intelligence, like Gates and Welch, have effectively integrated acquired companies and built a common culture. As much as Enron, they have recruited talent and supported entrepreneurial activity. They depend on innovation and recognize that the best way to kill it is overcontrol, and they understand that a strategy isn't worth much unless the organization can implement it. I am reminded of the philosophy expressed by Joe Gibbs, one of the most successful coaches in pro football. When Gibbs selected players from the draft for the Washington Redskins, he looked for two qualities: talent and character. He didn't care where the person had played and whether his team had won or lost. A talented player might have been on a team with less talented players or a poor coach. He believed—and his record supports his belief—that he could teach talented players who were also conscientious, hardworking, and honest. He couldn't make a slow player run 50 yards in 4.4 seconds or make a careless or dishonest player into someone responsible and honest. But he could mold the right kind of talent into a great team.

It is a mistake to take observations from one or even a number of companies and try to apply them across the board. Companies should be seen holistically as socioeconomic systems that need to adapt to particular markets. They can be typed in different ways. One of these is how much they depend on talented people to innovate and lead change. It is true that much of the damage done to companies has resulted from the arrogant, unethical behavior of corporate leaders. But it is also true that many leaders, even honest ones, don't pay enough attention to the social system. Building a great organization—one that is able to innovate—is not a question of talent vs. control systems. It requires leaders who know how to motivate talented and ethical people within a socioeconomic system that creates value for customers, employees, and owners.

The recent CEO scandals and the collapse of so many corporate visionaries has created a deep sense of distrust, a lack of faith in corporate leaders that has led to a new trend—reported in the August 19, 2002, *New York Times*—toward extensive background checks on potential candidates, especially those who are up for CEO or top management positions. Frank Renaud, the senior VP of a private investigation firm that screens executives, reports that "there is far more interest, post-Enron and post all these other corporate scandals, in checking people out." Certainly, an investigation of a candidate's record can reveal a pattern of illegal activity or unethical behavior, but there is no way that the details from a previous marriage, personal messages stored on an old hard drive, or interviews with estranged children will help determine a candidate's strategic intelligence, the best set of tools for predicting the success or failure of a CEO.

However, in the current climate, even the most productive narcissists may find it hard to gain leadership roles in companies. Many companies, even the most innovative ones, don't really want narcissists working for them. No matter how much they say that they encourage independent thinking and creativity, many businesses have little tolerance for true originals, preferring a marketing or obsessive personality who toes the company line. For the most part, people don't like narcissists and don't want to work around them even if they achieve better results than other personality types in an innovative business. This is clear in reactions to a fictional case study in the September 2001 issue of the *Harvard Business Review* titled "What a Star—What a Jerk," in which Jane, a manager at TechniCo, can't figure out how to handle her most talented employee. The problem with Andy is that he's a productive narcissist—alternately abrasive with colleagues, successful and seductive with potential clients. What should Jane do with someone who produces such stellar results but alienates the rest of the staff, even reducing one person to tears over a scheduling conflict? The four panelists—two psychologists, a business consultant, and an executive—who reviewed the case for the *HBR* advised Jane either to manipulate Andy ("As a manager, I would alternately stroke his ego . . . and hammer him hard—hard enough to really rattle him") or isolate him from the other members of the staff (". . . managers need to carve out places for unpleasant, highly productive people—places that keep them from poisoning everyone else's working environment"). Not one of the panelists said that Jane, as

Andy's direct manager, should work on developing his potential or partner with him to build a better team, both strategies I suggest in a follow-up commentary in the *HBR*. Too often, however, there is no room in many companies for a high-performing, creative visionary who isn't a team player, making it even more difficult for an up-and-coming productive narcissist to develop his skills and gut instincts (think back on the negative human resources report on the young Jack Welch, who was lucky to be promoted by an exceptional executive). Productive narcissists may be at the top of the most innovative companies—particularly if they started them, like Bill Gates, Steve Jobs, and Steve Case—but the corporate environment, even in fast-moving fields, is often inhospitable to narcissistic personalities who hold junior positions.

The lack of understanding of narcissistic leaders has already led to a backlash, a pendulum swing to conservative, value-based, bottom-line CEOs, the ones who are suited to their companies but cannot lead in innovative or change-based industries. Fear of risky, narcissistic CEOs can bring about knee-jerk appointments; for example, David Dorman, a telecom old-timer, has succeeded Mike Armstrong, signaling a return to the way things were always done at AT&T before Armstrong burst onto the scene. Some business theorists attribute AT&T's somewhat revived image to Dorman's conservative strategy for servicing customers, but this is wishful thinking; it's just that any surviving telecom company, including AT&T, looks good in comparison to an industry that has been pummeled by scandal and financial disaster. AOL Time Warner has turned the CEO position over to Richard Parsons, a marketing personality who is known for glad-handing the board and investors, fostering good relationships, and not making any waves. I expect other companies, traumatized by the wave of CEO flameouts, to follow suit, forgoing innovation for cost cutting and the hope of steady and predictable profits. This reactionary swing against visionaries is just as uninformed as our enthusiastic and uncritical embrace of visionary leaders in the late '90s.

Contrary to proclamations in the business pages that there is an end of arrogance, a return to the self-effacing, humble CEO who is touted as the be-all-and-end-all leader for large-scale businesses by Jim Collins, productive narcissists appear to be all around us, particularly in the arts (Wes Andersen, M. Night Shyamalan, and Paul Thomas Anderson in film, Dr. Dre and Russell Simmons in hip-hop music), fashion (John Galliano and Alexander McQueen), science (Rodney Brooks of MIT in AI and robotics, Scott Manalis of MIT Media Labs in biosensors, Leonard Guarente of MIT in genetics), and business (Steve Tuecke of Argonne National Lab and head software architect of Globus, and Tim Tuttle of Bang Networks). They continue to come up with new plans to change the world, for better or worse. Remember William C. Norris's vision of online learning in the late 1950s? Well, John Sperling has quietly, and quite efficiently, made it happen. Sperling, a productive narcissist who is now eighty-two, realized that the education system excluded a huge market—adults—and decided to offer continuing education courses in 1972 at San Jose University, where he was teaching history. The courses caught on, and Sperling believed that the next step was to set up a degree program for working adults. When the university board and state regulators resisted the expansion of Sperling's program, he went on to found the Apollo Group and later set up shop at the University of Phoenix—now the largest private university in the country, with a

2001 net profit of $108 million. In a time when other schools, including the University of California and New York University, have either closed or cut back on their online courses and adult education, the University of Phoenix Online now has 37,000 students enrolled—*and* turns a profit. Sperling, a former union organizer, shows a canny understanding of the social system that any educational program operates in, and keeps thirty-five lobbyists on retainer to negotiate with politicians as the university expands into more states around the country (it now offers courses in thirty-seven).

And consider the case of Craig McCaw, the billionaire who first made his fortune by cashing in McCaw Cellular, his wireless network, in an acquisition by AT&T for $11.5 billion. McCaw has started, and invested in, a series of telecommunications and technology companies—with varying degrees of success and failure—but his most ambitious project to date is Teledesic, which proposes to launch a network of satellites (the original plan called for 840; McCaw has now scaled back that number to 30) that "talk" to each other and communicate information to telecommunications companies, global corporations, and, most important for his overall plan, the U.S. government and military. In order to realize his vision, McCaw has raised an estimated $1 billion for the project through 2000 and has partnered with co-CEO Bill Owens, a former four-star Navy admiral and an expert on technology and military readiness. McCaw's long-term goals of the almost preposterous satellite system is to revolutionize the way we react to military engagement and terrorist attacks, on the one hand, and on the other, bring Internet service and increased literacy and communication to Third World countries. Wayne Perry, an adviser to McCaw and a colleague at McCaw's previous companies, is quoted in *Fortune* as saying, "Typical Craig. Leave it to him to try something greater than the sum of the whole world's experience."

Will John Sperling change the way we teach students of all ages? Will Craig McCaw spread the Internet to impoverished countries and redefine our defense systems? Will mass-produced "clean" cars make gas-powered cars obsolete? Will targeted gene therapy eradicate cancer before it occurs in high-risk patients? Will bioengineered seed technology work hand in hand with pharmaceutical advances, forever changing the way we take and administer drugs? Will Leonard Guarente of MIT identify and alter the genetic basis of aging, adding years to the human life span? I can't give a definitive answer to these questions, but I can say that productive narcissists are already working on each one of these challenges, and more are bound to appear in an economic and political landscape marked by disruptive change and upheaval. I have intended this book to give employees, board members, investors, and all of us—as members of a democratic society that is based on an electoral process—the tools to evaluate visionary leaders, to distinguish between the destructive demigods and the productive narcissistic leaders who combine the best of their personality type with developed strategic intelligence. I also hope that productive narcissists will use the book to understand themselves and recognize that their sustained success requires continual learning and practice of strategic intelligence. There is no question in my mind that narcissistic leaders will continue to emerge in this period of turmoil; it's our challenge as a society to be alert to the very real dangers of visionaries, while remaining open and aware of their power to change society for the better. It is only through a deep understanding of the personality of our leaders that we will recognize that there is a future for the productive narcissists; in fact, our progress as a society depends on them and how well they use their abilities.

INTERPRETING THE
QUESTIONNAIRE RESULTS

B elow is a key to scoring the personality questionnaire in Chapter One and two forms you can use to chart your results. One chart shows the degree to which your answers fit the four types: erotic, obsessive, marketing, and narcissistic. The other chart shows your profile for the productive aspects of these types: caring, systematic, self-developing, and visionary.*

---

* There are different approaches to psychological types. One test that is often used for team building is the Myers-Briggs, based on the theories of C. G. Jung. I have sometimes used this test with executive teams and have found it useful in describing differences in the way people think and feel. Jung based his types on inborn temperament. For example, he distinguishes between introverts, who live more in their heads, and extroverts, who are more outgoing. Also, he makes a distinction between intuitive people, who form new ideas, and those who need to see the facts before they believe an idea.

Write your answer (numerical score) to each question here:

1 _____	2 _____	3 _____	4 _____
8 _____	7 _____	6 _____	5 _____
10 _____	9 _____	11 _____	12 _____
13 _____	14 _____	15 _____	19 _____
16 _____	21 _____	18 _____	22 _____
17 _____	25 _____	23 _____	26 _____
20 _____	31 _____	28 _____	30 _____
24 _____	34 _____	29 _____	32 _____
27 _____	38 _____	37 _____	35 _____
33 _____	40 _____	41 _____	36 _____
39 _____	50 _____	44 _____	42 _____
43 _____	52 _____	45 _____	48 _____
47 _____	55 _____	46 _____	54 _____
49 _____	58 _____	53 _____	59 _____
51 _____	60 _____	57 _____	65 _____
56 _____	62 _____	61 _____	68 _____
63 _____	67 _____	64 _____	71 _____
66 _____	70 _____	69 _____	74 _____
72 _____	73 _____	75 _____	77 _____
78 _____	76 _____	80 _____	79 _____

In contrast, the Freudian personality types described in this book are to a large degree learned. I find them more useful than Jung's types, because they can be explained logically as a result of childhood experiences. Furthermore, they describe how people relate to others. In contrast to Jung's types, they come in both productive and unproductive versions.

However, this personality test is not meant to replace Myers-Briggs. There may even be some relationship between the two approaches. For example, productive narcissists tend to be introverted and intuitive because they create their own visions and don't listen to others. However, this and other relationships between the two sets of types remain to be studied. (To learn about the Myers-Briggs, see David Keirsey and Marilyn Bates, *Please Understand Me: Character & Temperament Types*, Del Mar, CA: Prometheus Nemesis Books, 1978.)

Add the numbers from each of the four columns on the previous page and write the totals here:

TOTAL

_____	_____	_____	_____
MARKETING	NARCISSISTIC	EROTIC	OBSESSIVE

Do the same for these questions:

1 _____	2 _____	3 _____	12 _____
10 _____	50 _____	37 _____	35 _____
51 _____	62 _____	46 _____	36 _____
63 _____	67 _____	53 _____	71 _____
66 _____	76 _____	57 _____	79 _____

TOTAL

_____	_____	_____	_____
SELF DEVELOPING	VISIONARY	CARING	SYSTEMATIC

We are all a combination of types, but one is usually dominant and colors the elements of the other types. Freud believed that a secondary type balances the extreme characteristics of the dominant type. Here are descriptions of each type and the combinations of types.

The Erotic Personality

The most important thing for erotics is loving and being loved. They want to help and care for people, but more than that, they want to be *seen* by others as helpers—that is, to be recognized for their help and good deeds, to be loved and appreciated more than respected or admired.

Erotics dominate the social services, or what I call the caring fields—teaching, nursing, social work, mental health, and therapy—and service industries, careers that involve personal management, nurturing creativity and growth, encouraging others to make more of their lives. They keep our social services running, on both an organizational and personal level, by teaching our children, caring for the elderly, helping displaced, homeless, or poor people, and, on a smaller scale, setting up this friend with that one, lending a hand with moving, or coming over to cook dinner for a sick colleague. They never like to say "no" to a favor, thriving on service and cooperation, trusting and relying on friends and family for a sense of security. If erotics rise to leadership positions, it's usually in the caring fields rather than innovative or high-tech companies. However, they can be found in executive roles as helpers to the boss. They also shine as musicians and performers who stimulate love in their coworkers and audiences.

STRENGTHS OF THE EROTIC PERSONALITY

- caring
- bringing people together
- reinforcing social interdependence
- service and cooperation
- trust
- stimulating love

WEAKNESSES OF THE EROTIC PERSONALITY

- dependency
- gullibility and disillusionment
- inability to make tough decisions
- fear of taking a stand
- excesses of emotion
- need for everyone to like them

Erotic Combinations

EROTIC-OBSESSIVE. The productive version is the prototype of the good mother, caring but hardworking and concerned with the health and well-being of her children. It could also be a loyal, caring, and efficient helper to someone, a boss or partner. The unproductive version is a type that worries obsessively about health issues or whether they are loved. This type can be too easily manipulated because they fear losing love.

EROTIC-MARKETING. The productive type is a receptive helper—empathic, sensitive to the needs of others, while also a self-developer. Many psychotherapists are this type. The unproductive types are constantly looking for a fulfilling relationship. They have many infatuations at work and love where they believe they have found themselves, but inevitably they decide they have lost themselves.

EROTIC-NARCISSISTIC. Narcissism is the dominant type. See narcissistic-erotic.

The Obsessive Personality

Obsessives exhibit an internal instead of an external dependence. They live by the rules, and the rules are usually determined by an internalized father figure, a strict conscience, or "the way things have always been done around here." They are motivated to live up to the high standards and ideals they set for themselves, to show, at all times, that they fit the specs of "good child" to an internalized father figure.

They are the conservatives who preserve order and maintain moral values, with a strong work ethic. Obsessives focus on the importance of right and wrong, whether at work or in their friendships. Once they believe in someone or something, they stick to it, displaying loyalty. They want good, orderly fashion in everything they do, whether it's in their well-kept closets or workspace or how they organize their time.

The most productive of these types should be called systematic rather than obsessive; they systematically break a task down into its components and set out to tackle it, one bit at a time.

They are the kind of people who say "If you're going to do anything, you should do it right." Expert obsessives see work as performance, meeting a standard, not helping anyone. In the past, they were the independent farmers and craftsmen. Today, they are doctors, engineers, financial experts, scientists, researchers, technicians, and craftsmen like electricians, bricklayers, and carpenters, as well as the majority of middle managers and some top managers, especially CFOs, COOs, and some CEOs.

Obsessives may make it to the top of a corporation and take on a leadership role, but they are most effective in a company that is itself obsessive—a company that is conservative, value-based, focused on the bottom line, whose goals are to cut costs and improve quality and profits.

STRENGTHS OF THE OBSESSIVE PERSONALITY

- systematic
- maintain order and stability
- preserve tradition
- loyal
- meet exacting standards, high-quality work
- disciplined and diligent
- determined
- responsible and accountable

WEAKNESSES OF THE OBSESSIVE PERSONALITY

- resisting anything new or different
- mired in details and rules, losing sight of overall goals
- more concerned with doing things in the right way than doing the right thing
- control freak; paper-pushing, bean-counting bureaucrat
- judgmental, stubborn, stingy, and extremely neat and clean: "anal" in exactly the way Freud described the character
- always right, a know-it-all

Obsessive Combinations

OBSESSIVE-EROTIC. The productive version makes the best clinician, the doctor who cares. Also, other professionals who are systematic and thorough but want to help people. The unproductive versions are the dependent but rigid types. As bureaucrats, they are servile to bosses but unbending to clients and subordinates.

OBSESSIVE-MARKETING. The productive version is similar to the marketing-obsessive, but the emphasis is on what they have to offer rather than what others need from them. They focus on developing their skills and looking good, adapting to the market in order to succeed. They are careful to walk the walk, talk the talk, and look the look that's in style.

OBSESSIVE-NARCISSISTIC. If you have this score, you may be a productive obsessive who believes that making the organization run more efficiently is a vision. It is not the kind of vision that real narcissists have. It is likely you are conscientiously attempting to improve the organization, not change the world. The unproductive version is rather stubborn and self-centered, the most difficult type to influence.

The Marketing Personality

Marketing personalities operate by radar, sensing what the market wants and needs, then conforming to it. Their self-esteem or self-valuation comes from what could be called a personal stock market that goes up and down depending on how they're viewed: their accomplishments, how well they align themselves with key people, a client or account base, good looks and style, new skills and expertise—or "whatever," as they are fond of saying. Everything they do is relative: it needs to meet the approval of other people.

They almost never use the words "right" or "wrong" (as do obsessives); they want to be "appropriate," as defined by the social group they want to impress. They intuitively know how to adapt to changes in the marketplace, and are not as unsettled by upheaval in the corporate or economic climate as obsessives are.

The most productive marketing personalities are the self-developers. They think of their life and career as continuing education, a chance to pick up new skills, to continually learn and grow, intellectually and emotionally. They are the types who want to do well, to feel and look good. They exercise, diet, talk to therapists, organize reading and study groups, and take classes. They are some of the most productive freelancers, setting their own goals and working well on their own; they are a big part of the current trend toward self-employment, and are excellent at self-promotion.

Marketing types do well in all manner of sales professions—real estate, public relations, advertising, publicity, event planning, venture capital, money raising. They are effective in consulting, technical design, acting, the arts, publishing, and entertainment. They increasingly play a part in the legal and medical professions because of their ability to bring people together and faciliate groups. They are often chosen as school principals and college presidents because they make all the different interest groups feel understood and supported; they build coalitions that don't insult anyone.

STRENGTHS OF THE MARKETING PERSONALITY

- intuitively adapting to changes in the marketplace
- superior networking skills
- continual reinvention
- self-marketing

WEAKNESSES OF THE MARKETING PERSONALITY
- no center, no inner core that directs them
- no lasting commitments to their work or to people
- anxiety hangs over them, the nagging questions "Is this the appropriate answer? Am I doing OK? Is this working?"
- pervasive anxiety turns into depression

Marketing Combinations

Note that marketing types often score every question "sometimes," since they can exhibit all behaviors if they feel they are appropriate.

MARKETING-EROTIC. This is the same as erotic-marketing. However, the productive type puts more emphasis on networking and gaining some economic and social advantage from helping others. They are particularly good at sales and PR. The unproductive types believe that if they look right and give others what they seem to want, they will be loved. They are the perpetual consumers who believe that they will find satisfaction through buying or experiencing what is fashionable.

MARKETING-OBSESSIVE. The productive marketing obsessive is especially effective as a technical consultant. Increasingly, professionals of this type are able to build useful networks and provide value for their clients because they listen well to problems and are systematic in following through. They keep up on the latest information and make good use of it. The unproductive types can be obsessive about getting more information than they can use. They compulsively surf the Internet or wade through the latest books, magazines, and newspapers in search of the "new."

MARKETING-NARCISSISTIC. This is another contradiction. See the narcissistic-marketing type. If you scored marketing-narcissistic, it means that you think you should be more independent and visionary and less concerned about what other people want you to be.

MARKETING-OBSESSIVE-EROTIC. The moderately productive version of this type is the average personality in the knowledge-service age. They smoothly fit right into the team-based organization of the modern office. The unproductive version suffers from the lack of focus and purpose that is expressed in countless hours of therapy, trying to find a center and commit oneself to something sustaining.

The Narcissist

The type of person who impresses us as a personality, who disrupts the status quo and brings about change.

Narcissists have very little or no psychic demands that they have to do the right thing. Freed from these internal constraints, they are forced to answer, for themselves, what is right, to decide what they value, what, in effect, gives them a sense of meaning. They create their own vision, a sense of purpose that not only engages them but also inspires others to follow them.

Narcissists train themselves from an early age to block out other voices, other opinions, so one of the few voices they trust is their own. They are accustomed to listening to themselves talk, debating different sides of the same issue, finally reaching a decision about what to do and the best way to do it.

Without the support of others, it's easy to see how narcissists have a highly developed "me against the world" way of looking at things. This often comes out as paranoia, a heightened awareness of danger that may be realistic, given narcissistic ambition, competitiveness, and unbridled aggressive energy. There's not a lot of gray area in the narcissistic view of the world—you are either a friend or a foe, for or against the vision.

Productive narcissists are not limited to any particular field; you can find them in almost any field, in any domain. They may not change the entire world (some notable narcissists do), but they may reinvent their part of the world.

STRENGTHS OF THE PRODUCTIVE NARCISSIST

- visioning to change the world and create meaning
- independent thinking/risk taking
- passion
- charisma
- voracious learning
- perseverance
- alertness to threats
- sense of humor

WEAKNESSES OF THE PRODUCTIVE NARCISSIST

- extreme sensitivity to criticism
- not listening
- paranoia
- extreme competitiveness
- anger and put-downs

- exaggeration
- lack of self-knowledge
- isolation
- grandiosity

Narcissistic Combinations

NARCISSISTIC-OBSESSIVE. The productive version is what Freud called the best leader, combining vision and systematic approaches to implementation. Jack Welch is a good example of this type. Freud also considered himself this type.

The unproductive version is the authoritarian bureaucrat, paranoid, hoarding, and without a creative vision. Rather, the vision is total control and domination.

NARCISSISTIC-EROTIC. The productive version is the creative musician or actor like Orson Welles or Marlon Brando. There are also organizational leaders of this type who need to partner with obsessives because they ignore processes and details, focusing on caring for the people who sign on to their vision. The unproductive is the Don Juan or Mata Hari type, seductive and exploitative.

NARCISSISTIC-MARKETING. This combination is a contradiction. The narcissist may use marketing traits in order to recruit or seduce without being controlled by others or trying to please them. Jan Carlzon was this type of leader at Scandinavian Airlines in the 1980s and 1990s.

NOTES

PREFACE

xiv *For a while, the new twenty-first century ideal became* . . . Jim Collins, *Good to Great: Why Some Companies Make the Leap . . . and Others Don't* (New York: HarperBusiness, 2001).

xiv *Steve Jobs, a prototypical productive narcissist,* . . . Fred Vogelstein, "Mastering the Art of Disruption," *Fortune*, February 6, 2006, 23.

xvi *This is a productive narcissist.* . . . Jack Welch and Suzy Welch, *Winning* (New York: Harper Business, 2005), 181–184.

xvii *Of all the personality types, the marketing type is* . . . An example is Malcolm Gladwell's statement, "I don't believe in character. I believe in the effect of the immediate impact of environment and situation on people's behavior." Rachel Donadio, "The Gladwell Effect," *New York Times Book Review*, February 5, 2006.

xviii *In contrast, unproductive people are less free . . .* See my discussion of the difference between developmental and addictive needs in Michael Maccoby, *Why Work?: Motivating the New Workforce*, 2nd ed. (Alexandria, VA: Miles River Press, 1995), chapter 2.

xix *According to Lyndon B. Johnson's brother Sam, . . .* "Lessons in Power: Lyndon Johnson Revealed: A Conversation with Historian Robert A. Caro," *Harvard Business Review*, April 2006, 47–52.

xxiii *For years he has teetered on the edge of disaster, . . .* "As Italy Votes, Golden Career of Berlusconi Is at Crossroads," *Wall Street Journal,* March 30, 2006.

xxiii *During the past twenty years, psychologists have . . .* See, especially, Robert J. Sternberg, *Beyond IQ: A Triarchic Theory of Human Intelligence* (New York: Cambridge University Press, 1985).

xxiii *When I compared those narcissistic business leaders who . . .* Before Fiorina was fired, I asked an HP manager what she thought of her. She wrote, "The people who work for her see her as an idea person who doesn't follow through or have deep knowledge. In psychological terms, she might be a productive narcissist. She has all the imperial accoutrements—limos, planes, etc. I get no sense that she is either an obsessive or erotic type—maybe also marketing."

xxiv *A group of consultants who read this book . . .* The consultants were Richard Greene, Richard Margolies, Edith Onderick-Harvey, Mark Paulson, Mark Paulson Jr., and Gary Wolford. This concept has provoked interest from both academics and consultants. I was invited to give a keynote address to the Strategic Management Society at its 2004 international meeting in San Juan, Puerto Rico.

xxv *A disastrous example of this weakness . . .* For warnings to managers, see Haruo Shimada and John Paul MacDuffie, "Industrial Relations and 'Humanware,'" working paper 1855-88, Sloan School of Management, Massachusetts Institute of Technology, Cambridge, December 1986. See also, Michael Maccoby, "Is There a

Best Way to Build a Car?" *Harvard Business Review*, November–December 1997, 161–171.

xxvi *In the exhibition of Daimyo Culture* . . . Shimizu Yoshaiaki, "Japan, the Shaping of the Daimyo Culture 1185–1868," exhibition catalogue, Washington, D.C., National Gallery of Art, 1988.

xxvii *A number of readers believe* . . . An enthusiastic reader from Buffalo, NY, summarized a number of positive comments about this book after giving it five stars in Amazon's customer reviews: "Wow! Now this is a book about what leadership really is! Real leaders are narcissists . . . Successful leaders are not warm and fuzzy types; they succeed because they can make tough decisions on difficult matters, often times ignoring or not listening to others . . . This book flies in the face of Daniel Goleman and others who have jumped on the emotional intelligence bandwagon (claiming that the stuff of leadership is empathy and emotional intelligence),"Amazon.com, January 2, 2005.

xxvii *Bill Clinton used empathy to charm and seduce, while Abraham Lincoln used* . . . Doris Kearns Goodwin writes that Lincoln "possessed extraordinary empathy—the gift or curse of putting himself in the place of another, to experience what they were feeling, to understand their motives and desires." See *Team of Rivals, the Political Genius of Abraham Lincoln* (New York: Simon & Schuster, 2006), 104. Lincoln also possessed an element of emotional intelligence that I haven't seen mentioned in books on the subject. That's a sense of humor, the emotional equivalent of a sense of reality.

xxviii *This is one of those crusades* . . . Michael S. Rosenwald, "J. Craig Venter's Next Little Thing. Tackling the World's Energy Problem," *Washington Post,* February 22, 2006.

xxviii *While the past few years have* . . . Charles O'Reilly and Michael L. Tushman, "The Ambidextrous Organization," *Harvard Business Review*, April 2004.

xxviii *Bala Chakravarthy and Peter Lorange* . . . Bala Chakkravarthy and Peter Lorange, "Leading for Growth: Managing Dilemmas" (paper presented at Strategic Society annual meeting, San Juan, Puerto Rico, November 3, 2004).

xxix *As you read this book,* . . . The best presentation of this theory is Marcus Buckingham and Donald O. Clifton, *Now, Discover Your Strengths* (New York: The Free Press, 2001). Right before he died, Donald Clifton sent me a note praising this book for pointing out the strengths of productive narcissists.

xxx *We also are better equipped to* . . . Jean Lipman-Blumen, *The Allure of Toxic Leaders: Why We Follow Destructive Bosses and Corrupt Politicians and How We Can Survive Them* (Oxford: Oxford University Press, 2004); Barbara Kellerman, *Bad Leadership: What It Is, How It Happens, Why It Matters (Leadership for the Common Good)* (Boston: Harvard Business School Press, 2004).

xxx *After the publication of this book,* . . . Michael Maccoby and Gerhard Gschwandtner, "Productive Sales Leaders," *Selling Power* 25, no. 1 (2005): 58–65.

INTRODUCTION: THE "CHANGE THE WORLD" PERSONALITY

2 *I was fresh from my experience interviewing* . . . *The Gamesman: The New Corporate Leaders* (New York: Simon & Schuster, 1976).

2 *I ended up working with Harman on a groundbreaking study of the humanization of his factory* . . . For a description of the Bolivar project and the subsequent project with Harman's factory in Coatbridge, Scotland, see my book *The Leader* (New York: Simon & Schuster, 1981).

3 *A consultant to Next said, "We signed up with Steve because we were going to revolutionize education . . ."* Alan Deutschman, *The Second Coming of Steve Jobs* (New York: Broadway Books, 2000), p. 46.

4 *Larry Ellison compares his misunderstood vision at Oracle to that of Galileo* . . . James Nicolai, "Oracle Takes Aim at .Net with Web Services," CNN.com/ITworld.com, December 13, 2000.

4 *Steve Case says that his special skill is "really believing in the medium . . ."* Ken Auletta, *World War 3.0* (New York: Random House, 2001), p. 91.

4 *Bill Gates rarely discusses profits with his staff and the public, preferring to say: "What we aim to do . . ."* Auletta, p. 249.

4 *Robert Shapiro, formerly CEO of Monsanto, described his vision of genetically altered crops as* . . . David Barboza, "Monsanto Faces Growing Skepticism on Two Fronts," *The New York Times*, August 5, 1999.

6 *The psychological portrait of today's business leaders . . . most closely fits the normal personality type that Freud called narcissistic.* Sigmund Freud, "Libidinal Types" (1931) from Standard Edition, Vol. XXI (London: The Hogarth Press, 1961), pp. 215–20.

6 *In other words, these are the type of people who are most likely to say that they want to change the world.* Ferenczi wrote that Freud typed himself as a narcissist with an "antipathy toward any weakness or abnormalities." *The Clinical Diaries of Sandor Ferenczi* (Cambridge: Harvard University Press, 1988), p. 62.

7 *This is one way of explaining Abraham Lincoln's early form of rebellion* . . . Douglas L. Wilson, *Honor's Voice: The Transformation of Abraham Lincoln* (New York: Alfred A. Knopf, 1998), pp. 56–58.

8 *Jim Clark was kicked out of high school* . . . Michael Lewis, *The New New Thing: A Silicon Valley Story* (New York: W.W. Norton & Co., 2000), p. 44.

8 *Steve Jobs talked his way into Reed* . . . Deutschman, pp. 26–27.

9 *Oprah Winfrey? She's so open about her doubts and fears* . . . A&E Biography Series: Oprah Winfrey.

11 *. . . Daniel Goleman's concept of "emotional intelligence."* Daniel Goleman, *Emotional Intelligence* (New York: Bantam Books, 1995).

11 *. . . strains of which can be found in business literature from Stephen Covey to Jim Collins* . . . Stephen R. Covey, *The 7 Habits of Highly Effective People* (New York: Simon & Schuster, 1989) and Jim Collins, *Good to Great: Why Some Companies Make the Leap . . . and Others Don't* (New York: HarperBusiness, 2001).

CHAPTER ONE: RECOGNIZING PERSONALITY TYPES

23 *It wasn't until I worked with the psychoanalyst Erich Fromm, whose books* . . . Erich Fromm, *Escape from Freedom* (New York: Rinehart, 1941), and Erich Fromm, *Man for Himself* (New York: Rinehart, 1946).

CHAPTER TWO: PATTERNS OF PERSONALITY

36 *. . . on July 4, 2001, reporters asked George W. Bush* . . . Frank Rich, "It's Good To Be the King," *The New York Times,* July 7, 2001.

37 *Under the title "Sea of Self-Love"* . . . Jon Pareles, "Sea of Self-Love, but Who's Drowning?" *The New York Times,* July 27, 2001.

38 *On September 26, 2001, Maureen Dowd wrote* . . . Maureen Dowd, "From Botox to Botulism," *The New York Times,* September 26, 2001.

39 *Every single one of these descriptive words and phrases is lifted from the DSM-IV* . . . *Diagnostic and Statistical Manual of Mental Disorders. Fourth Edition. DSM-IV*™ (Washington, DC: American Psychiatric Association, 1994), pp. 658–61.

40 *Freud said it best in the paper that is the basis for my understanding of narcissism.* Freud, "Libidinal Types," p. 217.

42 *The first time Freud named these repetitive patterns* . . . Sigmund Freud, *Character and Anal Eroticism* (1908), Standard Edition, Vol. IX (London: The Hogarth Press, 1957), pp. 167–77.

42 *Freud first treated narcissism as a personality type in his 1910 psychosexual biography* . . . Sigmund Freud, *Leonardo da Vinci and a Memory of His Childhood,* (1910) Standard Edition Vol. XI (London: The Hogarth Press, 1957), pp. 63–139.

43 *Freud added to and adapted his theories of narcissism* . . . Sigmund Freud, *On Narcissism: An Introduction* (1914), Standard Edition, Vol. XIV (London: The Hogarth Press, 1957), pp. 73–105.

43 *Freud's three normal personality types are: erotic, obsessive, and narcissistic. To these three, Erich Fromm added a fourth type, the marketing personality* . . . As categories, I've found them to be the most useful way to talk to CEOs and managers, starting with *The Gamesman* study when the head of systems development of IBM asked me to teach a group of their most promising managers about themselves. At that time, I gave these types psychosocial names, rather than the strict Freudian typologies, because I thought they were more easily accepted by the people I was studying. I called the obsessives craftsmen. The erotics were the company men, and I called the narcissists I encountered jungle fighters. The gamesmen were a productive version of the marketing and obsessive personalities combined. In *Why Work? Motivating the New Work Force,* 2nd edition (Alexandria, VA: Miles River Press, 1995), I called these types by their more productive values at work. The obsessives were experts, the erotics helpers, the narcissists innovators and defenders, and the marketing types were self-developers. In both books, I present examples of people working at all levels of business and government.

45 *"One of the Greek words for love,"* Erotic comes from *Eros,* the
winged youth who is the god of love in Greek mythology. Other
Greek concepts of love include *philos,* the more intellectual love as in
love of wisdom (*philosophy*) and brotherly love (*philadelphy*). Also
agape, the divine love described in St. Paul, *Corinthians I:13.*

49 *Freud describes obsessives as "dominated . . ."* Freud, "Libidinal
Types," p. 218.

51 *In Berkshire Hathaway's 2000 annual report, Buffet wrote . . .*
Floyd Norris, "Buffett Issues His Annual Report," *The New York
Times,* March 12, 2001.

52 *. . . men like Gillette's Colman Mockler, who put the company ahead
of his personal interests . . .* Collins, p. 61.

52 *Collins summarizes this leadership approach by saying that
"throughout our research, we were struck by the continual use of
words like* disciplined, rigorous . . ." Collins, p. 127.

53 *Glenn Kessler wrote in the* Washington Post . . . Glenn Kessler,
"First Impressions, Lasting Influence: O'Neill Has More Pull Than
Meets the Eye," *Washington Post,* October 7, 2001.

53 *Barrett described the symbiotic obsessive/narcissistic relationship
in* Fortune . . . Katrina Brooker, "The Chairman of the Board Looks
Back," *Fortune,* May 28, 2001.

54 *. . . in* Sports Illustrated, *Steve Rushin observes . . .* Steve Rushin,
"Grand Stand," *Sports Illustrated,* July 31, 2000.

55 *In an interview with Oprah Winfrey . . .* The Oprah Winfrey Show,
October 8, 2001, Harpo Productions.

56 *It speaks directly to a market of middle managers . . .* Spencer Johnson and Kenneth H. Blanchard, *The One-Minute Manager* (New
York: Berkley Publishing Group, 1983).

58 *This shift began in the 1950s, predicted with accuracy in . . .* David
Riesman, *The Lonely Crowd* (New Haven: Yale University Press,
1950). Also, for an analysis of how the socialization process forms
the marketing characters, see my article, "Toward a Science of

Social Character," *International Forum of Psychoanalysis*, 1001:11: 33–44.

58 *Two decades later, Daniel Bell* . . . Daniel Bell, *The Coming of Post-Industrial Society* (New York: Basic Books, 1973).

59 *The most productive marketing personalities are what I call self-developers*. See my book *Why Work?* for interviews with self-developers.

61 *Combs has created an empire* . . . "Michael Jordan, Master P, P. Diddy and Tiger Woods Named Among 40 Wealthiest Americans Under 40," *Jet*, October 1, 2001.

62 *It is the straightforward sale of ink and ink cartridges, which generates $9 billion annually.* Eric Nee, "Open Season on Carly Fiorina," *Fortune*, July 23, 2001.

64 *One of Bush's key advisers in his campaign was Governor William J. Janklow* . . . Richard L. Berke, "The Last (E-Mail) Goodbye from 'gwb' to His 42 Buddies," *The New York Times*, March 17, 2001.

68 *. . . but look at the existential questioning found in Napoleon's youthful diaries* . . . Robert B. Asprey, *The Rise and Fall of Napoleon Bonaparte* (New York: Basic Books, 2001), p.26.

68 *Steve Jobs, whose close friend Mike Murray was worried that Jobs would commit suicide* . . . Deutschman, p.16.

69 *"No commander in history has so inspired his troops . . ."* Asprey, pp. xix–xx.

70 *Oprah Winfrey says that she was harassed by the other kids in her schoolyard* . . . A&E Biography Series: Oprah Winfrey.

70 *Stephen King was holed up in his basement* . . . Stephen King, *On Writing* (New York, Scribner, 2000), pp. 41–50.

72 *. . . the Stephen King scenario . . . an absent or failed father who "piled up all sorts of bills and then did a runout."* King, p. 17.

73 *Jim Clark's father abandoned his family* . . . Lewis, p. 45.

73 *John D. Rockefeller's father, was, quite literally* . . . Chernow, in particular, pp. 6–13, 193–94, 463–65.

73 *Leonardo da Vinci was an illegitimate child* . . . Freud, Standard Edition, Vol. XI (London: The Hogarth Press), p. 81.

73 *The mother of William Durant, the founder of General Motors* . . . *To quote one of his mother's letters to Durant* . . . Axel Madsen, *The Deal Maker: How William C. Durant Made General Motors* (New York: John Wiley & Sons, 1999), p. 64.

73 *Duke Ellington's elegant and strong-willed mother* . . . "Jazz," A four-part documentary, by Ken Burns; Episode 2: "The Gift."

74 *James Carville says "anytime he was asked who was the most influential person in his life* . . .*"* Bonnie Angelo, *First Mothers: The Women Who Shaped the Presidents* (New York: William Morrow, 2000), p. 395.

74 *Richard Nixon's father was an unsuccessful lemon farmer.* Angelo, pp. 194–95, 210–11.

74 *Lou Cannon said that you would never have heard of Ronald Reagan* . . . Angelo, p. 330.

74 *Richard Branson's father was unsuccessful as a barrister* . . . Richard Branson, *Losing My Virginity: How I've Survived, Had Fun, and Made a Fortune Doing Business My Way* (London: Virgin, 1998), on p. 16, Branson describes his father as reluctantly reading law and on p. 19, writes that his parents had very little money when he was growing up. His father comes across as much softer than his mother, p. 20.

74 *There's another family scenario that's described by Heinz Kohut* . . . Heinz Kohut, M.D. *The Analysis of the Self* (New York: International University Press, Inc., 1971), pp. 143–44.

74 . . . *similar to Alexander the Great's mother* . . . Benjamin I. Wheeler, *Alexander the Great* (London: G. P. Putnam's Sons, 1900). "His mother, the fanatical, corybantic Olympias, had always been haunted with the delusion that her son was begotten of a god." p. 351.

75 *Welch writes admiringly of his mother's reaction when he was a sore loser* . . . Jack Welch with John A. Byrne, *Jack: Straight from the Gut* (New York: Warner Books, 2001), pp. 3–4.

75 *Douglas MacArthur's mother encouraged and promoted his military career . . .* "The American Experience: MacArthur," written, produced, and directed by Austin Hoyt, WGBH Educational Foundation, 1999.

75 *Frank Lloyd Wright's mother Anna decided, before he was born . . .* "Frank Lloyd Wright: Life and Work," a film by Ken Burns & Lynn Novick, The American Lives Film Project, Inc., 1997.

75 *. . . even going with Bill on his business trips.* Auletta, p. 145.

76 *As a child, Camille Paglia, a narcissist . . .* Camille Paglia, *Sex, Art, and American Culture* (New York: Vintage Books, 1992), p. 110.

76 *Freud was fascinated by the life of Hannibal . . .* Ernst Jones, *The Life and Work of Freud,* Vol. 2 (New York: Basic Books, 1955). Ernst Jones notes Freud's identifications with Hannibal (p. 19) and Moses (p. 365).

76 *At the height of Michael Saylor's career . . .* Evan Thomas, "Caesar and Edison and . . . Saylor?" *Newsweek,* January 1, 2000.

76 *John D. Rockefeller made a comparison between his corporate role and Napoleon's military command . . .* Ron Chernow, *Titan: The Life of John D. Rockefeller, Sr.* (New York: Random House, 1998), p. 223.

76 *Richard Nixon identified with Charles de Gaulle . . .* Harold Evans, "White House Book Club," *The New York Times,* January 14, 2001.

77 *John D. Rockefeller held intimate conversations with himself . . .* Chernow, p.67.

77 *This is the routine that Joe Klein noticed in Bill Clinton . . .* Joe Klein, "Eight Years: Bill Clinton and the Politics of Persistence," *The New Yorker,* October 16 and 23, 2000.

77 *In* Timeline, *Michael Crichton says more about the narcissistic leader in this one paragraph . . .* Michael Crichton, *Timeline* (New York: Ballantine Books, 2000), p.121.

78 *To quote Harold Bloom: "Hamlet, in his seven soliloquies, teaches us what imaginative literature* can *teach . . ."* Harold Bloom, *How to Read and Why* (New York: Scribner, 2001), p. 205.

79 *Andy Grove gave the high-tech world a slogan* . . . Andy Grove, *Only the Paranoid Survive* (New York: Doubleday, 1996.)

79 *This is exactly what David Dorman, then CEO of Pacific Bell, claims that Steve Ballmer said* . . . Auletta, p. 148.

CHAPTER THREE: THE PRODUCTIVE NARCISSIST

84 *I first put my understanding of "productiveness" to practical use in my work* . . . Erich Fromm and Michael Maccoby, *Social Character in a Mexican Village* (Englewood Cliffs, NJ: Prentice-Hall, 1970). Reprinted with new introduction by Michael Maccoby (New Brunswick, NJ: Transaction Publishers, 1996).

86 . . . *more than any other actor of the twentieth century* . . . Richard L. Sterne, *John Gielgud Directs Richard Burton in Hamlet: A Journal of Rehearsals* (New York: Random House, 1967), p. 338.

86 *Gielgud himself wrote about the role of Hamlet that "it is . . ."* Jonathan Croall, *Gielgud: A Theatrical Life* (New York: Continuum, 2001), p. 319.

86 *Gielgud, for example, had a disastrous stage debut* . . . Croall, p. 43.

87 *Dirk Bogarde told Gielgud's biographer* . . . Croall, p. viii.

91 *I applied it when I led a companywide program at AT&T* . . . My work with AT&T is described by Charles Heckscher, Michael Maccoby, Rafael Ramirez, and Pierre-Eric Tixier, *Agents of Change* (Oxford: Oxford University Press, 2003).

92 *Take, for example,* Who Moved My Cheese? . . . Spencer Johnson and Kenneth H. Blanchard, *Who Moved My Cheese? An Amazing Way to Deal with Change in Your Work and Your Life* (New York: Putnam Publishing Group, 1998).

96 *John D. Rockefeller consistently maintained that Standard Oil was more than a multinational corporation.* Chernow, pp. 153–54.

96 *In a letter to his colleague Henry C. Folger, Rockefeller wrote . . .* Chernow, p. 257.

97 *. . . whose vision of Standard Oil as "missionaries of light" . . .* Chernow, p. 154.

97 *. . . consider this quote from a journalist's interview with Rockefeller . . .* Chernow, p. 153.

99 *In an interview with the journalist Michael Specter in* The New Yorker . . . Michael Specter, "The Pharmageddon Riddle," *The New Yorker*, April 10, 2002.

99 *. . . a former executive at Monsanto said that "there was a real sense of noble purpose . . ."* Amy Barrett, "Rocky Road for Monsanto?" *Business Week*, June 12, 2000.

99 *Jack Welch not only wanted to "change GE from one of the great companies . . ."* Welch, p. 330.

100 *G. K. Chesterton pointed out how misleading it is to think that supreme self-confidence . . .* Gilbert K. Chesterton, *Orthodoxy* (New York: Dodd, Mead and Company, 1924), p. 22.

102 *Take, for example, Jim Clark. He told Michael Lewis that he felt like an absolute failure . . .* Lewis, p. 47.

102 *Clark became energized . . .* Lewis, p. 48.

103 *Robert Shapiro, who was general counsel at his father's company, General Instrument Corporation . . .* Specter, *The New Yorker.*

104 *. . . Ford jumped ship and started his third—and last—car company . . .* Jack Beatty, editor, *Colossus* (New York: Broadway Books, 2001), specifically the chapter by Richard S. Tedlow, "Like Trying to Screw an Elephant," p. 229. Additional Ford biographical material, Richard S. Tedlow, *Giants of Enterprise* (New York: Harper-Business, 2001), chapter on Henry Ford, pp. 119–78.

104 *As Marc Andreeson, the programmer who created Netscape with Jim Clark . . .* David Streitfeld, "Bill Gates's Executive Style Inspires a Cult Following," *Washington Post*, May 1, 2000.

105 *In an astute article, Michael Porter . . . asks . . .* Michael Porter, "What Is Strategy?" *The Harvard Business Review*, November/December 1996. The quote as well as the description of Southwest's business strategy draws on Porter's article.

105 *Kelleher's company embodies his own belief system and guiding principles . . .* Brooker, *Fortune.*

106 *When Jim Parker, the new CEO of Southwest, was asked . . .* Ibid.

107 *"My goal was to find a structure that would empower everybody on the team, not just the stars . . ."* Phil Jackson with Hugh Delanty, *Sacred Hoops* (New York: Hyperion, 1995), p. 63. The biographical material on Jackson, and his description of his coaching philosophy, are drawn from *Sacred Hoops.*

108 *He had seen other coaches try, and "unless they're incredibly gifted psychologists . . ."* Jackson with Delanty, p. 152.

108 *When the Bulls won the 1991 NBA championship . . .* Jackson with Delanty, p. 145.

109 *"The first time we practiced meditation, Michael [Jordan] thought . . ."* Jackson with Delanty, p. 173.

109 *Jackson said that it "embodied the Zen Christian attitude."* Jackson with Delanty, p. 87.

110 *Brian Shaw, one of the Lakers, says about Jackson . . .* Michael Wilbon, "Zelig or Zen Master? Either Way, Jackson's Act Is Hard to Match," *Washington Post*, May 22, 2002.

110 *Rockefeller told his children: "Never mind the crowd . . ."* Chernow, p. 30.

112 *When he was interviewed for* Black Enterprise *magazine, Robert Johnson . . .* Joyce Jones, "Betting on Black," *Black Enterprise,* January 2001.

116 *Garry Wills writes that "genius . . ."* Garry Wills, *Confessions of a Conservative* (New York: Penguin, 1979), p. 230.

117 *Alan Deutschman reports that "he tormented Heidi Roizen . . ."* Deutschman, p. 250.

117 *One of the engineers on the job recalled that "there was a rocking chair . . ."* Robert Lacey, *Ford: The Men and the Machine* (Boston: Little, Brown & Co., 1986), p. 91.

117 *"We often wondered when Henry Ford slept."* Lacey, p. 43.

117 *When Jim Clark was cooking up Netscape . . .* Lewis, pp. 80–83.

117 *William Durant would call meetings any time inspiration struck.* Madsen, p. 6.

118 *Jürgen Schrempp calls ten to fifteen people on weekends to bounce ideas off them.* Jürgin Grasslin, *Jürgen Schrempp and the Making of an Auto Dynasty* (New York: McGraw-Hill, 2000), p. 188.

118 *Harry Bennett, Ford's sidekick, received a phone call . . .* Harry Bennett as told to Paul Marcus, *We Never Called Him Henry* (New York: Fawcett Publications, 1951), p. 38.

119 *Rockefeller was said to have a "magnetic power over workers."* Chernow, p. 177.

119 *Durant was legendary for his ability to talk his way into anything. Walter Chrylser wrote . . .* Madsen, p. 149.

119 *I thought of this when I read that Jürgen Schrempp said that . . .* Grasslin, p. 129.

121 *Churchill, who knew a thing or two about perseverance, said it best . . .* David Gergen, *Eyewitness to Power* (New York: Simon & Schuster, 2000), p. 317.

121 *When a reporter asked him about another one of his financial fiascos in 1921, he said: "Forget mistakes . . ."* Madsen, p. 215.

121 *. . . reduced to managing a bowling alley, with all his auto industry years behind him and he still boasted . . .* Madsen, p. 276.

121 *Susan Barnes, a former employee, said that no matter what happened to Jobs . . .* Deutschman, p. 298.

122 *Rockefeller's response to his anxious colleagues was to point solemnly upward and say . . .* Chernow, p. 283.

123 *Just look at this statistic from Ken Auletta's account . . .* Auletta, p. 267.

123 *Freud's motivation? His "greed for knowledge."* From page x of

"Sigmund Freud: A Brief Life," an introduction, by Peter Gay, in Sigmund Freud, *Leonardo da Vinci and a Memory of His Childhood* (New York: W.W. Norton & Co., 1964).

124 *To quote Freud's description of Leonardo da Vinci, they have "an insatiable . . ."* Standard Edition, Vol. XI, p. 75.

125 *Napoleon was never a star pupil . . . but he pored over history books . . .* Asprey, p. 26.

125 *Rockefeller was nicknamed "the Sponge . . ."* Chernow, p. 95.

125 *Bud Tribble said the same thing about Steve Jobs . . .* Deutschman, p. 44.

125 *Bill Clinton's childhood friends used to say . . .* Angelo, p. 367.

125 *Henry Ford learned by doing. . . . His first hands-on experience with an internal combustion engine . . .* Lacey, p. 38.

126 *For example, David Gergen writes that "when [Clinton was] elected . . ."* Gergen, p. 320.

126 *Jack Welch may well say that "business is a game" . . .* Welch, p. 267.

126 *We can see this in Rockefeller, who never let anyone sneak up on him . . .* Chernow, p. 263.

127 *Rockefeller himself defended his questionable business practices as the only way to survive . . .* Chernow, p. 143.

127 *Jim Clark has his own spin on this . . .* Lewis, p. 66.

128 *Rockefeller almost never used the word "I" . . .* Chernow, p. 228.

128 *Martha Stewart appeared as herself on David Letterman . . .* A&E Biography, "Martha Stewart: It's a Good Thing," 2000–2001, A&E Television catalogue number AAE-18236.

129 *David Gergen noted that "humor was the one place where [Ronald] Reagan might easily talk . . ."* Gergen, p. 234.

130 *Steve Case said of Microsoft: "Their greatest vulnerability is themselves."* Auletta, p. 371.

133 *In the midst of huge losses at Chrysler, management turnover, and an onslaught of bad press, Jürgen Schrempp boasted . . .* Edmund

L. Andrews, "No Apologies from Stuttgart: DaimlerChrysler Chief Defends His Strategy," *The New York Times*, December 2, 2000.

133 *Rockefeller called his critics "blackmailers . . ."* Chernow, p. 155.

133 *Gates calls his critics liars.* Auletta, p. 241.

134 *Shapiro ignored the outcry and pursued his own strategy without any regard for the fears of the market. After he was fired, Shapiro conceded . . .* Specter, *The New Yorker.*

134 *The former vice president Michael Winkel commented: "We bought too many companies . . ."* Barrett, *BusinessWeek.*

135 *A dose of paranoia can be useful, an awareness of the market or personal threats . . .* An erotic CEO I coached said he always tried to have a paranoid sidekick around, because he wasn't suspicious enough.

135 *Ron Chernow notes that "Rockefeller made a fetish of secrecy . . ."* Chernow, p. 161.

135 *. . . and recounts a story of a friend of a Standard Oil employee dropping by . . .* Chernow, p. 161.

135 *Joe Klein points out that one of Clinton's most annoying qualities . . .* Klein, *The New Yorker.*

135 *Lyndon Johnson's tapes reveal a deep paranoia about his supposed enemies . . .* See, for example, *Reaching for Glory: Lyndon Johnson's Secret White House Tapes, 1964–1965,* Michael R. Beschloss, editor (New York: Simon & Schuster, 2001), p. 157.

136 *Henry Ford built elaborate tunnels . . .* Bennett, p. 82.

136 *Rockefeller installed a series of tricky locks . . .* Chernow, p. 223.

137 *. . . to which Jobs responded: "Nothing you say means anything to me. . . ."* Deutschman, p. 290.

137 *Gates is famous for blurting out "That's the stupidest thing I've ever heard . . ."* Mark Gimien, "Smart Is Not Enough," *Fortune*, January 8, 2001.

138 *It's worth quoting this passage on Henry Ford from David Halberstam to make my point . . .* Beatty, p. 234

139 *Ford's sidekick, Harry Bennett, said that he lasted so many years . . .*
Bennett, p. 5.

139 *This was an accusation Ray Lane, on leaving Oracle, made about Larry Ellison . . .* Lee Gomes, "Oracle Ex-President Criticizes Former Employer," *The Wall Street Journal*, August 24, 2000.

142 *Nacchio complained to institutional investors, "Anything I tell you, you're not going to believe. . . ."* Peter Elstrom, "On the Firing Line," *BusinessWeek*, October 29, 2001.

142 *Bill Gates rationalizes his exclusionary practices and financial favoring as essential . . .* Auletta, p. 242.

143 *After Miramax Films announced the biggest cutbacks in their history . . .* Harvey Weinstein told *The New York Times . . .* Laura M. Holson, "Miramax Films Cuts 75 Jobs After Some Recent Setbacks," *The New York Times*, March 16, 2002.

144 *(I have edited the translation and modernized the language used by Gummere, e.g., "your" for "thy"). Gummere, Francis Barton (1855– 1919) Translator, Project Gutenberg Etext #981, First Release, July 1997, ID: 1001).*

CHAPTER FOUR: STRATEGIC INTELLIGENCE

146 *Here's an actual report from human resources about a guy who is up for a promotion . . .* Welch, pp. 41–42.

148 *. . . in a study reported by* The Economist *. . .* "Marked by the Market: A Global Ranking of Companies," *The Economist*, December 1, 2001.

149 *Goleman offers this advice to managers who need to deliver critiques . . .* Goleman, p. 154.

149 *This is very similar to the advice you will find in Stephen Covey's . . .* Covey, p. 240.

150 *Anne Jardim, a Ford biographer, wrote that . . .* Tedlow, *Giants of Enterprise*, p. 146.

150 *And compare the qualities of emotional intelligence with Welch's description of his own managerial style* . . . Welch, pp. 42–43.

151 *The Level 5 executives, Collins claims, are not celebrity CEOs* . . . Collins, p. 27.

151 *One such Level 5 leader that Collins singles out in the political field is Abraham Lincoln* . . . Collins, p. 22.

151 . . . *eagerness to fit a fairy-tale model of Lincoln's "personal modesty* . . ." Collins, p. 22.

151 *According to Lincoln's law partner, William Herndon* . . . William H. Herndon and Jesse W. Weik, *Herndon's Life of Lincoln* (New York: Da Capo, 1943), p. 304.

151 *Lincoln even pushed the limit of legality during the 1858 senatorial race* . . . Abraham Lincoln: *Speeches and Writings, 1832–1858* (Library of America, 1989), p. 824.

152 *In his review of* Jack: Straight from the Gut, *Joseph Nocera writes* . . . Joseph Nocera, "The Customer Is Usually Right," *The New York Times*, October 14, 2001.

153 *Collins writes: "Throughout our research, we were struck* . . ." Collins, p. 127.

154 *Even Welch himself wrote that he's glad* . . . Collins, p. 42.

154 *I summed up my own leadership theories in my 1981 book* . . . *The Leader*, p. 51.

161 . . . *how do you craft a strategy especially when there are so many different definitions of strategy* . . . I find the most satisfying definition of business strategy in the writings of Michael Porter: "Strategy is the creation of a unique and valuable position, involving a different set of activities"; "strategy is a whole system of activities, not a collection of parts"; "competitive advantage comes from the way the activities fit and reinforce each other." Porter, *The Harvard Business Review*.

164 *Welch himself says: "More often than not, business is smell, feel, and touch* . . ." Welch, p. 18.

164 *Henry Ford knew what every single car part did and where it went, as seen in this astute comment from Richard Tedlow* . . . Tedlow, *Giants of Enterprise*, p. 149.

165 *. . . Jim Clark's vision for interactive television before Clark changed his mind, switched visions (in what Michael Lewis calls* . . . Lewis, pp. 82–83.

166 *[Sidney Harman] now says that "the discrete, multiple channel surround sound* . . . This quotation is taken from a letter that Harman wrote me in response to a draft of this chapter.

166 *Edison's technological history is riddled with errors and missteps. He may have invented* . . . Steven Johnson, *Interface Culture: How New Technology Transforms the Way We Think and Communicate* (New York: HarperEdge, 1997), pp. 145–46.

166 *Welch said: "Now, just think: Ten years from now, as we're sitting there out in the middle of the 1990s* . . ." Holly Peterson, "Jack Welch," *Talk*, December 2000/January 2001.

168 *This is one of the many lessons about the interdependent nature of systems thinking that I learned from Russell Ackoff* . . . See Russell L. Ackoff, *Creating the Corporate Future* (New York: John Wiley & Sons, Inc., 1981).

168 *In an article in* Business Week, *Larry Ellison said that a lot of companies* . . . Steve Hamm, with Jay Greene and David Rocks, "Oracle: Why It's Cool Again," *Business Week*, May 8, 2000.

169 *Another example of a highly successful business system is Southwest Airlines; as Michael Porter describes* . . . Porter, *The Harvard Business Review*.

172 *In order to accomplish this massive restructuring of business priorities, Welch needed to break down the barriers* . . . Welch, p. 96.

172 *This systemic vision of the company finally came together in his clearly articulated theory of the "boundaryless organization."* Welch, p. 186.

173 *Another CEO who understands the critical importance of a contin-
ually evolving vision is Bill Gates* . . . Jay Greene, with Steve Hamm
and Jim Kerstetter, "Ballmer's Microsoft: How CEO Steve Ballmer
Is Remaking the Company That Bill Gates Built," *Business Week*,
June 17, 2002; Jay Greene, Mike France, Amy Borrus, and Peter
Burrows, "Microsoft: How It Became Stronger Than Ever," *Busi-
ness Week*, June 4, 2001; Don Clark, "Microsoft Advances on
Game, TV Fronts," *The Wall Street Journal*, January 5, 2001; Alex
Pham, "The Cutting Edge: Focus on Technology; Gates Hopes Xbox
Is Key to the Living Room," *Los Angeles Times*, January 8, 2001; P.
J. Huffstutter, "Xtreme Xpectations: Xbox," *Los Angeles Times*, May
13, 2001.

173 . . . *which* Business Week *reports is more than AOL, Sun
Microsystems, and Oracle combined.* Greene, France, Borrus, and
Burrows, *Business Week*.

174 . . . *to compete with the Japanese in that $9.4 billion market.* Susan
Stellin, "Good Year for Games," *The New York Times*, February 18,
2002.

174 *When Ford's son, who had been running the company, died of
cancer in 1943* . . . Tedlow, *Giants of Enterprise*, p. 173.

175 *The Fordist production system became the model for the auto industry until Toyota's management* . . . See my article, "Is There a Best
Way to Build a Car?" *Harvard Business Review*, November/Decem-
ber, 1997.

175 *Russell Ackoff makes a useful distinction among three kinds of systems* . . . Ackoff, *Creating the Corporate Future*.

179 . . . *according to Michael Jordan, "Phil gets under your skin when
he needs to . . ."* Wilbon, *Washington Post*.

179 *In Jackson's defense, Bryant said, "It's the combination . . ."* Ibid.

180 . . . *management knew it was a stretch of Ruth's abilities: "It was
manager Ed Barrow . . ."* Thebaseballpage.com.

180 *This is the goal of Steve Ballmer's management initiative at Microsoft* . . . Greene, Hamm, and Kerstetter, *Business Week*.

181 *Welch drilled managers in his way of seeing things, saying that* . . . Welch, p. 194.

181 *My view of this was confirmed in an interview with Jack Welch in the* Harvard Business Review . . . Harris Collingwood and Diane L. Coutu, "The HBR Interview: Jack on Jack," *The Harvard Business Review*, February 2002.

184 *Learning from Welch, Ballmer has instituted a rigorous set of meetings* . . . Greene, Hamm, and Kerstetter, *Business Week*.

187 *An internal memo from the bank's Middle East and North Africa department* . . . "Wolfensohn Stirs Hornet's Nest of Criticism," *Financial Times Ltd.*, January 31, 2001; also, Stephen Fidler, "Wolfensohn: A Benevolent Dictator," *FT.com* site, February 2, 2001.

188 *This is a classic case of the pitfalls of narcissistic leadership, or, as Stephen Fidler of* Foreign Policy *puts it* . . . Stephen Fidler, "Who's Minding the Bank?" *Foreign Policy*, September/October, 2001.

191 *Andy Grove was able to dominate* . . . James Moore, *The Death of Competition* (New York: HarperBusiness, 1996), pp. 208–28.

191 *Right after his departure, Lane said, "The difference between us was good for shareholders."* William Santiago, "A Much Calmer Life After Oracle," *The New York Times*, October 1, 2000.

191 *Observers think that Michael Eisner* . . . Marc Gunther, "Has Eisner Lost the Disney Magic?" *Fortune*, January 7, 2002.

192 *Jeffrey Sonnenfeld, a dean at the Yale School of Management, singled out partnering failures* . . . Sonnenfeld, *The New York Times*.

192 Information on Durant's business practices draws on Beatty, ed., *Collossus*, pp. 234–36, as well as Madsen.

196 *Venter told Andrew Pollack of* The New York Times . . . Andrew Pollack, "Genome Pioneer Will Start Own Center," *The New York Times*, August 15, 2002.

CHAPTER FIVE: WORKING WITH A
PRODUCTIVE NARCISSIST

203 *In like manner, Ray Lane left Oracle with a net worth of $850 million.* Santiago, *The New York Times.*

206 *A former Apple executive said about Steve Jobs: "Quite honestly . . ."* Deustchman, p. 292.

206 *Regis McKenna, who was a marketing consultant to Jobs . . .* Deutschman, p. 67.

207 *Consider this passage from* Dialogue with Myself, *an internal dialogue committed to the page, between Augustine . . .* Garry Wills, *St. Augustine* (New York: Lipper/Viking Books, 1999), p. 54.

208 *Rockefeller, for example, was extremely focused on whom he was talking to . . .* Chernow, pp. 105–6.

208 *Henry Ford had his right-hand man, Bennett, take meetings with people.* Bennett, p. 41.

208 *Patty Stonesifer, the cohead of the Gates Foundation, says that "Bill by his own admission . . ."* Auletta, p. 155.

214 *Harry Bennett sums up his most important job at Ford . . .* Bennett, p. 120.

217 *As a coach, I was able to get one CEO to listen . . . by engaging him and his top team in an exercise called Desert Survival.* Desert Survival Situation TM, Plymouth, Michigan, Human Synergistics, 1974. Scoring is based on ratings by an expert.

222 *Heed the advice of Harry Bennett, who responded to a silly command from Henry Ford . . .* Bennett, p.19.

225 *When asked by Diane Coutu of the* Harvard Business Review *if he has any tragic flaw . . .* Hollingwood and Coutu, *Harvard Business Review.*

227 *In an excellent four-part series in the* Washington Post *in January 2002, Mark Leibovich describes . . .* Mark Leibovich, "MicroStrategy's

CEO Sped to the Brink," January 6, 2002; "At the Height of a Joy Ride, MicroStrategy Dives," January 7, 2002; "Once Defiant, MicroStrategy Chief Contritely Faces SEC," January 8, 2002; "'Maybe an Older, Wiser Visionary'"; "Chastened Boy Wonder Back to Business Roots," January 9, 2002, *Washington Post.*

CHAPTER SIX: THE PROMISE AND PERIL OF VISIONARY LEADERSHIP

230 *The first time I observed this correlation was not in a business setting. In 1965, Erich Fromm and I . . .* Fromm and Maccoby, *Social Character in a Mexican Village.*

232 *Napoleon took the inchoate stirrings of equality that found expression in the French Revolution . . .* Asprey, p. xix.

232 *What historian Garry Wills calls the "refounding" of the American ideal . . .* Garry Wills, *Lincoln at Gettysburg* (New York: Touchstone, 1992), p. 147.

236 *Armstrong boasted: "We, against all public and industry knowledge, believed that space would commercialize."* Rebecca Blumenstein and JoAnn S. Lublin, "Armstrong Pays $110 Billion in Effort to Transform AT&T," *The Wall Street Journal,* November 5, 1999.

236 *Within a few years, the company controlled over half the direct-broadcasting market . . .* Ibid. Additional AT&T material from Jeff Cole and Paul B. Carroll, "GM's Hughes Division Hires Armstrong, IBM's Heir Apparent to Become Chief," *The Wall Street Journal,* February 20, 1992; Jeff Cole, "Change Masters: Outsiders Who Transform Companies," *The Wall Street Journal,* March 30, 1993; Floyd Norris, "AT&T Realigns Its Planet," *The New York Times,* October 26, 2000.

237 *This is exactly the fictional scenario imagined by Stephen Vincent Benét . . .* "The Curfew Tolls," originally published in *The Saturday Evening Post,* October 5, 1935.

238 *"Revolutions are ideal times for soldiers with a lot of wit . . ."* Alan Schom, *Napoleon Bonaparte* (New York: HarperPerennial, 1998), p. 12.

239 *We need visionary leadership for what Michael Lewis brilliantly writes is the "idea . . ."* Lewis, p.15.

240 *The engineers at Intel had the circuitry, the chips, the power source, everything they needed to make a relatively cheap home computer . . .* Johnson, *Interface Culture*, p.148.

242 *Between 1900 and 1908, more than 60 percent of the auto manufacturers went out of business.* Madsen, p. 88.

242 *Even with such a high attrition rate, money continued to pour into the car industry, prompting a speaker at a bankers' convention . . .* Ibid, p. 127.

246 *The recent CEO scandals and the collapse of so many corporate visionaries has created a deep sense of distrust, a lack of faith in corporate leaders that has led to a new trend . . .* Alex Kuczynski, "Companies Dig Deeper Into Executives' Pasts," *The New York Times*, August 19, 2002.

247 *This is clear in reactions to a fictional case study in the September 2001 issue of the* Harvard Business Review *. . .* Sarah Cliffe, "What a Star—What a Jerk," *Harvard Business Review*, September 2001. See my response to the case in my letter published in the *Harvard Business Review*, October 2001.

249 *Well, John Sperling has quietly, and quite efficiently, made it happen.* "Teaching the World a Lesson," *The Economist*, June 8, 2002.

250 *And consider the case of Craig McCaw, the billionaire who first made his fortune by cashing in McCaw Cellular . . .* Christine Y. Chen, "The Man Who Would Save Satellites," *Fortune*, July 8, 2002.

aggression in, 137
celebrities and entertainers as, 46–47, 87
combinations with other types, 256
empathy and, 150, 179
motivation for, 177, 178
professions, 45, 79, 255
projects, 203
sense of security, 67
social or internalized controls, 66, 100
strengths, 46–47, 255
weaknesses, 47–49, 129–30, 134, 256
workaholism in, 116
in workplace and management, 48–49
working with narcissist, 211
Escape from Freedom (Fromm), 23
Ethics (Aristotle), 82–83
Exaggeration and lying, 141–42, 224

F
Fidler, Stephen, 188
Fiorina, Carly, 15, 61–63
Ford, Henry, 16, 94, 99, 102–5, 109–10, 114, 117, 118, 125, 133, 136, 138–39, 150, 163, 164–65, 169, 174–75, 208, 214–15, 221, 222, 227, 240, 241, 242
Foreign Policy (Fidler), 188
Fortune magazine, 4–5, 62
Francis, Saint, 80
Franklin, Benjamin, 51
Fraser, Claire, 141, 167, 195, 209
Freedom, internal and external, 110–13
Freud, Sigmund, 5, 6, 25, 76, 79, 103
on narcissism, 35–36, 40–43, 96, 123, 126, 127, 211, 231, 264

on obsessives, 49, 55
personality types, 43, 221, 253n
"social control" model, 72–73
Frisinger, Hakan, 196
Fromm, Erich, 6, 23, 25, 83–84, 205, 230

G
G. D. Searle, 103
Galliano, John, 249
Gamesman, The (Maccoby), 2, 12, 48, 167, 202
Gandhi, Mohandas, 10, 231
Garland, Judy, 46
Gates, Bill, 4, 8, 9, 75–76, 79, 94, 117, 123, 125, 127, 133, 135, 137–38, 140–43, 150, 156, 164, 173–74, 183–84, 191, 208, 220, 221, 244, 245, 248
Gehry, Frank, 79
General Electric (GE), 99–100, 148, 166, 171, 180–82, 225, 245
General Motors, 73, 192–93
Gergen, David, 126, 129
Germs (Miller), 38
Gerstner, Louis V., 156–57
Gibbs, Joe, 245–46
Gielgud, John, 85–86, 87
Gillette, 52
Gladwell, Malcolm, 243–44
Global Crossing, 192
Goldman Sachs, 54
Goleman, Daniel, 11, 124, 148, 149
Good to Great (Collins), 52, 150–51, 249
Gore, Al, 56, 137
Grandiosity, 143–44, 227–28
Grove, Andy, 4, 79, 127, 191, 221
Guarente, Leonard, 249, 251
Guevera, Che, 231
Gyllenhammar, Pehr, 3, 12, 131, 143–44, 196–97

MICHAEL MACCOBY, PH.D., is president of the Maccoby Group and director of the Project on Technology, Work, and Character, a nonprofit research center. A psychoanalyst, anthropologist, and consultant, Dr. Maccoby has advised leaders at numerous corporations, from AT&T to Volvo, as well as institutions such as the World Bank and the State Department. From 1970 to 1990 he led a research program on leadership and work at Harvard's Kennedy School of Government. He is the author of the best-seller *The Gamesman*, and author or coauthor of seven other books, most recently *Why Work? Motivating the New Work Force.* He lives in Washington, D.C.